The Authors

DR. RACE FOSTER

Dr. Race Foster is a practicing veterinarian with a special interest in canine and feline medicine and surgery. He has practiced in Northern Wisconsin since receiving his DVM from Michigan State University. In addition to veterinary practice, he is co-owner of Drs. Foster and Smith, Inc., a leading catalog of products for pets and their owners that is known throughout the world.

Dr. Foster is a member of the Michigan and Wisconsin Veterinary Medical Associations and lives in Rhinelander, Wisconsin, with his wife and four children.

In his free time, Dr. Foster writes veterinary articles and books and, of course, enjoys being with animals. He has a unique interest in consulting and working with professional dog and cat breeders, especially in the area of animal health, and is a consultant on pet health nationwide.

DR. MARTY SMITH

Dr. Marty Smith's interests in veterinary medicine have included canine and feline medicine and surgery along with many hours devoted to wildlife treatment and rehabilitation. He received his DVM at Iowa State University and is a member of the Wisconsin Veterinary Medical Association.

Dr. Smith, his wife and their five daughters enjoy a wide range of outdoor activities including camping, hiking, boating, wildlife photography and skiing. Today he is a part owner of one of America's largest pet supply mail order catalog companies, Drs. Foster and Smith, Inc. He divides his time between his family, practicing, writing and consulting with other writers, organizations and pet breeders across the United States.

Acknowledgments

It is appropriate to give a special thank you to employees who were instrumental in preparing this text. Sue Ellen Hopp spent countless hours proofing and organizing this writing. Tanya Frisque provided expertise in typing and data entry. Patricia Dinda, our illustrator, worked diligently to provide clear and concise drawings throughout the text. Marcy Zingler of Howell Book House was instrumental in providing direction when it was needed.

Additionally, we would like to thank all of the employees of Drs. Foster and Smith, Inc. as they have provided endless hours listening to pet owners and breeders about their concerns, thus enabling us to assemble a meaningful book.

Lastly, it is a true honor to be allowed to work so closely with owners, breeders, groomers and other pet enthusiasts. Without you the veterinary profession does not exist. We do not view the profession as simply being a group of veterinarians; rather, it is a relationship made up of responsible pet owners, loved pets and veterinarians. By reading this book you have allowed us to become a part of your pet's life. For that we are forever grateful.

To our wonderful families, who have provided love and support throughout our professional careers.

Contents

Introduction

RESPONSIBLE PET OWNERSHIP BEGINS WITH AN UNDERSTAND-ING OF VETERINARY HEALTH CARE. As advances in medicine continue by leaps and bounds, it becomes apparent that for one to stay informed, an organization of common disorders of the canine is needed.

We have spent over thirty-one combined years owning and operating veterinary hospitals dedicated totally to dogs and cats. As our practice grew in patient numbers, coupled with an influx of health discoveries and information, we found pet owners would often become confused or not be quite clear about their pets' ailments. Veterinary medicine, with all its advances, is more complicated than ever. Through medical ignorance our practice used to be easy and routine; now modern medicine has provided us with new diseases and diagnostics. The practice of veterinary medicine is now more complicated, yet rewarding and concise.

To practice "good medicine" veterinarians need to educate pet owners, as well as ourselves. Additionally, we need to hear their concerns and adjust our practices accordingly. The goal of this book is to provide information about pet health care in an organized fashion. This knowledge will enhance the bond between veterinarian, client and patient, hopefully with the end result being quality pet care through understanding.

This book was written with the intention of providing a better understanding of disorders affecting the canine. Some ailments are serious, others are not, but most disorders found in this text are common. If a disease or syndrome is not common, then chances are it is not included in this text. This book was meant to be an extension of the veterinary practice and our link to you as a pet owner. No pet remains healthy forever and in time of need this book will help you understand: What can be expected? What can be done? Why is this happening? What can I do? This is not just a "What is it?" book. Once you know what the diagnosis is, this will help you understand and, together with your veterinarian, decide on the necessary therapy. Treating an ailment is not just the job of the veterinarian. The owner provides most of the love and care needed for recovery. The owner, therefore, must comprehend the problem. This book will accomplish that.

What's the Diagnosis?

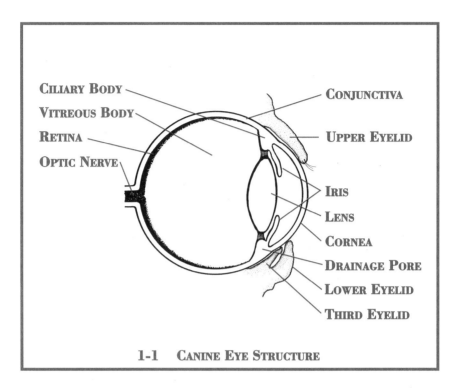

CILIARY BODY

VITREOUS BODY

RETINA

OPTIC NERVE

CONJUNCTIVA

UPPER EYELID

IRIS

LENS

CORNEA

DRAINAGE PORE

LOWER EYELID

THIRD EYELID

1-1   CANINE EYE STRUCTURE

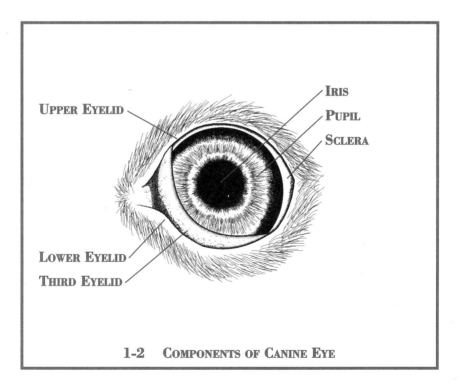

UPPER EYELID

IRIS

PUPIL

SCLERA

LOWER EYELID

THIRD EYELID

1-2   COMPONENTS OF CANINE EYE

The Eye, Eyelids and Surrounding Tissue

INTRODUCTION

The visual system provides one of the most important senses available to the canine. The eyeball gathers light and converts it into electrical impulses which are transmitted to and interpreted by the brain, which then forms images. The eye is protected by being sealed in a strong bony eye socket supported by lubricating tissues, muscles and eyelids.

The eyeball is formed by several layers of tissue. (See figure 1-1.) The white part, called the **sclera,** is made of tough fibrous tissue rich in blood vessels, which transport oxygen and nutrients to the contents of the eye. The clear outer portion of the eye that the dog sees through is the **cornea** and is made up of extremely thin layers of cells arranged in a unique fashion so as to be transparent. The cornea allows light to enter unaffected into the eye. Inside the eyeball are specialized structures bathed in a liquid called vitreous fluid, which keeps the eyeball "inflated" so that it maintains its shape. Additionally, this fluid supplies nutrients and oxygen to the various parts of the inner eye. In the interior of the eyeball is the colored portion, called the **iris**. As in humans, dogs have different-colored eyes. This is determined by the color of the iris, in the center of which is an opening called the **pupil**. This opening can be made larger or smaller by muscles, called **ciliary bodies**, that attach to the colored iris, causing it to expand or contract. In dim light, the pupil is made larger to let more light enter the eye. Conversely, in extremely bright situations, the pupil becomes smaller. This is important because too much light, as in humans, can cause pain or damage to the inner structures of the eye. Behind the pupil lies the **lens**, a pea-sized organ that is normally clear. The lens bends, concentrates and focuses the light rays entering the eye so they will land on the rear surface of the eyeball, which is called the **retina**. The retina contains nerve cells referred to as **rods** and **cones**. The rods are sensitive to light and the cones to color. Unlike humans, the canine possesses very few cones; that is why *domestic* dogs are color-blind. It is believed they only see shades of gray, white and black. Dogs do, however, have many rods and other reflective cells that enable them to see in very dim light. The nerve cells within the retina transform the light into nerve impulses. These are concentrated and leave the eyeball by the **optic nerve** and are then carried to the brain. The brain translates the impulses into images, creating vision.

The eyeball is surrounded by a soft pinkish tissue called the **conjunctiva**. The conjunctiva connects the eyelids to the eyeball. There are three **eyelids** in the canine: the *upper, lower and nictitating membrane.* (See figure 1-2.) The latter is commonly referred to as the third eyelid. The third eyelid functions in the production of tears, but also has lymphoid tissue within that is an important part of the system. Canines blink about three times per minute as blinking helps spread tears and other lubricating oils over the cornea plus clean it of dust and microscopic debris. The lids and surrounding tissue contain lubricating structures called tarsal and lacrimal glands, which produce a fluid called tears to bathe the eye. The upper lids also contain eyelashes, which help prevent dirt and other particles from falling upon the cornea. Tears provide moisture to the eye and help flush out dust, pollens and other fine particles.

The three eyelids and the surrounding conjunctiva therefore lubricate, nourish and protect the eyeball. The **tear glands** supply the tears to continually flush and cleanse the eye surface. Tears exit the eye and its related structures through a small duct or opening at the inside corner of the eye, called the lacrimal or tear duct. (See figure 1-3.) Tears are also protective in that they are bactericidal (i.e., they kill bacteria that could possibly infect the eye). Disorders of these tissues usually result in a very reddened eye and, frequently with excessive or altered tear production, hence the term "red, runny eyes." In reality the eyeball may be fine, but the tissues around the eye are irritated and inflamed. Disorders of the eye and its surrounding tissues are common and are the topics covered in this chapter.

CONJUNCTIVITIS

Conjunctivitis is an inflammation or infection of the conjunctiva, the tissue lining the eyelids and attaching to the eyeball near the cornea. The conjunctiva can become irritated due to allergies induced by pollens, grasses,

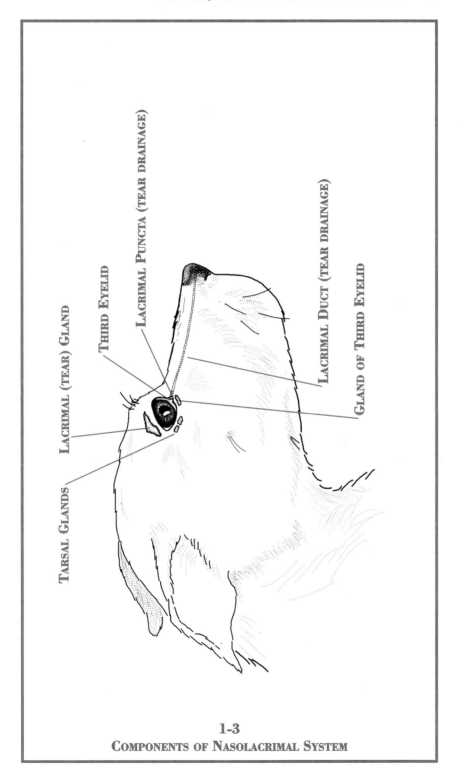

1-3
COMPONENTS OF NASOLACRIMAL SYSTEM

etc., or from infections caused by viruses, bacteria or fungi. If the white portion of the eyeball (sclera) is also inflamed, this condition is occasionally referred to as "Pink Eye." Conjunctivitis is the most common ailment affecting the eye of the dog.

What are the symptoms?

The symptoms vary depending on the cause. Typically both allergies and infections cause a severe redness or "meaty" appearance of the conjunctiva. This is caused by edema or fluid build-up and an increase in the size and number of blood vessels within the tissue. Either allergies or infections cause the eye to discharge or "weep," with the consistency of the discharge often helping to determine which is the cause. Usually infections caused by bacteria, fungi, etc., create a thick yellow or greenish eye discharge. The eyelids may actually stick together when held shut. This results from the accumulation of white blood cells (or "pus") excreted into the area in an effort to fight off the infection. Allergies, on the other hand, generally cause a clear or "watery" discharge. Regardless of the cause, a patient with conjunctivitis will often squint and/or keep the third eyelid elevated, thereby partially covering the eyeball. This condition is often painful, causing a dog to paw at or rub the eye against objects such as your leg or the carpet.

What are the risks?

Normally conjunctivitis is not life-threatening; however, in advanced cases of infection the organisms can spread and affect other structures of the eye. Vision could become impaired. As in humans, some infections can be transmitted to other individuals or littermates. Allergies are not contagious and therefore pose no threat to other canines.

What is the treatment?

All cases of conjunctivitis should be *treated at once*. A culture and sensitivity test may be necessary to determine if bacteria are the cause and if so, what medication should be used for treatment.

Usually eye drops or ointments are the drugs of choice. Eye drops are watery solutions that must be applied every few hours, while ointments last longer and are usually only applied two to three times per day. If the cause is suspected to be allergy, then various medications are available containing anti-inflammatories, usually hydrocortisones. If the cause is an infection, then bactericidal or fungicidal ointments or solutions may be applied. In severe cases, oral antibiotics are used in addition to the topical preparations. Most cases will respond to treatment; however, it may take one to two weeks to fully recover. Many eye ointments containing hydrocortisones and antibiotics are available and are frequently used when the exact cause cannot be determined.

MEIBOMIAN CYSTS

These are small cysts arising from glands lining the upper and lower eyelids. The lids each contain about forty such glands. (See figure 1-4.) Meibomian glands provide an oily lubricant that spreads over the eyeball to help keep it moist. Occasionally these glands plug up and become enlarged. When this happens, a small, dark-colored mass, usually pea-sized or smaller, forms on the lid margin. Since these growths arise from the meibomian glands, they are termed meibomian cysts. About 90 percent will occur on the upper lid versus the lower. Geriatric patients have a much higher incidence of these structures than younger patients.

What are the symptoms?

Generally a small cyst (BB-size) will appear on the lid margin. Untreated, it will grow and occasionally ulcerate, thereby releasing a brown, oily secretion. Larger cysts may rub against the cornea or interfere with normal blinking and lubrication, causing the eye to become red and inflamed.

What are the risks?

Meibomian cysts are not cancerous and pose no threat to the individual's life. As they grow, they do prevent the eye from being properly lubricated so infections become common. It is possible for these infections to enter the deeper eye tissues.

What is the treatment?

Surgical removal is the only sure cure for meibomian cysts. Occasionally they can be squeezed or lanced and may decrease in size temporarily; however, recurrence is likely. Surgery involves a removal of a portion of the affected lid, so it is best if these cysts are removed before they become excessively large.

CHERRY EYE

This condition affects the third eyelid (nictitating membrane) of the canine. This structure's normal functions include both lubrication for the eye and defense of it. The third eyelid has lymphoid tissue that releases white blood cells and antibodies to ward off infection. Cherry eye can occur in any breed. However, Cocker Spaniels, Beagles, Bloodhounds, Bulldogs, Bull Terriers, Chinese Shar Peis, Lhasa Apsos and Saint Bernards seem to be the most susceptible. The tear gland on the third eyelid becomes enlarged, often to the size of a marble, and appears as a "cherry" in the eye, hence the name "Cherry Eye." It will be on the nasal side or inside corner of the eye where the third eyelid is found.

What are the symptoms?

A marble-sized red growth will suddenly appear in the corner of the eye closest to the nose. Some patients may squint and have difficulty with

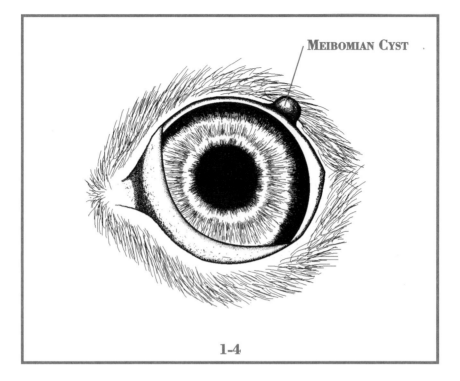

MEIBOMIAN CYST

1-4

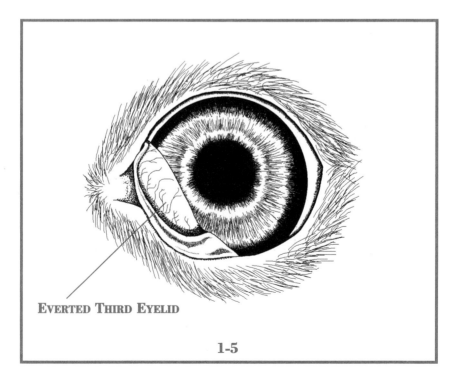

EVERTED THIRD EYELID

1-5

vision while others will seem oblivious to the growth. In those dogs that show some sort of reaction to the cherry eye, it is because the mass can cover a portion of or irritate the cornea; however, the mass is not attached to it. The mass is nothing more than an enlarged tear gland located on the back of the third eyelid. Secondary eye infections may develop as the mass prevents normal blinking and lubrication of the eye surface.

What are the risks?
Cherry Eye is not a serious disorder, however, it should be corrected so it will not interfere with vision. Additionally, the patient cannot blink normally until the cystic gland is corrected.

What is the treatment?
Cherry Eye is corrected with the aid of surgery. It should be noted that the third eyelid or the gland within it *should not be removed* as they are necessary for normal eye lubrication and are a part of this immune system. In the past, the treatment was to remove the gland surgically, but this was found to result in "dry eye" (keratoconjunctivitis sicca). Surgery is aimed at *repositioning* the gland, *not removing* it. This is done by tucking the enlarged gland into a cut made in the base of the third eyelid. This in effect buries it deeper within the nictitating membrane without impairing the gland's function. Eye drops may be used in addition to surgery to control inflammation or infection.

DISTICHIASIS
Distichiasis is a condition in which small hairs abnormally grow on the inner surface or very edge of the eyelids. (See figure 1-6.) Both upper and lower lids may be involved. Some breeds are affected more commonly than others, suggesting that it is probably an inherited trait. Cocker Spaniels, Golden Retrievers, Boxers and Pekingese are among those most commonly affected.

What are the symptoms?
The abnormally placed hairs growing from the lids irritate the cornea as they rub against it. The affected eye will become red, inflamed and may develop a discharge. Quite often the patient will squint or blink often, much like a person with a hair or other foreign matter in the eye. The animal will often rub the eye against objects such as the furniture or the carpet. In severe cases, the cornea may become ulcerated and appear bluish in color from the aberrant hair or from self-mutilation by the pet.

What are the risks?
Left untreated, severe corneal ulcerations and infections usually develop. The hairs can cause severe irritations and without treatment they usually worsen. As stated, the animal may further irritate the eye through scratching

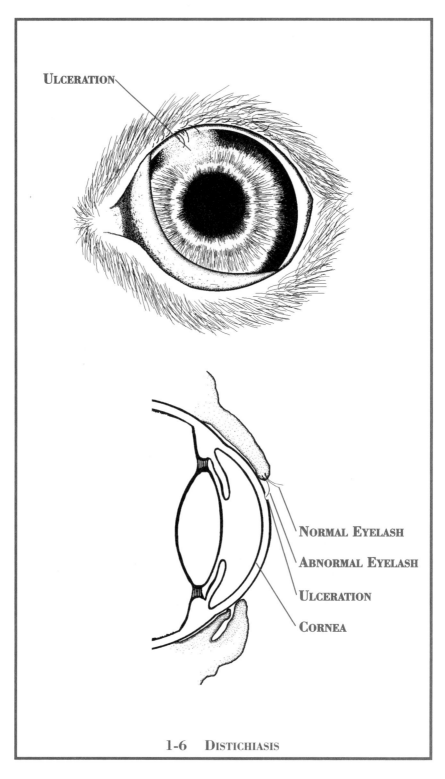

1-6   DISTICHIASIS

or rubbing against it to the point of self-mutilation. Blindness can also result if infections develop.

What is the treatment?

The abnormal hairs are best removed through the use of surgery or electro-epilation. With electro-epilation, a fine needle is passed into the hair follicle and an electric current destroys the hair and its roots. If surgery is performed, the lid is actually split and the areas where the abnormal hairs grow are removed. Both procedures require anesthesia and a full recovery is expected. Antibiotic eye drops may be used following surgery to eliminate infections.

ENTROPION

This is a condition in which the lower lid margins roll *inward* to the extent that hair rubs on the surface of the eyeball. In rare cases the upper lid can also be affected to some degree. One or both eyes may be involved. (See figure 1-7.) This condition can occur in all breeds; however, most kinds of Spaniels, Great Danes, Chinese Shar Peis, Poodles and Saint Bernards seem to be the most frequently affected, suggesting an inherited trait.

What are the symptoms?

Most patients with entropion will squint and have a reddened, inflamed eye. Because of the pain involved, dogs will scratch at the eye with a paw, possibly doing further damage. Examination of the lower eyelid will confirm the diagnosis.

What are the risks?

Left untreated, *severe* eye infections may develop. The cornea can become severely irritated or damaged as the chronic abrasion by the inverted lower lid wears away at its surface. In some cases, deep ulcers form in the cornea, even to the point of rupturing through its surface. This quickly leads to intraocular infections and potential blindness.

What is the treatment?

Once diagnosed, surgery is the only treatment. There are several different techniques, but typically a small incision is made below the lid and when sutured, it pulls the border of the lid downward into a normal position. Antibiotic ointments may be applied if infections are present.

ECTROPION

Ectropion is used to describe a condition where the lower lids are loose, causing a drooping of the eyelid's margins. (See figure 1-8.) The lower lids actually turn outward. One or both eyes may be involved. It can occur in any breed, but it is inherited in American Cocker Spaniels, Saint Bernards, Mastiffs and Bloodhounds.

What are the symptoms?

As the lower lid sags downward, the underlying conjunctiva is exposed. This forms a pouch or pocket, allowing pollens, grasses, dust, etc., to accumulate and rub against the sensitive conjunctiva. This is a consistent source of irritation in these patients, leading to occasional watering of the eye which then spills out over the lower lid and face.

What are the risks?

Many patients live normal lives with ectropion. However, some develop repeated eye infections due to the collection of dirt, dust, etc., within the eye. Therefore, the risks are minor except in severe cases, where secondary eye infections may develop.

What is the treatment?

Some patients require no treatment; however, if eye irritations develop, medical attention is advisable. Mild cases can be treated with eye drops or salves to alleviate irritations and/or infections when they occur. In severe cases a surgical procedure is preferred which removes excess tissue, thereby tightening the lid and removing the abnormal pocket.

EVERTED THIRD EYELID

Occasionally the third eyelid will fold over on itself, causing an *eversion*. Great Danes, Golden Retrievers and Saint Bernards appear to have inherited traits for this condition; however, all breeds can be affected. The third eyelid contains a cartilage support structure that may be defective or injured, thus allowing the folding to occur. (See figure 1-5.) When this happens the entire third eyelid will actually appear folded forward over itself. Occasionally the cornea can become irritated and an eye discharge may then be apparent.

What are the risks?

An everted eyelid poses no great threat to health, except in rare instances where corneal irritation or infection develops. For both cosmetic and health reasons, most veterinarians recommend correction.

What is the treatment?

Eversion is corrected by surgery. The defective cartilage within the third eyelid is dissected out and removed, allowing the lid to unfold and return to its normal position.

PROMINENT NASAL FOLDS

Nasal folds arising from the muzzle immediately in front of the eye may be so pronounced as to rub against the cornea. (See figure 1-9.) Usually

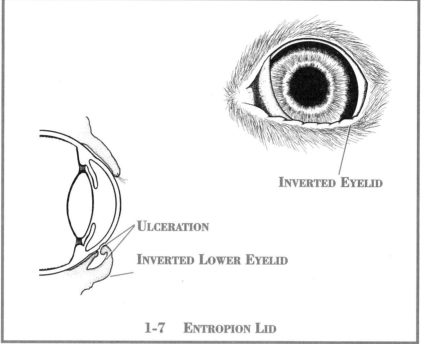

INVERTED EYELID

ULCERATION

INVERTED LOWER EYELID

1-7 ENTROPION LID

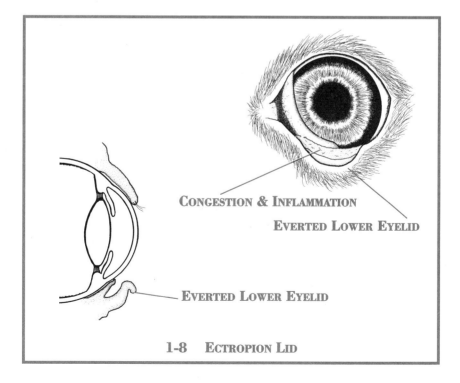

CONGESTION & INFLAMMATION

EVERTED LOWER EYELID

EVERTED LOWER EYELID

1-8 ECTROPION LID

short-muzzled (brachycephalic) breeds are most affected, for example, Pekingese, Bulldogs and Pugs.

What are the symptoms?
Patients affected will have watery eyes due to the irritation. The cornea may become very irritated and/or infected. A simple examination will reveal the prominent nasal folds of the skin and/or their hair actually touching the surface of the eye.

What are the risks?
Cases can vary from mild to severe and eye irritation can become extensive. Usually the patient experiences discomfort, even in the more mild cases. Treatment is recommended.

What is the treatment?
Treatment involves surgery to simply remove or decrease the size of the folds. The extent of surgery depends on severity, but complete correction is expected.

RETROBULBAR ABSCESS
Occasionally abscesses (pockets of infection) will develop behind the eyeball. Usually only one eye is involved. Generally the cause cannot be determined, but it is suspected that bacteria enter through the mouth and gum line and cause a pocket of infection to become trapped behind the eyeball. Dogs that chew sticks, straw, etc., are at greater risk.

What are the symptoms?
Retrobulbar abscesses usually cause the eyeball to protrude or bulge from the socket. The eye may be repositioned at a strange angle, causing the affected eye to be "looking off to the side." Almost always, the patient will experience pain when the mouth is opened. When the animal pants, barks or attempts to eat or drink, the jaw bone places increased pressure behind the eye; if an abscess is present within that area, severe pain may result. Most patients will stop eating as a result of the pain.

What are the risks?
Any suspected cases should be treated at once. Not only are the pain and discomfort a concern, but any infection this close to the eye and its nerves can potentially spread and involve these structures.

What is the treatment?
Surgical drainage of the abscess is the quickest and surest way to treat the condition. An incision is made inside the mouth immediately behind the last molar. Once the abscess is drained, the patient will recover quickly. Following surgery, oral antibiotics are used to treat the bacteria.

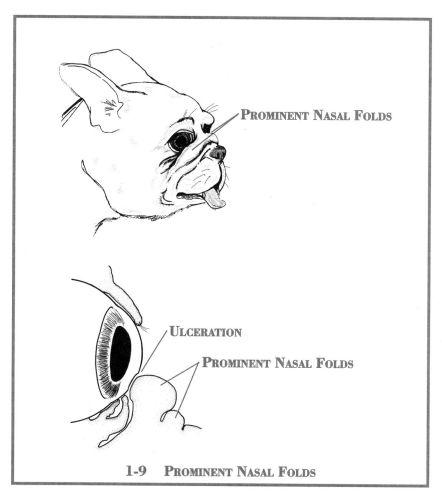

1-9   PROMINENT NASAL FOLDS

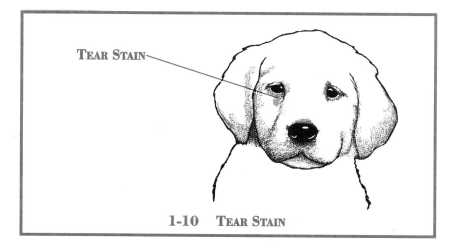

1-10   TEAR STAIN

PLUGGED LACRIMAL DUCT

After they flow across and lubricate the surface of the eye, the tears produced by the glands drain from the area via the lacrimal or tear duct, located in the lower eyelid at the inside corner of the eye. Tears travel through the lacrimal duct, which passes to the nasal cavity. They are deposited on the end of the nose, giving the animal a "wet nose." There the fluid may evaporate, be inhaled back through the nasal passageway to be swallowed, or be licked off by the tongue. Bacteria, dust, debris or excretions from the eye can occasionally clog this duct and prevent normal drainage.

What are the symptoms?

Patients with plugged tear ducts will appear to have an excessively watery eye. In reality, the tear production is normal, but since drainage is impeded, tears build up, spill over the lower lid and drain down the face from inside the cover of the eye. This usually discolors the hair a dark brown color. If the duct or eye is infected by bacteria, a thick yellow discharge may appear within the eye.

What are the risks?

For the eye to be properly lubricated, the ducts need to function correctly. If the ducts are plugged this does not occur, but this is certainly not life-threatening. Rather, the eye is more prone to infection, the hair becomes discolored and in some cases the skin below the eye becomes irritated from the chronic, moist exudate lying against it. Bacteria can invade and clog these ducts and cause severe and painful infections. If this is suspected, treatment should begin at once.

What is the treatment?

The lacrimal duct is "reopened" by flushing and forcing out the restrictive material. A small needle is placed into the opening of the duct and saline is flushed downward (through the end of the nose), providing cleansing action. Anesthetic may be required. If an infection is suspected, then oral antibiotics and eye drops are used following the flushing. This problem may recur in animals with abnormal or thickened tear secretions or in cases where the duct is abnormally formed or has been damaged.

TEAR STAINING—EPIPHORA

In some dogs, especially Poodles, tears drain down the face causing a pink to brown discoloration of the hair under the eye. (See figure 1-10.) Many Poodles, and occasionally other breeds, do not have adequate tear drainage and therefore the excess spills over the lower lid. *It is not a problem of too much tear production, but rather improper drainage.* This can be a result of clogged lacrimal ducts, abnormal conformation that prevents the tears from opening the duct or the tears produced from being too thick to make their way into the duct opening. Poodles are the breed most commonly affected. Occasionally this condition is called "Poodle Epiphora."

What are the symptoms?

Generally the hair becomes stained a pink to light brown color. As normal facial bacteria react with clear tears, a stain is formed that colors the hair. In white or light-colored dogs, the stain is more pronounced. In severe cases a thick crust may form in the corner of the eye and over the skin. This can be quite irritating, causing small ulcers on the skin over which it forms.

What are the risks?

The risk is minor unless a severe crust forms, causing a skin irritation. Tear staining is considered normal in Poodles, but other breeds such as German Shepherd Dogs can also be susceptible.

What is the treatment?

Unless it is secondary to a clogged lacrimal duct, nothing can be done to prevent the tear spillage. The hair should be trimmed below the eye to reduce crust formation. Common stain removers are available to remove the discoloration. However, this is not a treatment, but rather a cosmetic measure. Antibiotics can be used to reduce the bacteria count and therefore the staining, but this usage of antibiotics is questionable. Ninety percent of patients require no treatment whatsoever.

KERATOCONJUNCTIVITIS SICCA (KCS)

Keratoconjunctivitis sicca is the technical term for a condition also known as "dry eye." Inadequate tear production is the cause. This may be due to injuries to the tear glands, such as infections or trauma. The nerves of these glands may also become damaged. Eye infections and reactions to drugs such as sulfonamides can impair the nerves and/or the glands. Some cases are also the result of the gland of the third eyelid being surgically removed by mistake. Many cases have no known cause; the glands simply cease to function at their normal levels.

What are the symptoms?

The eyes typically develop a thick, yellowish discharge. Infections are common as the lack of the bactericidal tears allows bacterial organisms to overgrow the eye. Additionally, inadequate lubrication allows dust, pollen, etc., to accumulate. As a result the eyes lose their ability to flush away foreign particles and protect themselves from bacteria. To confirm a case of "dry eye," a measurement of tear production is performed. Veterinarians utilize a small piece of absorbent material called a Schirmer tear test strip.

This small strip is placed in the eye. Over a period of usually one minute, the tears soak and migrate up the strip. The wet area of the strip is then measured and compared to normal values. If inadequate tear production is found, then "dry eye" is diagnosed.

What are the risks?

Left untreated, the patient will suffer painful and chronic eye infections. Repeated irritation of the cornea results in severe scarring which will become apparent. *Corneal ulceration may develop, and will lead to blindness.*

What is the treatment?

If the cause can be identified, treatment should be aimed at eliminating it. An evaluation to determine infection should be performed. A thorough history may reveal past infections that could have damaged the tear glands or their nerves. *If the patient is receiving sulfa drugs, they should be stopped at once.* From our clinical experience, it is very rare that the cause can be identified, in which case therapy is aimed at replacing tears rather than correcting the cause.

Artificial tear solutions available for humans and sold in pharmacies can be used in canines. Depending on the severity, these drops are placed in the eyes at regular intervals throughout the day. These artificial tears provide the needed lubrication and flushing for the corneas. Antibiotic preparations are often used simultaneously to provide protection from bacterial organisms. In very severe instances, a surgery can be performed which transplants a salivary duct into the upper eyelid area. Saliva then drains into the eye, providing lubrication. This procedure is rarely utilized, but is an option.

DISORDERS OF THE EYEBALL

The eyeball is made up of several structures including the **cornea, iris, lens, chambers and the retina.** Although the eyeball is protected by three lids and placed within a bony socket, it is still an organ subject to injury and disease.

FOREIGN BODIES IN THE CORNEA

Any abnormal objects within and potentially causing injury to the body are referred to as foreign bodies. The front portion of the eyeball, called the cornea, is particularly exposed and subject to injury. Foreign bodies such as sticks, seeds, weeds and dirt frequently cause damage to and/or become lodged within the cornea. The foreign body can be visible or may be hidden behind the lids, most commonly the third eyelid. In these cases, as the animal blinks, the material will cause an abrasion on the cornea.

What are the symptoms?

Most patients with a foreign body injury experience some pain and tend to squint or blink excessively. They may rub the eye either with a forepaw or slide the entire head across the carpet in an effort to remove the offending material. This causes further damage.

What are the risks?

The cornea is easily damaged, leading to a corneal ulcer. This in itself requires treatment, but the problem may not stop there. Loss of vision is a real possibility if the cornea is severely damaged and especially if it is punctured. This would allow bacteria or other organisms to gain access to the inside of the eyeball.

What is the treatment?

If the foreign body is lodged in the eye, *it must be removed at once.* Flushing with warm water or saline may wash away the particles. More severely lodged foreign bodies, such as sticks or splinters, may require surgical removal. Antibiotic ointments are usually applied to minimize infections. It is important to examine behind the third eyelid for foreign material. This is a common place for bits of weeds or seeds to be hidden from view. *No eye exam is complete without examining behind the third eyelid.*

ULCERS OF THE CORNEA

Occasionally viruses, bacteria or traumatic injury can result in damage to the cornea. A corneal ulcer is an area of damage in which the outer layers of cells are removed or destroyed, forming a pit-like structure.

What are the symptoms?

The ulcer may not be detectable with the naked eye, or it may appear as a hazy or bluish area on the otherwise clear cornea. In chronic cases, pink scar tissue and blood vessels may appear on the eye's surface. Squinting is common as most ulcers are very painful.

What are the risks?

Ulcers of the cornea are always serious. Ulcers may become so deep as to puncture the eyeball, allowing the internal fluids to rupture out through the opening. Blindness (or at the very least, impaired vision) is always possible.

What is the treatment?

To identify an ulcer, veterinarians frequently stain the eye with a green fluorescent dye. When the dye is flushed from the cornea, any area that remains green is an ulcer. The dye adheres to the deeper, exposed layers of the cornea. Ulcers are usually treated with ointments or drops. These protect the deeper areas and allow healing to occur as new cells spread back over the area. However, **it is very important not to use medications containing steroids (cortisones) in an ulcer.** Steroids have a melting effect on the inner layers of cells within the cornea, resulting in permanent scarring. Solutions containing only antibiotics should be used. In very severe instances, surgery may be required to clean and cover the ulcer.

PANNUS/CORNEAL OPACITY

Pannus is a general term used to describe an inflammation within the cornea. The exact cause is unknown; however, it is more common in German Shepherd Dogs than other breeds. It is probably an inherited trait, as certain lines have a higher incidence than others. Both eyes are usually involved.

What are the symptoms?
The cornea becomes covered by a thick film of cells that form a membrane. Initially this appears as a gray to bluish deposit. Blood vessels, as well as a dark pigment, may later cover all or a portion of the cornea.

What are the risks?
Pannus is usually chronic and progressive. If both eyes are involved, blindness may result. Blindness occurs because the cornea becomes so inflamed that scar tissue and pigment cover its surface, blocking vision.

What is the treatment?
Treatment generally does not provide a total cure; however, the progression can be slowed. Steroids such as cortisone help fight inflammation. These may be applied topically, as in ointments, or injected directly into the scleral area. Cyclosporine has also been used. Surgery to remove excess scar tissue is occasionally performed.

KERATITIS (CLOUDY EYE)

Keratitis is a general term used to describe an inflammation of the cornea. Causes may be injury, viral, bacterial, fungal or unknown.

What are the symptoms?
An inflamed cornea will appear bluish or hazy rather than clear. In advanced cases, the cornea will be opaque, making it impossible for light to pass through.

What are the risks?
All forms of keratitis are serious and can result in blindness. A mild keratitis may heal by itself while severe forms cause destruction or breakdown of the structures involved.

What is the treatment?

The proper treatment depends on the cause. The eye should be examined by a veterinarian to determine the exact cause. Usually drops or ointments are used to clear an inflammation and/or infection.

HEPATITIS BLUE EYE

"Blue eye" is a term used to describe cloudy corneas as a result of an adenovirus type 1 infection. Adenovirus type 1 is a severe viral disease affecting dogs of all ages. Usually the liver is affected, hence the name hepatitis, but occasionally the eye is also involved, forming the term "Hepatitis Blue Eye."

What are the symptoms?

About ten days after exposure to the virus, the corneas appear blue or very hazy. Most patients squint and the eye may tear excessively. Puppies are more commonly involved than adults. With some vaccines for adenovirus, the vaccination itself could actually cause the blue eye, hence the popular name "Blue Eye reaction." This reaction is seldom seen with modern vaccines. Signs such as lethargy, poor appetite, nausea, jaundice (a yellowing of the skin, eyes and membranes), bloating or even death may be noted if the liver is severely affected by an adenovirus infection.

What are the risks?

Once the patient's body fights off the viral infection, the eyes will clear. Several weeks may be required for the eyes to become normal again. In severe cases involving the liver, death can occur.

What is the treatment?

Fortunately, excellent and safe vaccines for adenovirus type 1 are available and usually administered yearly to prevent this disease. In animals not protected, life-saving treatments may be needed, including hospitalization and intravenous fluids.

DERMOID CYST

Dermoid cysts are hair-covered growths that form on the lids, the conjunctiva and/or the cornea. They tend to be darkly pigmented and are usually found in young dogs. Dalmatians, German Shepherd Dogs and Saint Bernards are the most commonly involved, but other breeds are also affected. It appears that these cysts may be inherited, at least in the above breeds.

What are the symptoms?

Dermoid cysts usually appear as dark, hair-covered growths and usually cover a large portion of the cornea and sclera.

What are the risks?

Dermoids are not a form of cancer and pose little risk to the health of the patient. The main concern is that they tend to cover the surface of the cornea, thus limiting vision. They do irritate the surrounding lids.

What is the treatment?

Surgery is the only means of correction. Usually the entire cyst can be removed; once healed, vision is restored. If totally removed, regrowth is unlikely.

DISORDERS OF THE LENS

The lens is found inside the eyeball and is a small marble-like structure that is responsible for focusing. By changing shape, it focuses images, projecting them to the surface of the retina to be visualized. The lens is normally clear so any disturbance of the lens will cause images to be blurred, cloudy or difficult to see.

NUCLEAR SCLEROSIS

This is a normal change associated with aging. As one grows older, the lens takes on a hazy appearance.

What are the symptoms?

When the patient is viewed straight on and we look into the pupil, a hazy or blue-gray color will be seen. In severe cases, the patient may have difficulty seeing small objects at rest, but can usually detect motion. In most cases, vision will be only slightly affected and objects will appear as if one is looking through a dirty window.

What are the risks?

There is little risk to the patient. With age, nuclear sclerosis will progress, however, *seldom to the point of severely affecting vision.*

What is the treatment?

Usually treatment is not necessary in nuclear sclerosis. Total removal of the lens would be possible, but is not warranted.

CATARACTS

The marble-like lens is made up of water and protein. The normal lens contains about 66 percent water and 34 percent protein. If this delicate balance of water and protein is upset, cataracts can form. In these cases excess levels of protein cause deposits that create small dense areas within the normally clear lens. These are termed cataracts. A patient with cataracts will therefore not have a clear lens. In fact, it will appear cloudy and often with an internal latticework of lines similar to that seen in ice cubes. There are several types of cataracts. Juvenile cataracts develop in young puppies, while adult cataracts come with age. Cataracts are routinely seen in patients suffering with the disease affecting blood sugar levels, diabetes mellitus.

JUVENILE CATARACTS

Juvenile cataracts are those that occur at less than three years of age. Inheritance plays a role as Standard Poodles, Afghan Hounds, Miniature Schnauzers, Cocker Spaniels, Golden Retrievers, Boston Terriers, Labrador Retrievers and Staffordshire Bull Terriers have a higher incidence than other breeds. All breeds, however, can be affected. It is not uncommon to detect juvenile cataracts as young as two months of age.

ADULT CATARACTS

Adult cataracts develop as the pet ages. Some books refer to adult cataracts as senile cataracts; however, the authors do not prefer this term as it implies senility or extreme age. Adult cataracts typically develop after six years of age. They generally appear as small white areas within the lens; if the changes are not severe, they may not deter vision. In other cases, the lesion is progressive and without treatment leads to total blindness.

DIABETIC CATARACTS

As in humans, pets with Diabetes Mellitus often develop cataracts. In this instance the abnormally elevated blood sugar will cause sugar deposits to occur within the lens. This abnormal concentration of sugar attracts excess fluid, causing a breakdown of cell membranes, resulting in protein deposits, forming cataracts.

What are the symptoms of cataracts?

Regardless of the cause, cataracts can appear quite similar. Other than the age and medical history, there is no easy way to determine the cause or type of the cataract. Most cataracts are clearly visible to the naked eye. When viewing the patient from the front, one may notice small white to milky gray lines or areas throughout the lens. In more severe instances, the patient may have a vision defect serious enough to cause bumping into objects. Mild or early stage cataracts may not be visible without the aid of an ophthalmoscope used by an experienced veterinarian.

What are the risks?

The risks vary with the cause. Both juvenile and diabetic cataracts may progress to the point of causing total blindness. Adult cataracts tend to develop slowly, and in some instances pose no real threat to the animal's vision. Abnormalities in these areas should always be referred to your veterinarian as soon as they are noted.

What is the treatment?
Once the cause or type of cataract has been identified, the appropriate therapy can be selected. In severe instances, cataract surgery may be an option, in which case the entire lens is removed. Vision will be present, but slightly impaired. Diabetic cataracts are very difficult to resolve. Correcting the blood sugar with insulin (see Chapter 7) may help discourage further development, but will not affect changes that have already occurred. Most adult cataracts require no treatment as they tend not to progress rapidly. It is not recommended to breed animals with a known history of juvenile cataracts. Obviously, the issue of cataracts and treatment is a complex subject. A thorough understanding must be developed between the veterinarian and pet owner. Once accomplished, the patient can be evaluated and the proper treatment selected.

LENS LUXATION

Luxation of the lens is a common abnormality seen in all breeds; however, it is most common in the small terrier breeds such as the Sealyham, Fox, Tibetan and Welsh Terriers. The lens is held in place by small fibers within the inner eye. In these breeds, the fibers seem to be reduced in number and/or prone to an early degeneration. As the fibers weaken, the lens is no longer held in place and it moves from its normal position behind the pupil. (See figure 1-11.) The fibers holding the lens can also be damaged as a result of head trauma. Lens luxation can therefore be inherited or a result of injury. One or both eyes may be affected.

What are the symptoms?
Usually as the lens falls from its normal position, vision is disrupted. This is a problem, but the greatest danger of a luxation of the lens is that it may block drainage of the inner eye fluid (vitreous). This causes the fluid to accumulate within the eye, causing increased intraocular pressure. This extremely painful condition is referred to as glaucoma. (See page 25.)

What are the risks?
A luxation of the lens affects vision, but if glaucoma develops and goes untreated, blindness will almost certainly result.

What is the treatment?
Generally surgery is recommended to remove the lens entirely. Once removed, vision is impaired, but present.

DISORDERS OF THE EYE CHAMBERS

The eyeball is a hollow structure divided by the iris into two distinct chambers, the anterior and posterior. (See figure 1-12.) Both chambers are filled with what is called vitreous fluid, which bathes and nourishes the inner eye structures. Vitreous fluid is produced within the eyeball and drains outward into the veins. The amount of vitreous fluid production precisely equals what drains out, so as to maintain a consistent shape and fluid pressure within the eyeball.

GLAUCOMA

Glaucoma is a term used to describe increased pressure within the eye. When vitreous production no longer is equal to drainage, fluid builds up within the eye, causing increased pressure. Glaucoma may be primary or secondary. Primary glaucoma is one in which it is not caused by another unrelated condition. There is simply too much vitreous fluid, either from an excess production or decreased drainage. Secondary glaucoma is an increased pressure due to other eye disorders such as lens luxation. Primary glaucoma can be inherited and is seen frequently in Cocker Spaniels, Afghan and Basset Hounds, Wire Fox Terriers, Dalmatians and Poodles, as well as other breeds. One or both eyes may be involved.

What are the symptoms?
Regardless of cause, a patient suffering with glaucoma will have a swollen and very painful eye. The pupil will be large (dilated) and unresponsive to light. In other words, it will not constrict when a bright light is directed into the eye. Squinting is common and the pain may be so great as to cause depression and a lack of appetite. The animal will often rub its eye against the carpet or furniture. The cornea may appear bluish and the white portion of the eye will be reddened with enlarged blood vessels. Vision is generally greatly impaired.

What are the risks?
All causes of glaucoma are medical emergencies. As the pressure builds within the eye, blood vessels, nerves and other structures within the eye become damaged and total blindness results.

What is the treatment?
Eye pressure is measured with a veterinary device called a tonometer. The exact extent of increased pressure is determined and the proper treatment is selected. Therapy is aimed at decreasing vitreous production and increasing vitreous drainage, thus decreasing and stabilizing the inner eye pressure. Veterinarians use a variety of drugs, such as Pilocarpine and Daranide, to accomplish this. Surgery may be indicated in cases of primary or secondary glaucoma.

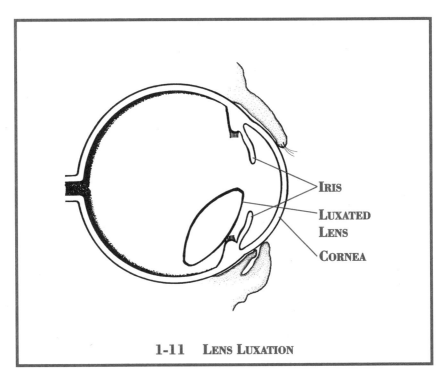

1-11   LENS LUXATION

- IRIS
- LUXATED LENS
- CORNEA

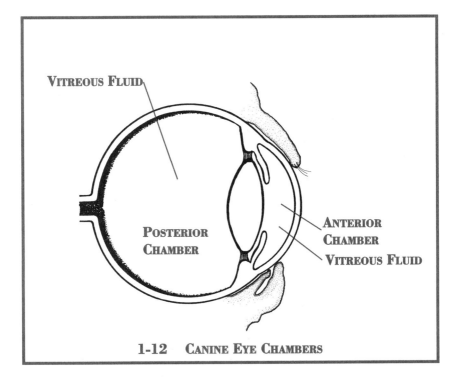

1-12   CANINE EYE CHAMBERS

- VITREOUS FLUID
- POSTERIOR CHAMBER
- ANTERIOR CHAMBER
- VITREOUS FLUID

UVEITIS

Uveitis is an inflammation of the anterior chamber of the eye including the iris and ciliary body (tissue supporting the lens). Bacteria and fungus are often the cause. They may enter the eye through the bloodstream or by an injury to the cornea or other eyeball surface.

What are the symptoms?

Uveitis causes the eye to become shrunken and soft, just the opposite of glaucoma. The patient will squint, usually with excess tearing. The pupil is usually small (constricted), the opposite of glaucoma. Pain is severe. Usually only one eye is involved.

What are the risks?

All cases of uveitis are medical emergencies. Left untreated, blindness is the end result.

What is the treatment?

The underlying cause (i.e., injury or infection) must be identified. If bacteria or fungus is the reason, then specific drugs such as antibiotics and antifungals must be used. Cortisones are used in many cases to fight inflammation. Atropine is administered to dilate the pupil. Proper treatment requires the examination and care of a veterinarian.

DISORDERS OF THE IRIS

The colored part of the eye is the iris. Its main function is to expand or contract to alter the size of the pupil in response to changes in light conditions.

IRIS CYSTS

Occasionally the iris may develop small, round, dark spots that are not firmly attached. These are iris cysts. The cause is unknown and generally no treatment is used, as they do not affect the iris' function.

IRIS ATROPHY

Certain breeds such as Chihuahuas, Miniature Poodles and Miniature Schnauzers may develop iris atrophy. This is simply a condition in which the iris degenerates. The iris may actually develop holes within it, occasionally affecting the entire iris. Patients with iris atrophy may avoid bright light, as too much light passes through the holes onto the retina, causing pain. The cause is unknown, but probably inherited. There is no known treatment.

DISORDERS OF THE RETINA

The retina is the very back portion of the eyeball. A complex layer of cells compose a membrane which transforms light into electrical impulses that are passed through the optic nerve to create vision. Disorders of the retina greatly affect the quality of vision.

Collie Eye Anomaly (CEA)

Collie eye anomaly is an inherited condition originally discovered in the Collie breed, but it also affects other breeds including Shetland Sheepdogs, Australian Sheepdogs and German Shepherd Dogs. It is inherited and as many as 90 percent of all Collies in the United States are said to be affected to some degree.

What are the symptoms?

In severe cases, vision may be greatly impaired; however, in most instances, the lesions can only be identified by an exam with an ophthalmoscope. CEA actually comprises several eye defects. A patient with CEA may have a detached retina, optic nerve abnormalities and/or a loss of retinal cells.

What are the risks?

Vision is always somewhat impaired, but the extent depends on the severity of the defects. It is inherited and should be selected against in any breeding program.

What is the treatment?

There is no treatment to eliminate CEA. Breeders typically select against this condition by having puppies examined at a very young age (six weeks), then periodically afterwards. Veterinarians can detect lesions early on in which the retina has not developed correctly or lacks normal pigmentation. Small lesions, however, may become pigmented with age. Breeders refer to puppies with disappearing lesions as "go normals." Despite the term "go normal," these puppies are not normal and should not be bred. They carry the genes for CEA.

Progressive Retinal Atrophy (PRA)

Progressive Retinal Atrophy is an inherited eye condition seen most frequently in Collies, Norwegian Elkhounds, English and American Cocker Spaniels, Golden Retrievers, Irish Setters, Toy and Miniature Poodles and Miniature Schnauzers, as well as other breeds.

What are the symptoms?

Initially, as the retina degenerates, patients have difficulty seeing in dim light, and if progressive, daytime vision is also affected. A veterinary eye exam will detect the characteristic lesions of PRA, usually with areas of hyper-reflectivity. Lesions may appear at any age, even as young as six weeks in some patients.

What are the risks?
The condition is progressive and therefore worsens over time. Total blindness may result.

What is the treatment?
There is no treatment for PRA. Breeders, through testing, generally remove individuals with PRA from their breeding programs. Depending on diagnostic equipment used, PRA can be detected before one year of age and occasionally as young as six weeks.

CENTRAL PROGRESSIVE RETINAL ATROPHY (CPRA)

Central Progressive Retinal Atrophy is very similar to PRA. It is inherited in Labrador Retrievers, Border Collies, Shetland Sheepdogs, Golden Retrievers and others. In this condition, the center part of the retina begins to degenerate first. A blind spot develops in the central portion of the patient's field of vision. Moving objects will be visualized better than those at rest. There is no treatment for this disorder and those carrying this trait to any degree should not be bred.

RETINAL DETACHMENT

Retinal detachment is a condition in which the retinal layer of cells becomes separated from the underlying tissues. The cause may be injury, cysts, tumors or inflammations within the eye. Some will reattach with no treatment; others may respond to medications such as diuretics and cortisone. Some cases, however, are untreatable and may lead to either partial or total blindness.

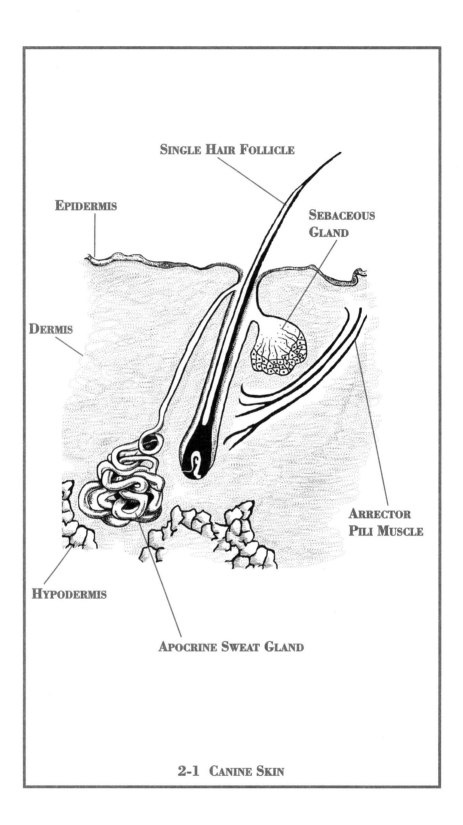

SINGLE HAIR FOLLICLE

EPIDERMIS

SEBACEOUS GLAND

DERMIS

ARRECTOR PILI MUSCLE

HYPODERMIS

APOCRINE SWEAT GLAND

2-1 CANINE SKIN

Skin, Hair and Nails

INTRODUCTION

The skin is the largest and one of the most important organs of the body. It forms a barrier to protect the dog from infections, parasites and the elements. It also maintains the body's internal environment, preventing loss of moisture and other body constituents. Because the skin is on the outside of the body and therefore exposed, it is easily susceptible to injury and disease. It is also very visible, so disorders are readily detected during an examination.

The skin is made of layers of cells, lubricating glands (sebaceous), hair and follicles, blood vessels and nerve endings. (See figure 2-1.) The skin cells form layers, namely the tough outer covering called the epidermis and the deeper layer called the dermis.

The **epidermis** is composed of older cells that form a tough, almost impervious, protective outer barrier. As the cells erode, other cells mature and move up to replace them. The epidermis varies in thickness, being thicker on the more exposed areas such as the head and back and thinner in other areas, such as the armpits and belly.

The deeper layer (**dermis**) contains hair follicles, blood vessels, nerves and sebaceous (oil) glands. Hair follicles and sebaceous glands are more prevalent on the back than on the belly. Dogs generally have two layers of hair, a long, stiff outer coat and a shorter, softer inner layer for insulation. The hair coat and the variations between the two layers vary tremendously depending on breed and climate. Both hair and nails are formed from dead cells hardened with keratin.

HOT SPOTS—ACUTE MOIST DERMATITIS

"Hot spots" are discrete, well-defined areas of inflamed skin caused by excessive scratching and/or chewing the affected area. Any cause of itching, such as fleas, allergies, ticks, burrs, ear infections, etc., can result in excessive scratching and the formation of a "hot spot."

What are the symptoms?

The main symptom is a circular lesion that is moist, raw, inflamed and devoid of hair. The patient will generally scratch or chew excessively upon the area. Hair surrounding the lesion may mat due to the irritated skin exuding fluid or "weeping." The lesion can increase rapidly in size. They are commonly found on the skin over the hip, the back legs and the sides of the face and body. (See figure 2-2.) In severe cases, an elevated temperature may develop.

What are the risks?

Once initiated, hot spots spread very rapidly, causing considerable pain and discomfort. Secondary bacterial skin infections frequently result and can develop into equally serious disorders. Because hot spots advance quickly, often doubling or tripling in size in 24 hours, they should be treated at once.

What is the treatment?

The treatment for hot spots is twofold. Most importantly, the cause of the itching must be identified. Check about the head for ear infections. If near the tail base, infected anal glands may be the cause. If the itching occurs all over the body, then suspect fleas, mange mites or an allergic reaction to pollens, grasses, etc. Eliminate the underlying cause once identified. The hot spot lesion should be thoroughly clipped of surrounding hair. Then clean the area vigorously to remove all of the crust and dirt. Hydrogen peroxide or tamed iodine solutions can be used to cleanse; however, it must be remembered that these lesions are often very painful and in some cases a veterinarian may use tranquilizers to calm the patient. Once the area is cleaned, topical anti-inflammatory sprays should be applied. It is important to keep the area dry, so do not place heavy salves or creams such as Vaseline on the hot spot. Oral antihistamines, such as Benadryl, and antibiotics may be given. In severe cases veterinarians may prescribe cortisones to suppress the itching.

Hot spots are more prevalent in long-haired breeds. It is therefore suggested to have long-haired pets clipped and groomed regularly, especially during the hot summer months when skin problems are most common. Medicated shampoos designed for pets also greatly reduce skin irritations and should be used on a regular basis, weekly if necessary.

ALLERGIES—THE MOST COMMON SKIN DISORDERS OF DOGS

By definition, if you see inflamed and itchy skin, your pet probably has an allergy to something. Dogs may be allergic to pollens, grasses, fleas and other insects, plastics, cigarette smoke, medications, carpet fibers, mites, detergents, foods and many other things. Some allergies are due to things the pet inhales. Pollens and smoke fit this category and are termed **inhalation allergies**. If the allergy is due to something **ingested,** we call it a **food allergy**. Allergies caused by carpet fibers, grass and plastics are termed **contact allergies**. Those due to fleas are referred to as **flea allergies** or **flea bite dermatitis**.

Whether the allergy is an inhalation, contact, food or bite allergy, the principles are the same. The item the pet is allergic to is called the **allergen** and allergens stimulate histamine release from within cells and cause the patient's skin to itch excessively. Itching, with the scratching and chewing that it causes, is the hallmark of an allergy.

Depending on the cause, the patient may suffer allergies throughout the year or these can be short-term or seasonal. Seasonal allergies are the most common and are worse in the summer and fall when the grasses, weeds, etc., produce the most pollen. This is also true in humans with "hay fever," which is really a pollen or grass allergy.

The average canine typically does not develop allergies until about three years of age; however, younger patients are occasionally seen.

Allergies rarely are life threatening, but can make the patient miserable. A pet with allergies will be preoccupied with the itching sensation and will not be happy. Additionally, the appearance of the coat and skin will be poor and they may produce an offensive odor.

What are the symptoms?

As previously mentioned, most patients with allergics suffer from excessively itchy skin. The skin may also be pink and inflamed, occasionally to the point of hair loss and bleeding. The areas most commonly affected will be the feet and sides of the body and in the case of flea bite dermatitis, over the back in front of the tail. These animals will also have frequent ear infections. With food allergies, the patient may also vomit or suffer from diarrhea.

What is the treatment?

The treatment varies depending on severity. Occasionally veterinary dermatologists can perform allergy tests to identify the cause and through injections, desensitize the patient. Allergy testing, although useful, is expensive and not always successful. From a practical standpoint, the allergic condition is seldom cured, but becomes more manageable, much like "hay fever" in people.

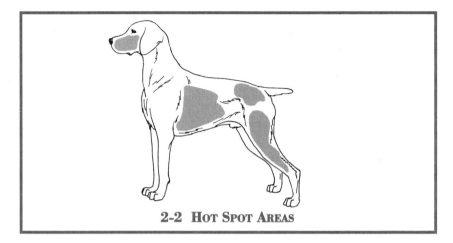

2-2 HOT SPOT AREAS

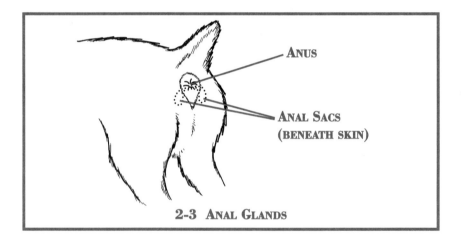

ANUS

ANAL SACS
(BENEATH SKIN)

2-3 ANAL GLANDS

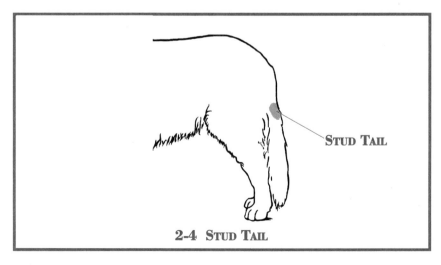

STUD TAIL

2-4 STUD TAIL

Antihistamines such as Benadryl can be useful. In more severe cases, veterinarians may use potent anti-inflammatories such as cortisones to alleviate the itching and provide comfort for the patient. Medicated shampoos, such as oatmeal, melaleuca and hydrocortisone, are an aid in the patient with mild allergies. They will not eliminate all signs, but do help in the overall treatment.

Changing the diet may be beneficial in food allergies; however, food allergies are infrequently encountered. In instances of flea or mange mite allergies, it is very important to practice strict parasite control.

It must be understood by both owner and veterinarian that the exact cause of the allergy usually will not be determined. *Treatment is aimed at controlling the allergic response, not necessarily finding a cure.* Improving the quality of life for the allergy patient is the primary goal of therapy.

ANAL GLANDS

All carnivores including dogs (both male and female) possess two anal glands. As the dog is viewed from behind, the glands are found just under the skin at the four and eight o'clock positions, immediately adjacent to the anus. (See figure 2-3.) Sometimes referred to as pockets or sacs, they are about one inch in diameter in a forty pound dog.

Through a tiny duct, the glands secrete a thick brownish substance giving each dog a characteristic odor, easily detected and identified by other canines. This is why dogs frequently smell this area on other dogs, especially at their first meetings. It serves as a method of identification. The glandular secretion is excreted when the pet defecates, as the act of defecation places pressure upon the glandular muscles. This secretion is therefore on every stool and is a mechanism of territory marking. Dogs may also scoot or drag their rear ends in an effort to empty the glands. The glands commonly become impacted and/or infected and require medical attention.

What are the symptoms?
Dogs suffering with malfunctioning anal glands, either from infection or impaction, may have several symptoms, typically seen when the glands become plugged. This may include dragging the rear end across the ground or carpet. Most people refer to this as scooting. The pet may lick or chew excessively about the rump, tail and anal area. With infections, the area about the anus will become swollen, red and painful. The gland may actually rupture and drain if an abscess forms. A fever may also be present.

What are the risks?
Impactions when the anal glands are simply too full are less of a problem than actual bacterial infections. With impaction, the glands need to be

forced open. Infections, however, can cause considerable discomfort and may damage nerves and muscles about the anal area. Impactions can lead to infections, so any disorder of the anal glands should be attended to at once.

What is the treatment?

Veterinarians and experienced pet owners can manually squeeze the glands to clean them of any excess material or infection. This is generally referred to as "expressing" the anal glands. Some dogs may need this done on a monthly basis. In cases of infections, antibiotics such as amoxicillin may be needed to kill the bacteria. In chronic cases, surgical intervention may be necessary, in which case the glands can be entirely removed. Done properly, this surgery is an excellent choice and 100% curative.

TAIL GLAND HYPERPLASIA (STUD TAIL)

All dogs have a small oval gland on top of the tail about 3 inches from the anus. (See figure 2-4.) This area of skin is rich in oil glands, specifically sebaceous and perianal glands. In addition, the hair over this area arises from single rather than multiple follicles. (See figure 2-5.) Occasionally the glands in this area increase in size (hypertrophy) and the area loses its hair. This condition is often referred to as "stud tail"; however, *both* males and females are affected.

What are the symptoms?

Generally the area loses all hair and the glands increase in size, forming a bald protruding mass of tissue. Some dogs chew at the area, causing raw tissue to be exposed, which can allow secondary infections to develop.

What are the risks?

In most patients, the lesion will be unsightly, but pose no medical risk. Infrequently the dog may bite and traumatize the area, occasionally culminating in infection.

What is the treatment?

In most patients treatment is not necessary and is largely cosmetic. The affected tissue can be surgically removed, usually leaving only a slight scar. In more severe instances, especially if infected, surgical removal of the entire tail may be needed. Castration of the male may slow the progression.

STAPHYLOCOCCAL PYODERMA

Staphylococcal bacterial infections are usually simply referred to as **staph** infections. Staph bacteria are widespread and cause mild to severe skin infections in dogs of all ages. (See figure 2-6.)

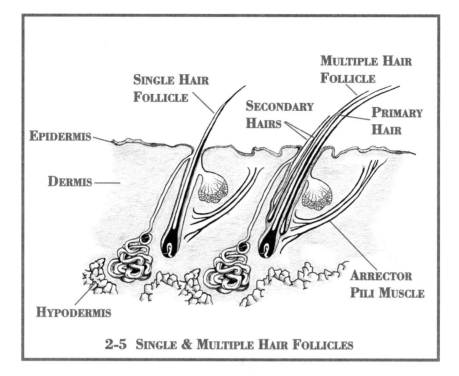

SINGLE HAIR FOLLICLE
MULTIPLE HAIR FOLLICLE
SECONDARY HAIRS
PRIMARY HAIR
EPIDERMIS
DERMIS
ARRECTOR PILI MUSCLE
HYPODERMIS

2-5 SINGLE & MULTIPLE HAIR FOLLICLES

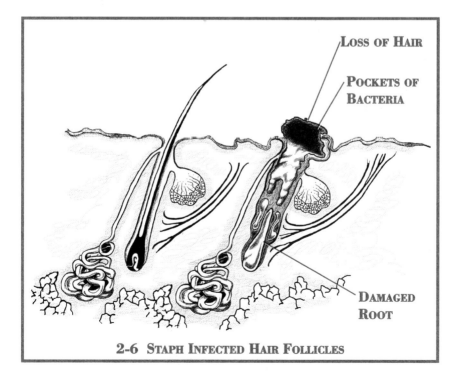

LOSS OF HAIR
POCKETS OF BACTERIA
DAMAGED ROOT

2-6 STAPH INFECTED HAIR FOLLICLES

What are the symptoms?
Symptoms depend on severity. Mild skin infections may appear as crusty skin lesions, frequently about the belly area. More advanced cases will manifest draining areas and can cause severe itching.

In puppies, the infection may develop to the extent of causing severe facial swelling and swollen lymph nodes about the neck. In this case the staph bacteria have invaded the hair follicles. This condition in puppies is termed "puppy strangles." Occasionally, usually in adults, individuals are actually allergic to the staph bacteria. These patients have severely reddened and itchy skin.

What are the risks?
The risk depends on the severity of the individual case. *Puppies* especially are vulnerable and *may actually die* as the infection worsens. All cases of staph pyoderma can progress and should be treated as soon as possible.

What is the treatment?
The skin is usually biopsied and/or cultured to confirm the diagnosis. Oral antibiotics are selected based on test results. Usually medicated shampoos, such as tar and sulfur, are used in conjunction with oral antibiotics. In the rare case of a staph allergy, steroids or hyposensitization ingestion may be indicated along with the antibiotics.

VULVAR FOLD DERMATITIS
The folds of skin surrounding the vulva of the female create an excellent environment for bacteria. Overweight pets and those with tucked-in (inverted) vulvas (see figure 2-7) have a higher incidence of infections in these areas.

What are the symptoms?
Females so infected will lick excessively about the vulva and surrounding area. Examinations of the vulvar folds will reveal reddened tissue, frequently with a thick discharge. The vulva may be swollen and traumatized due to the excessive licking.

What are the risks?
Seldom life threatening, this condition can become chronic and painful. It rarely goes away without treatment.

What is the treatment?
The folds of skin must be washed and cleansed thoroughly. Medicated shampoos will help reduce the bacteria. Antibiotic ointments applied to the infected areas are beneficial. More severe cases will require oral antibiotics. In obese animals and those with an inverted vulva, surgery and weight loss will be beneficial. Surgery is aimed at removing the folded

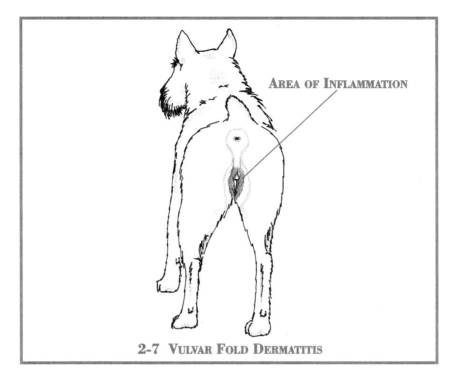

2-7 VULVAR FOLD DERMATITIS

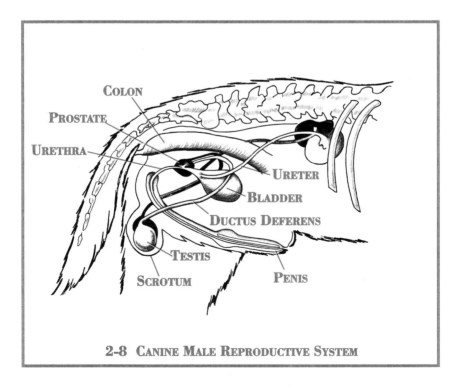

2-8 CANINE MALE REPRODUCTIVE SYSTEM

tissue so bacteria do not have a place to colonize. Pets prone to vulvar fold dermatitis should have the creases about the vulva cleansed regularly, daily if needed, to prevent recurrence.

SCROTAL DERMATITIS

Infections and irritations of the scrotum are not infrequent in the male dog. Usually this is secondary to trauma from brush, grasses, bug bites, crusty snow, etc. Outdoor and Sporting dogs are at particular risk.

What are the symptoms?
The scrotum will usually develop crusty areas surrounded by red, inflamed tissue. (See figure 2-8.) Most dogs will chew and lick excessively, often making the condition worse.

What are the risks?
Left untreated, the scrotum and testicular area may become severely infected and traumatized. *Treatment should begin at once.*

What is the treatment?
As previously mentioned, this condition usually begins due to abrasions or trauma to the scrotum. The pet should rest in a clean, dry area to prevent further damage. Anti-inflammatory sprays or creams can be applied daily to the affected area. Oral antibiotics and anti-inflammatories may be needed in some instances. Recovery may take two to three weeks. In severe cases, the scrotum may have to be surgically removed.

ABSCESSES

Abscesses under the skin are one of the most common ailments seen in dogs. An abscess (sometimes referred to as a boil) is an area of infection, usually characterized by a painful swelling filled with fluid, occasionally referred to as pus. Any material that irritates the skin may cause an abscess to develop. Bite wounds from other dogs are a cause, but thorns, scratches, hay, sticks, bee stings, and flea and other insect bites can all break the skin, allowing bacteria to enter, and result in an abscess formation.

What are the symptoms?
Usually the abscessed area will be swollen, reddened and painful to the touch. A visible wound may or may not be present. Most abscesses seen in dogs tend to be about the head and neck. This may be caused by animals inflicting wounds on each other, chewing on sharp objects or due to the fact that the head and neck area are frequently exposed to the elements. Ninety percent of the time the actual cause will not be determined.

What are the risks?

An abscess is an area of infection. Left untreated, it can spread to other areas of the body. *The infectious bacteria can leave the abscessed area and enter the bloodstream, and death could result.* This is seldom the case, however, and most abscesses remain in the local area.

What is the treatment?

The abscess, filled with fluid, will occasionally rupture and drain. Once drained, they usually heal rapidly. If the abscess is large and *not* draining, veterinary intervention may be required. The abscess should be lanced and drained. Oral antibiotics may be required to fight infection. However, antibiotics will seldom work without sufficient drainage.

ACRAL LICK GRANULOMA

An acral lick is a reddened area on the skin devoid of hair. The cause is excessive licking by the pet. The area is simply licked excessively, resulting in a skin irritation. High-strung, nervous or bored dogs seem to have the most problems. This condition is similar to nail biting in humans. It is simply a habit and not a disease or disorder.

AREA AFFECTED
BY PUPPY ACNE

2-9 PUPPY ACNE

What are the symptoms?

The pet will have one or more areas of skin that appear raw with no hair covering. The lesion may even be thickened. Most frequently the lesions are found on the top of the front legs or about the hock area of the rear leg. These areas are easy to lick, especially when the pet is lying down.

What are the risks?

Acral lick granulomas pose no health risk whatsoever. The main concern is that they appear unsightly, but they do not harm the pet. Rarely, if ever, do they become infected.

What is the treatment?

The initial cause, if there is one, is rarely known. It is more of a habit than a medical problem. The treatment therefore must be aimed at the mind, not the lesion. Occasionally bandaging the area may help create a physical barrier, but is seldom a long-term solution. Cortisone creams may help, but again are not usually curative. DMSO (dimethyl sulfoxide) solution works on some dogs, as do commonly prepared bitters, such as apple and orange, that may help discourage licking. It is best if the pet can be distracted by providing chews, toys and treats to chew on rather than the skin.

Puppy Acne (Impetigo)

This skin infection is usually seen in puppies less than one year of age. The areas most often involved are the chin and/or abdomen. (See figure 2-9.)

What are the symptoms?

In the dog, acne is the term used to describe small white pustules usually located on the lower chin. These may actually form a whitehead and drain, much like acne in humans. Impetigo is used to describe small areas of infection found on the hairless area of the abdomen (belly).

What are the risks?

As in humans, acne in puppies seldom creates more than a localized area of infection. It is not life threatening, but can be irritating and itchy, causing the puppy to scratch excessively.

What is the treatment?

No matter where the pustules are located, the treatment is the same. Hydrogen peroxide or benzoyl peroxide applied twice daily will usually clear the condition. Excellent benzoyl peroxide shampoos are available to treat this condition. In severe cases your veterinarian may prescribe antibiotics, either orally or as a cream. Most puppies actually outgrow the condition; however, in Doberman Pinschers, Bulldogs, Boxers and Chinese Shar Peis, the condition may persist into adulthood.

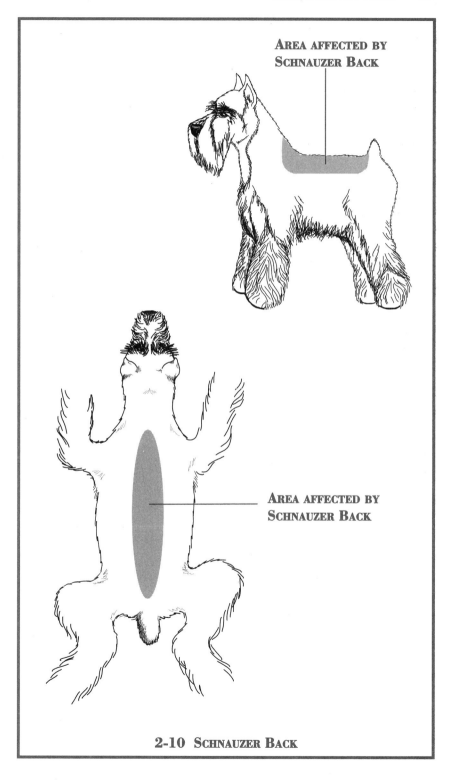

AREA AFFECTED BY
SCHNAUZER BACK

AREA AFFECTED BY
SCHNAUZER BACK

2-10 SCHNAUZER BACK

SCHNAUZER COMEDO SYNDROME (SCHNAUZER BACK)

This skin condition is seen in adult Miniature Schnauzers. Although other breeds may be involved, it is typically seen in Miniature Schnauzers, suggesting a genetic predisposition.

What are the symptoms?

Generally the area along the spine is the most affected. (See figure 2-10.) Raised, black, crusty bumps similar to "hives" will develop all along the back area. These may be up to one inch in diameter or longer. Patchy hair loss will be evident and the skin may become thickened and red. In some, the skin takes on an oily nature with a strong odor.

What are the risks?

Although not life threatening, this condition affects the appearance and smell of the animal.

What is the treatment?

Treatment is aimed at managing the condition; comedo syndrome usually persists in varying degrees for the life of the pet. Medicated shampoos such as tar/sulfur and benzoyl peroxide work well and should be used on a regular basis, often at least weekly. Although not usually curable, the condition can be successfully managed.

NUTRITIONAL DANDRUFF

This condition is characterized by excessively dry, flaky skin which can be the result of a zinc or fatty acid deficiency. Although not all cases of dandruff are caused by diet, most can be at least partially resolved with corrective nutrition. Both zinc and fatty acids are important to maintain proper skin.

What are the symptoms?

The symptoms include dry, flaky skin, dull hair coat and thin or brittle hair. The patient will usually itch as a result of dry skin with excessive flakiness.

What are the risks?

There is usually no serious medical risk; however, the patient may suffer from scaly, cracking skin. Additionally, the hair coat will be poor and not of good cosmetic appearance.

What is the treatment?

Nutritional supplements are available to help add oils back into the skin. Body chemistries differ, so not every patient will respond to nutritional therapy, but most will. Excellent balanced supplements are available that contain not only zinc and fatty acids, but other necessary vitamins as well. Fatty acid quality and digestibility varies greatly and one may need to try several different nutritional supplements before determining which is right for a particular patient.

SKIN CALLUS

Dogs, much like humans, develop calluses in areas of pressure. In the canine, calluses develop over bony areas such as the elbows and/or hocks. (See figure 2-11.) The weight of the body, when at rest, applies great pressure to the skin over these areas. Consequently, the skin will become thickened, rough and devoid of hair. Large dogs, particularly those sleeping on hard surfaces, tend to develop calluses at a young age, occasionally by a year old. With age, the calluses become harder and more pronounced.

What are the symptoms?

A circular area without hair develops on the outer surfaces of the elbows or hocks. Calluses may form in other areas, but the elbows are the most common sites. The calluses may become raw and occasionally will crack and bleed. *Calluses are frequently confused with or misdiagnosed as mange.* The location and skin scrapings will verify the diagnosis.

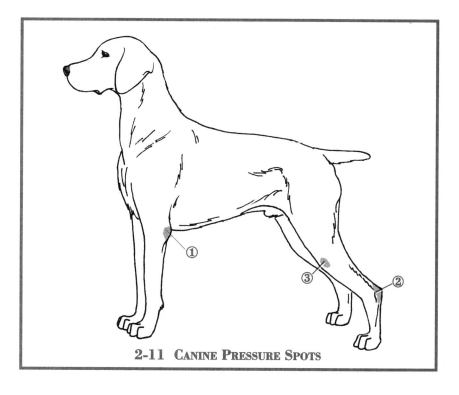

2-11 CANINE PRESSURE SPOTS

What are the risks?

Calluses do not present a medical risk. On very rare occasions, they may become infected, but these instances are minor. Calluses are considered normal in the canine.

What is the treatment?

Bandages on these areas are usually not practical. The calluses are normal and generally do not require medical treatment. Even with treatment, they will not go away. If they become cracked or irritated, antibiotic skin salves may help them heal. However, they will always be present.

COLLIE NOSE (NASAL SOLAR DERMATITIS)

"Collie nose" is used to describe a condition in which breeds with little or no pigment develop lesions, usually on the nose, eyelids and lips. The lesions are caused by a hypersensitivity to sunlight. Despite the term "Collie nose," breeds other than Collies are also involved, especially Shetland Sheepdogs. Collie nose definitely has an inherited component and is worse in areas with sunny climates. Sunlight is a triggering factor; however, the condition has a genetic predisposition.

What are the symptoms?

Usually the lesions appear as pink, raw areas about the nose and occasionally on the eyelids. (See figure 2-12.) The hypersensitive areas may actually ulcerate and develop a crusty scab-like covering. The condition may vary from mild irritation to severe ulcerating lesions that hemorrhage.

What are the risks?

Left untreated, severe discomfort can result. As the nasal tissues become deeply irritated, they may crack, bleed and impair breathing. All cases should begin treatment in the early stages. *Advanced stages may develop into a form of cancer which can be deadly.*

What is the treatment?

Before treatment can begin, this condition must be differentiated from various autoimmune disorders such as Lupus Erythematosus or skin cancer, which may cause similar lesions. Biopsies are usually warranted to help confirm the diagnosis.

Collie nose can be managed several ways; however, a complete cure is seldom attained. Exposure to sunlight should be kept to a minimum. Sunscreen lotions help, but have limited effectiveness due to a canine's licking behavior. The treatment of choice is tattooing. A permanent black ink is tattooed into the affected areas. The black ink serves as a shield against sunlight. It is best if young dogs with lightly pigmented noses are tattooed before any lesions develop.

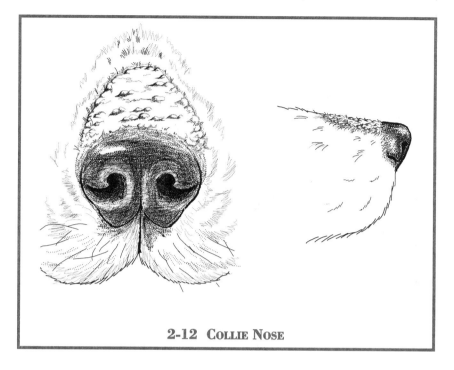

2-12 COLLIE NOSE

INFECTIONS OF THE SKIN

The skin, being the outermost covering of the body, can occasionally be invaded by organisms, both **bacterial** and **fungal**. Bacteria belonging to the genus Staphylococcus are frequent pathogens. In addition to bacteria, various fungi can invade the skin. Fungi affecting the skin are termed "ringworm" because the lesions appear circular. There actually is no worm involved.

What are the symptoms?

A patient suffering from a skin infection will generally have areas of hair loss with small to large scabs. Ringworm lesions are usually circular and dry, whereas bacterial infections often vary from numerous small lesions similar to acne, to large diffuse areas affecting only the hair follicles.

What are the risks?

All cases of skin infection should be treated at once. There always is the potential for the organisms to enter the deeper skin layers, causing severe illness. The zoonosis of ringworm and some bacterial conditions shows that they can be spread to humans.

What is the treatment?

Skin biopsies, coupled with cultures and sensitivities, are very important in determining the exact cause. Without these, treatment is often no more than a hopeful shot in the dark. Ringworm must be differentiated from bacteria, as they respond to different medications. Oral antibiotics will be required to kill bacteria, including staph. Antifungal dips with or without oral medications will be necessary to treat ringworm.

TUMORS AND CYSTS OF THE SKIN AND UNDERLYING TISSUE

Tumors of the skin and underlying tissue are common in the canine. Most are benign and present no significant health risk. There are, however, more severe types of skin cancer. The common tumors are discussed here.

SEBACEOUS CYSTS

These are the most common skin cysts encountered in dogs. The canine's skin, especially along the dorsal (neck and back) area, contains many glands called sebaceous glands. (See figure 2-13.) These glands arise from the deep layers of tissue and open by tiny pores to the skin surface.

Sebaceous glands provide oils, called sebum, for the hair coat and skin. Sebum is needed to keep the skin surface lubricated and moist. Occasionally the tiny pores that open to the skin surface become clogged. The glands continue to produce oils and they swell in size, forming a lump in the skin. This lump is called a sebaceous cyst. Sebaceous cysts are not life threatening; however, they may become as large as an orange, causing pain and discomfort, and can become infected with various bacterial organisms. Surgical removal is the treatment of choice.

LIPOMAS—FATTY TUMORS

These are not really skin tumors, but arise from the fatty tissue beneath the skin layers. They are discussed here because they must be differentiated from the more serious skin cancers. Lipomas are very frequently encountered in middle-aged and older patients. They are most common along the rib cage and chest area. They vary from marble-sized to as large as a basketball. Small fatty tumors are generally left untreated. Larger fatty tumors, especially if located where the leg joins the body, may interfere with normal movement. Surgery is the best option, at which time the tumor can be completely removed. Fatty tumors generally do not spread to other organs and pose little health risk.

DERMOID CYSTS

Dermoid cysts are small benign cysts encountered in younger dogs. They arise from the dermis layer and are generally covered with hair.

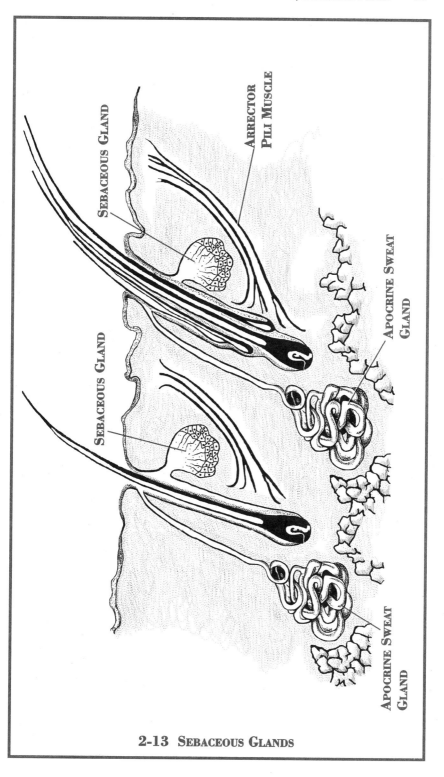

2-13 SEBACEOUS GLANDS

Boxers and Rhodesian Ridgebacks have a higher incidence than other breeds, suggesting an inherited component. Usually these are left untreated; however, they can be removed surgically. They pose no health threat.

PERIANAL ADENOMAS

Perianal adenomas are tumors arising from the glands around the anus. They often bleed and look like a small clump of grapes immediately next to the anus. Generally they are not life threatening; however, they can be very irritating and cause intermittent bleeding. They should be surgically removed when first encountered; however, regrowth is likely. Neutering (castration) of the male dog while young will usually prevent these from forming. Neutering of older dogs will in some instances slow the regrowth. Occasionally hormones such as estrogens are administered to decrease the recurrence.

PAPILLOMAS (WARTS)

As in humans, many dogs develop small skin nodules called warts. They most frequently develop in older patients, especially on the muzzle, head and back. Poodles have a higher incidence than other breeds. No treatment is necessary unless the warts ulcerate and cause discomfort. In these cases they can be surgically removed.

SQUAMOUS CELL CARCINOMA

This is a malignant form of skin cancer which can cause serious health problems. This skin tumor will grow, ulcerate and cause considerable discomfort. In some instances, it can spread to other organs such as the lungs and liver. However, this is relatively rare. Surgical removal is the treatment of choice. If surgery is not curative, then chemotherapeutic agents and/or radiation therapy may be required.

DISORDERS OF THE HAIR

In some instances the skin may be relatively normal, but the hair coat thins. **Alopecia** is the term used to describe a hair loss.

BLUE DOBERMAN SYNDROME (COLOR MUTANT ALOPECIA)

This is an example of color mutant hair loss. It affects blue Doberman Pinschers and sometimes red ones. Despite the name, other breeds can have a hair loss linked to coat color. Most notable are blue Chows Chows, Dachshunds, Whippets, Standard Poodles and Great Danes.

What are the symptoms?

Most color mutant canines are born with (except for color) a normal-appearing coat. As they grow and mature, they develop brittle hair, followed by patchy hair loss sometimes referred to as a "moth-eaten" coat. Only the blue portions of the coat are affected, other colored areas remaining normal.

What are the risks?

Initially the patient will appear quite normal, but with a thin coat in the blue areas. As the condition advances, the skin also becomes involved and becomes very dry, scaly and itchy.

What is the treatment?

The condition is incurable; however, treatment may help alleviate some of the symptoms. *Thyroid hormone supplementation* will help some patients even though their thyroid is functioning normally. High levels of zinc supplementation have been reported to alleviate some scaling. Medicated shampoos such as benzoyl peroxide and tar/sulfur products will help reduce scaling and itching.

DISORDERS OF THE NAILS

The **nails of the canine are basically extensions of the skin**. Nails are composed of cornified epithelial cells arising from the ungual crest. (See figure 2-14.)

TORN NAIL

The nails of dogs frequently become traumatized from breakage. Patients commonly catch a nail in rugs, carpets, decks, etc., and the nail can actually be broken or torn.

What are the symptoms?

A torn nail will usually be intensely painful. All limping dogs should first be examined for a traumatized nail. If the nail is torn near the base (by the toe), one may see bleeding, sometimes profuse.

What are the risks?

Torn nails may bleed profusely for short periods of time; however, they are not serious. Only rarely do infections develop.

What is the treatment?

Generally the fractured nail is removed entirely. Anesthesia may be required in some patients. Hemorrhage should be controlled either with styptic powder, bandage or cautery. As intense as the bleeding may seem, the normal dog will not lose a significant amount of blood. Once the nail is

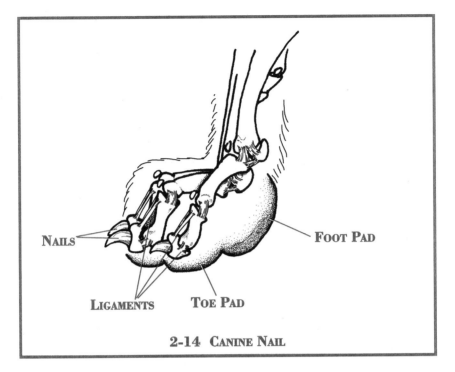

NAILS

FOOT PAD

LIGAMENTS   TOE PAD

2-14 CANINE NAIL

removed, healing will begin. Eventually a new nail will regrow. This may take months.

ONYCHOMYCOSIS

Occasionally a patient will be examined suffering from a fungus infection of the nail and/or toe. This is termed onychomycosis.

What are the symptoms?

Usually every toe on the foot is involved and occasionally all four feet. Where the nail meets the body, a thick crust will form and may ooze or bleed. The patient may or may not limp. In advanced cases the nail will grow in a deformed fashion and will be soft or spongy.

What are the risks?

Left untreated, the fungus (ringworm) can spread throughout the skin, posing a severe health threat. Some forms of ringworm can also be spread to humans. *Once diagnosed, treatment should commence at once.*

What is the treatment?

A fungal culture usually is performed to confirm the diagnosis. Treatment is best accomplished with long-term oral antifungal medication. Ketoconzole (Nizoral) tablets have been widely used. Antifungal lotions or creams may work in minor cases where only one toe is involved.

The Nervous System

INTRODUCTION

The nervous system forms a complex network of electrical transmissions similar to a computer. Electrical impulses travel through **nerve fibers** which deliver messages to, and control functions of, other cells and organs within the body. Chemical reactions are also utilized for communication between different **nerve cells** and other tissues they communicate with.

In the canine, the nervous system is divided into several segments. The **central nervous system (CNS)** is made up of the brain, brain stem and spinal cord. (See figure 3-1.) The **peripheral nervous system (PNS)** includes the nerves that run from the brain to areas of the head and neck, and also those nerves exiting and entering the spinal cord. These nerves carry messages from the CNS to other body areas. Nerve impulses travel from the brain down the spinal cord, out the peripheral nerves, to the tissues and back again. (See figure 3-2.)

Peripheral nerves that go from the brain or spinal cord are called motor nerves as they affect muscles, i.e., they control movements, posture and reflexes. Peripheral nerves that return to the brain or spinal cord are referred to as sensory nerves as they carry information from the body's structures back to the central nervous system.

Another set of nerves comprises the **autonomic nervous system (ANS).** The ANS (which arises from the CNS) contains nerves which control involuntary movements of organs such as the intestines, heart, blood vessels, bladder, etc. Canines have no voluntary control over the autonomic nervous system; it functions automatically.

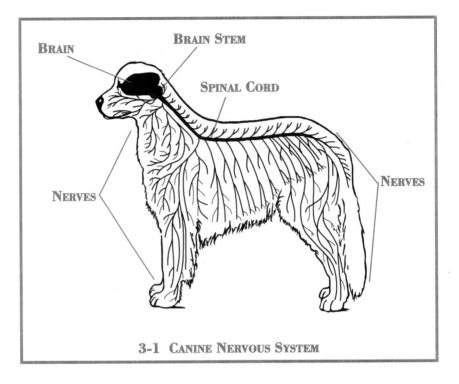

3-1 CANINE NERVOUS SYSTEM

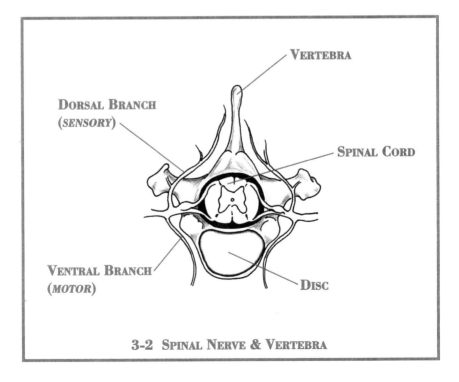

3-2 SPINAL NERVE & VERTEBRA

HEAD TRAUMA

In the canine, trauma to the head can result from automobile accidents, falling, being struck by an object, etc. Neurologically, the main problem is an injury to the brain.

What are the symptoms?

Damage to the brain may be mild or severe; hence the symptoms may vary. Additionally, different areas of the brain are responsible for different functions. An injury to one area will affect the patient in one way, whereas injury to another area will probably have a completely different result even in the same dog. (See figure 3-3.)

There is a wide range of symptoms that indicate injury to the brain has occurred. **Nystagmus** is a term used to describe rapid, uncontrolled eye movements. The eyes will appear similar to those of a person who is looking rapidly and repeatedly from side to side without moving the head. Nystagmus indicates a problem with the brain. **Anisocoria** is a term used to describe a patient having one large pupil and one smaller. In other words, the eyes are not functioning together. This can also indicate a problem within the brain. Pinpoint pupils or an extreme reduction in the size of the pupillary opening typically indicates a concussion of the brain.

Head tilt is another indicator that something may be wrong with the brain. If a canine receives injury to the left side of the brain, then the head may tilt to the left. Circling is yet another indicator of a possible brain injury. The pet will walk in small tight circles and circle towards the damaged side. In some cases, head tilt and circling will be seen simultaneously. Seizures or convulsions commonly are noted when the brain is damaged or irritated. In severe injuries, the patient may actually lie unconscious or be in a comatose state. In very mild injuries, there may be no noticeable signs. A headache in a dog would probably go unnoticed.

Regardless of which signs are observed, they rarely indicate the seriousness of the injury, and do not relate to the probability of recovery.

What are the risks?

Trauma to the brain is always serious. Damage to the brain tissue may be transient or permanent. Death can easily result if the condition is left untreated.

What is the treatment?

Always see your veterinarian at once if damage to the brain is suspected. Your veterinarian will administer drugs such as dexamethazone (an injectable steroid) and/or mannitol (an intravenously administered sugar solution that draws excess fluid from the central nervous system) to minimize brain swelling and inflammation.

Rest is also important. Generally if brain damage occurs, the healing process can and probably will take weeks to months to complete. It is usually very difficult to predict the final outcome when the patient is first examined. In a few cases it may take months before a veterinarian can predict if the patient will recover completely or to what extent recovery will take place.

Tumors of the Brain and Spinal Cord

Tumors of the central nervous system are rare, but occasionally a patient is diagnosed with brain cancer.

What are the symptoms?
The symptoms are much like those of a brain injury except they develop slowly over time and usually progress despite treatment. Typically tumors of the brain or spinal cord are fatal. An accurate diagnosis is finally made from sophisticated tests and not clinical signs.

What are the risks?
In all cases, tumors of the brain and spinal cord are serious and life threatening. Early treatment should be sought.

What is the treatment?
In the dog, rarely does medical treatment provide a cure for cancer involving the brain or spinal cord. It may control clinical signs, but the disease still progresses. Most university veterinary hospitals have a doctor on staff specializing in this area. Consultation with a specialist is advised. In these types of institutions, surgery may be done, but the prognosis is still very poor.

Infections of the Brain, the Spinal Cord and Related Structures

Infections of brain are called **encephalitis**, while those that involve the spinal cord are referred to as **myelitis**. A tough protective layer of connective tissue called the **meninges** covers the central nervous system. An infection of this tissue is termed **meningitis**.

An infection of the central nervous system can involve any or all of these structures. Many different viruses and bacteria can enter the central nervous tissue and cause an infection. The most notable central nervous system diseases are rabies, distemper, parvovirus and Rocky Mountain Spotted Fever. The first three are viruses while the latter is a bacteria.

Bacteria that are more typically associated with infections in other areas of the body, such as Staphylococcus, Streptococcus, E. coli, Pseudomonas, etc. can also infect areas of the central nervous system.

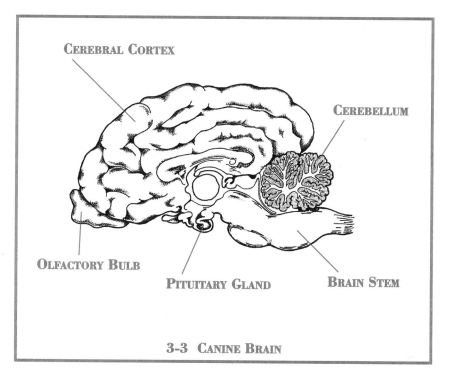

CEREBRAL CORTEX

CEREBELLUM

OLFACTORY BULB

PITUITARY GLAND

BRAIN STEM

3-3 CANINE BRAIN

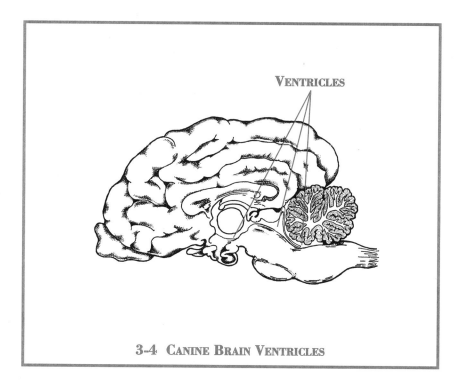

VENTRICLES

3-4 CANINE BRAIN VENTRICLES

What are the symptoms?

Symptoms vary greatly, but may include fever, disorientation, confusion, blindness, staggering, vomiting, seizures and loss of consciousness.

What are the risks?

All instances of a central nervous tissue infection are serious. Death will likely result if left untreated. If suspected, call a veterinarian at once.

What is the treatment?

With any central nervous system infection, the affected tissue is irritated and swollen. This swelling can cause irreversible damage because these tissues are encased within the skull and back bones. As the nervous tissue expands, individual cells are damaged or destroyed as they are crushed against the surrounding bone.

Therefore, in all cases of central nervous system infection much of the therapy is aimed at controlling the swelling of the tissues. Intravenous solutions, such as mannitol, or corticosteroids are used. Whenever a bacterial infection is present, as in the case of Rocky Mountain Spotted Fever (that is caused by a rickettsial bacterium), high levels of antibiotics are used. There are no specific medications that can eliminate or destroy viruses and these must therefore be allowed to run their course (with the exception of rabies).

The patient will be supported with intravenous fluids, often nourished through feeding tubes and protected from alterations in body temperature. Because of the human risk of rabies and other organisms causing infections of the central nervous system, treatment must always be weighed against the probability of cure and the risk of infection to others.

HYDROCEPHALY

Hydrocephaly is a congenital condition in which excessive fluid is found within and around the brain. Within the brain are fluid-filled spaces called **ventricles**. (See figure 3-4.) In a hydrocephalic patient, the ventricles contain too much fluid, become swollen and the increased pressure damages and/or prevents development of brain tissue. The body may form too much fluid or, as occurs in most cases, the fluid that is produced cannot drain from the central nervous system as it normally does. Toy breeds such as Maltese, Yorkshire Terriers, Pomeranians, and Chihuahuas are commonly affected. It does occur in other breeds as well.

What are the symptoms?

Generally the patient is young, usually less than four months of age, when first diagnosed. The head takes on a dome-shaped appearance and the skull bones at the top of the head fail to close. This is termed "open fontanel" and a soft spot may be noticed on the top of the head. The affected patient may be blind, have seizures or have an altered gait. Different levels of severity exist.

What are the risks?

In the canine, the hydrocephalus patient typically has a very limited life span. Severity differs, but few dogs with this condition live to be over two years of age.

What is the treatment?

Most cases go untreated. Veterinary neurologists can be consulted and occasionally the excess fluid can be drained. However, the patient rarely will live a normal life. Treatment is often unsuccessful and expensive. *Hydrocephaly is a congenital disease and dogs with this condition should be removed from any breeding program.*

SEIZURE DISORDERS

Any insult to the brain such as trauma, infection or drug overdose can cause a seizure. Most instances of seizures in the canine are not due to any detectable cause and are termed **idiopathic epilepsy.** Generally, veterinarians refer to the condition only as epilepsy. The exact cause of this epilepsy is not known, but whether the cause is unknown or trauma-induced, the condition results in an uncoordinated firing of the neurons (nerves) within the brain. Normally the neurons transmit impulses in a uniform or coordinated fashion, allowing precise and timed movements and thoughts.

During an epileptic seizure, the neurons are functioning independently of each other; therefore there is no coordinated effort. Patients may lose consciousness or be unaware of their surroundings and have rapid, uncoordinated body movements.

While some epilepsy may be the result of trauma, infections, etc., most canine epileptics are believed to have inherited this condition from their parents. It has a much higher incidence in certain lines of several breeds.

What are the symptoms?

Normally the epileptic patient will have the first seizure between two and three years of age. This may vary, but *seldom is epilepsy seen in the very young.* Seizures will vary in severity and are usually described utilizing three terms; petit mal, grand mal, and status epilepticus.

Petit mal seizures are the mild form. The patient may simply develop a blank stare, shake one leg or cry out as if in pain. The seizure length is usually less than one minute. The **grand mal** seizure is the most common. This seizure is characterized by the following: the patient will fall to one side, urinate or defecate uncontrollably, paddle the feet as if swimming, froth at the mouth and may cry out. This patient will be unaware of surrounding activities. Grand mal seizures usually last five minutes or less. **Status epilepticus** is the most severe form. It appears exactly like a grand mal seizure, but it may last for hours or more; or, as soon as the dog seems to recover, it immediately degenerates back into the seizure.

What are the risks?

Epilepsy is a chronic disorder and usually not curable, but it can be controlled. The petit and grand mal seizures, in most cases, are not life threatening unless they occur at a time when the dog could be in danger. For instance, a swimming patient that suffers a seizure may drown.

Status epilepticus is a very serious seizure state. With the body convulsing violently for hours, the internal body temperature will become critically high. Organ damage and death can result. All seizure instances, when first noted, should be reported to your veterinarian; however, therapy is not always indicated.

What is the treatment?

In most instances epilepsy is not life threatening unless status epilepticus develops. Anticonvulsant medications are used in chronic cases. *It must be completely understood that drug therapy is not a total cure*, but rather controls the severity and frequency of the seizures. Anticonvulsant drugs include phenobarbital, Dilantin, Primidone and others. These drugs provide a sedative action on the nerves within the brain.

The goal of therapy is to stabilize the nerves and membranes within the brain, but not to a point where the patient appears or acts sedated. Generally, anticonvulsant drugs are not given unless the patient has more than one seizure per month or the seizures last more than half an hour. This is a general guideline only. Known epileptic dogs should not be bred, as epilepsy can run in genetic lines.

HERNIATED DISC (SLIPPED OR RUPTURED DISC)

As in humans, the canine **vertebrae**, which extend from the skull through the tail, are separated from one another by flexible cartilaginous **discs.** (See figure 3-5.) These discs provide a cushioning effect and permit the neck, spine and tail to bend, allowing changes in positioning and posture. Above the discs and running through the bony vertebrae is the **spinal cord.** The spinal cord extends from the brain and ends in the sacral area, near the base of the tail.

As the cartilaginous discs become weakened from age, disease or trauma, they may herniate or rupture, causing portions of disc to protrude upwards, placing pressure upon the spinal cord. This pressure may cause

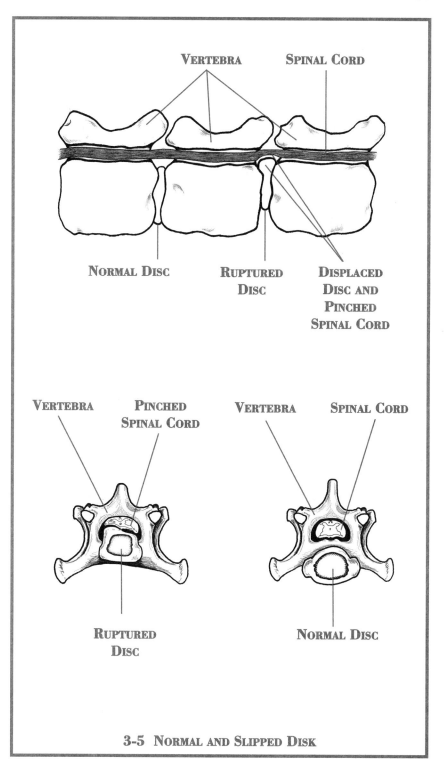

VERTEBRA   SPINAL CORD

NORMAL DISC   RUPTURED DISC   DISPLACED DISC AND PINCHED SPINAL CORD

VERTEBRA   PINCHED SPINAL CORD

VERTEBRA   SPINAL CORD

RUPTURED DISC

NORMAL DISC

3-5 NORMAL AND SLIPPED DISK

damage to the spinal cord and/or prevent nerve transmission through it. When a disc herniates, the damage to the cord may be severe or very slight depending on the extent of the abnormal disc movement. Any injury to the spinal cord can result in pain, weakness or paralysis. Also, the location of the disc disease will affect the cord differently. A disc herniation in the neck (cervical) area will affect the entire body from the neck down. A herniated disc in the lower back (lumbar) area will only affect the rear limbs and loin or hip area. Severe cases affect the dog's control over urination and defecation as well. Breeds with very long backs, such as Dachshunds, have a greater incidence of **lumbar disc disease** than other breeds. Similarly, Beagles tend to have a higher occurrence of herniated discs in the neck (cervical) area.

What are the symptoms?

When a disc herniates, it causes intense pain. Patients with herniation in the neck (cervical) area will hold the head lower than normal, not be willing to flex it upwards or from side to side, and may have difficulty eating. A severe herniation in the neck area can cause enough damage to the cord to cause complete paralysis in all four limbs.

The most common disc herniation occurs in the lumbar (back) area. Generally these patients will hump their backs in response to the pain. In severe lumbar disc herniations, the rear limbs will be partially or completely paralyzed. Depending on the degree of damage to the cord, this may be temporary or permanent. Nerves to the anus and bladder may also be affected.

As you can see, the symptoms very greatly depending on the location and extent of disc herniation.

What are the risks?

Injuries to the spinal cord are always serious. Complete or partial paralysis can result. The risks of long-term irreversible paralysis are greatly reduced if treatment begins at once, i.e., within hours. Spinal injuries are an emergency.

What is the treatment?

Treatment almost always involves the use of anti-inflammatories such as cortisones. These medications cause the herniated disc and swollen tissue to shrink and relieve swelling and inflammation within the spinal cord. Surgery to remove the disc or surrounding bone is a viable option; however, it is best if surgery is performed within the first 24 hours following the injury. The recovery period may take from weeks to months. *In severe disc herniations, a full or even partial recovery will not always be possible.* The degree of recovery is never predicted and only time will reveal the extent of a recovery.

WOBBLER SYNDROME

This is caused by a malformation of the vertebrae within the neck. The **spinal canal** is the opening within the vertebrae in which the **spinal cord** lies. In affected dogs, this opening is smaller than normal, causing pressure on the spinal cord. This prevents neural impulses from passing through the spinal cord. (See figure 3-6.) Additionally, as the animal matures, the space within the vertebrae continues to shrink in relation to the spinal cord. Instability between the individual neck vertebrae is generally noted in addition to the narrowing of the spinal canal. As a result, this disease has several names, among them **cervical vertebral instability** and **cervical spondylomyelopathy**. Any breed can be affected; however, over 80 percent of all cases reported are in Great Danes and Doberman Pinschers. *Genetics definitely play a role.*

What are the symptoms?

Usually symptoms appear before four years of age and on average, earlier in Great Danes than in Dobermans. An unwillingness to bend the neck is usually the first sign, followed by weakness and lack of coordination in the rear limbs, progressing to weakness in the front limbs as well.

What are the risks?

This condition is always serious and can progress to complete paralysis. A veterinary examination should be performed at once in animals of these breeds showing the above signs.

What is the treatment?

Occasionally anti-inflammatory medications provide relief, but they do not correct the abnormal spinal canal within the vertebrae. Surgery can be performed to stabilize the vertebrae and/or to remove a portion of the vertebrae, allowing more room for the spinal cord. A full recovery is not always achieved.

GERMAN SHEPHERD DOG PROGRESSIVE MYELOPATHY (DEGENERATIVE MYELOPATHY)

This disorder is characterized by a progressive degeneration of the spinal cord. It is not known why this occurs; however, almost all instances occur in the German Shepherd breed. Most patients are over five years of age.

What are the symptoms?

Patients present with a weakness of the limbs. The weakness often presents itself in the front limbs, and progresses to affect the rear legs. The condition is progressive; eventually the patient may not be able to bear weight on the rear limbs.

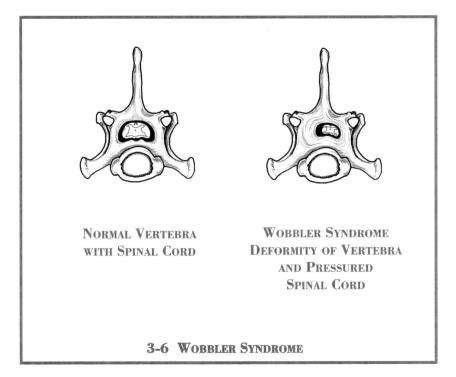

NORMAL VERTEBRA
WITH SPINAL CORD

WOBBLER SYNDROME
DEFORMITY OF VERTEBRA
AND PRESSURED
SPINAL CORD

3-6 WOBBLER SYNDROME

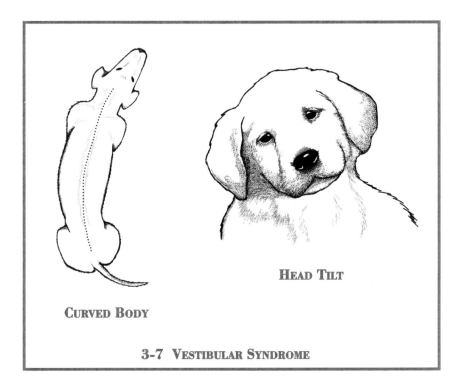

CURVED BODY

HEAD TILT

3-7 VESTIBULAR SYNDROME

What are the risks?

The condition is progressive with no complete cure. Eventually the patient will be unable to walk and function normally. The progression may, however, take years.

What is the treatment?

There is no proven treatment. The progression has been slowed in some patients by administering a drug called E-aminocaproic acid, or EACA (Amicar, Lederle). The drug, however, is expensive. Increasing exercise is beneficial. B-complex vitamins may help some patients. Even with treatment, a slow progression of the disease is expected.

DISORDERS OF THE NERVES

As with the central nervous system, there are various conditions which can affect the nerves once they leave the brain or spinal cord.

VESTIBULAR SYNDROME

Vestibular syndrome is a term used to describe a patient having difficulty with balance. A lesion on the brain, on the nerves exiting the brain or on structures within the inner ear are the most common causes.

Specifically, the **eighth cranial nerve** is the nerve responsible for balance (equilibrium). The eighth cranial nerve exits the brain and communicates with the **inner ear**. Any abnormality involving the **middle** or **inner ear** can cause a disruption of this nerve, thereby disturbing balance. Certain drugs can also cause a deterioration of the eighth cranial nerve. Therefore the causes of vestibular syndrome may be infections, tumors, trauma, drugs and in some instances, a deterioration of the brain itself. Most cases are either inflammatory or infectious in nature.

What are the symptoms?

Usually the patient has a **loss of equilibrium** (balance). **Head tilt and walking in a circle** may be present. (See figure 3-7.) The eyes may also move in a back-and-forth, uncoordinated fashion (**nystagmus**). Frequently these signs are confused with or compared to a stroke as it occurs in humans, but these are two totally different conditions. That of humans is related to ruptured blood vessels within the brain, while Vestibular syndrome of the dog is caused by abnormalities with the ear or the nerve going to it.

What are the risks?

As stated, there is a multitude of abnormalities that may cause a vestibular syndrome. If a malignant tumor is the cause, death may eventually result.

Most cases, however, are due to infections or inflammations of the ear. These are generally treatable and recovery is expected.

What is the treatment?
One must first attempt to isolate the cause. Vestibular syndrome caused by ear infections or inflammations generally responds well to oral antibiotics and/or anti-inflammatories such as cortisone. Recovery may take several weeks and recurrence is common. Cases involving tumors may require surgery and a full recovery is not usually expected.

POLYRADICULONEURITIS (COON HOUND PARALYSIS)

Polyradiculoneuritis is a neurologic disease seen in all breeds, but most commonly in those involved in raccoon hunting. The complete cause is unknown; however, it sometimes follows the bite of a raccoon. Some dogs seem to be immune while others are not. The raccoon saliva is the suspected cause, but why remains a mystery. Other cases occur without any known exposure to raccoons or their bites.

What are the symptoms?
Generally the symptoms begin to develop about seven to ten days after a raccoon bite. The legs become weak and the rear limbs have an exaggerated reflex. The weakness progresses rapidly until the legs become limp and the patient is unable to walk.

What are the risks?
Most patients recover; however, this may take up to three months.

What is the treatment?
Treatment involves good nursing care until the patient recovers on its own. The affected pet must be hand fed and sanitation becomes a chore. No drugs are beneficial.

TICK PARALYSIS

This is a paralyzing condition attributed to ticks. Wood ticks are the most common cause. Saliva of wood ticks contain a neurotoxin that once injected into the canine can cause a paralysis. It is not known why some dogs are immune and others are not.

What are the symptoms?
Symptoms begin as a lack of coordination progressing within seventy-two hours to paralysis.

What are the risks?

In severe cases involving paralysis of the chest muscles, death due to suffocation may result. All suspected cases should be treated immediately to halt progression. Most patients recover fully with proper treatment.

What is the treatment?

Treatment involves the immediate removal of all visible ticks. Insecticides (tick-killing products) should be applied to kill all ticks not seen. Animals in respiratory distress will need assisted ventilation. Once ticks are removed, a complete recovery is expected within three days.

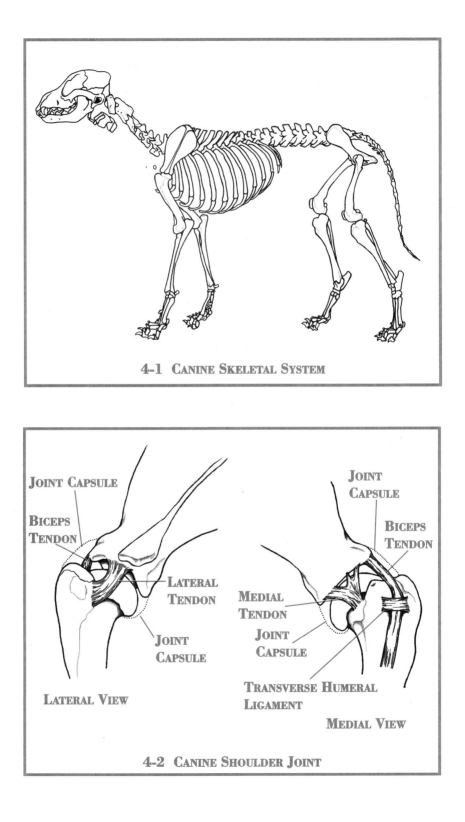

4-1 CANINE SKELETAL SYSTEM

JOINT CAPSULE

BICEPS TENDON

LATERAL TENDON

JOINT CAPSULE

LATERAL VIEW

JOINT CAPSULE

BICEPS TENDON

MEDIAL TENDON

JOINT CAPSULE

TRANSVERSE HUMERAL LIGAMENT

MEDIAL VIEW

4-2 CANINE SHOULDER JOINT

Bones, Joints, Muscles, Ligaments and Tendons

INTRODUCTION

The skeletal system and its interconnecting tissues—the muscles, ligaments and tendons—compose the bulk of the dog's body mass. Between many bones are complex areas of articulation. Each of these areas forms a joint.

Allowing for variations in tail length, there is an average of **319 bones** in the canine skeleton. (See figure 4-1.) Bones are complex, rigid, living organs that have their own supply of blood vessels and nerves.

They are composed of minerals, especially calcium and phosphorus. They provide both the framework for the body and protection for many delicate organs and structures. For example, the bones of the skull protect the brain and eyes while the breast plate (sternum) helps protect the heart and lungs. Other bones, such as those of the limbs, function to provide support and locomotion. Bones of the internal ear structures function for neither protection nor support, but rather in sound transmission, allowing the dog to hear.

Muscles primarily bring about movement of all or a part of the dog's body. *Smooth muscles* are found within the internal organs such as the intestines, stomach and bladder. These are not subject to voluntary or conscious control by the individual. They function automatically to satisfy the body's needs. *Striated muscles* are predominantly attached to the skeleton. All of their movements are under the conscious control of the individual.

They are involved with such things as walking, eating, wagging the tail, moving the eyes, etc. The *skeletal or striated* muscles will be discussed in the remainder of this chapter. *One half of the dog's total weight is skeletal muscle.*

Skeletal muscles are connected to the bones by tough fibrous bands called **tendons**. Tendons begin on a muscle and end on a bone. A good example is the Achilles tendon, which connects the muscle of the lower rear limb (calf) to the bones forming the ankle.

Ligaments connect bone to bone and are generally found spanning across joints. **Joints** are places where two bones meet or articulate with their ends covered by a layer of smooth cartilage. A joint by itself is not considered an organ. It consists of bones, muscles, ligaments, cartilage and a lubricating joint fluid all enclosed by a tough joint capsule. (See figure 4-2.)

DISORDERS OF THE BONES AND JOINTS

Bones and joints frequently are damaged or become diseased. Even normal aging can have a profound effect on the joints. Arthritis is an example of a disease that can actually be a normal component of aging.

OSTEOCHONDRITIS DISSECANS (OCD)

This describes a condition in which joint cartilage develops abnormally. Normally, the cartilage within a joint covers the ends of the bone where they may have contact with each other.

In OCD, the joint cartilage separates from the underlying bone, forming a rough, crater-like fault, thus preventing normal movement of the joint. (See figure 4-3.) The cause for the abnormal cartilage development is unknown; OCD may affect many joints including the shoulder, elbow and knee. The shoulder joint has the highest incidence. Large breeds are more commonly affected than small breeds.

What are the symptoms?
Lameness of the affected limb is almost always a sign not only of OCD, but other joint diseases as well. With OCD the lameness will be most pronounced upon or following exercise. This is usually first noticed at about six months of age.

What are the risks?
Dogs will not die from OCD; however, they will experience extreme pain while walking or running. Pieces of the diseased cartilage may actually break from the bone and float around within the joint. These free-floating

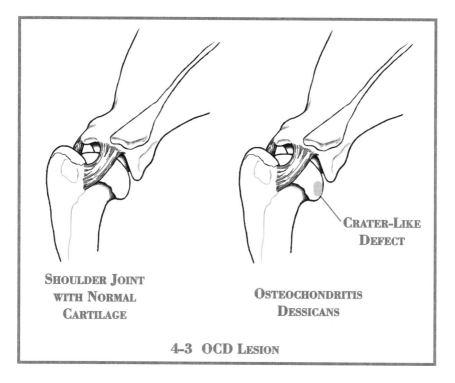

SHOULDER JOINT
WITH NORMAL
CARTILAGE

CRATER-LIKE
DEFECT

OSTEOCHONDRITIS
DESSICANS

4-3 OCD LESION

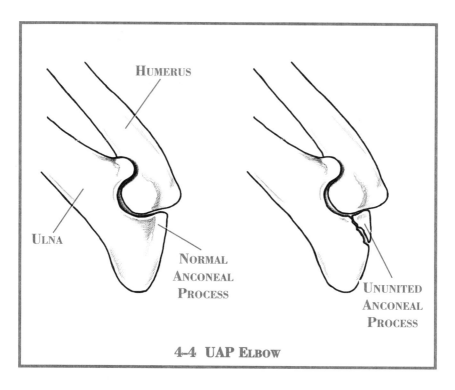

HUMERUS

ULNA

NORMAL
ANCONEAL
PROCESS

UNUNITED
ANCONEAL
PROCESS

4-4 UAP ELBOW

pieces of cartilage remain alive and grow in size. They are called joint mice. Joint mice interfere with normal movements and cause pain if caught between the two bones.

Left untreated, the joint will usually become very inflamed and small growths of bone called bone spurs will develop. As the animal ages the joint will become increasingly painful and immobile. There are some cases of OCD that do heal spontaneously on their own.

What is the treatment?
Usually an examination and radiographs (X rays) are needed to confirm the diagnosis. Occasionally with two to three weeks of strict rest, the abnormal cartilage will heal and become stable. Rest should be tried when OCD is first diagnosed. Most OCD cases will, however, require surgery. Surgery is utilized to remove the diseased cartilage and joint mice if present. Typically with surgery, the joint will heal and return to normal function. Surgery is most successful when performed early in the disease process.

UNUNITED ANCONEAL PROCESS (UAP)

UAP is a disorder of the elbow. A small bony process called the anconeal bone fails to unite and fuse with the ulna, the smaller of the bones making up the foreleg. (See figure 4-4.) Generally the anconeal bone and ulna fuse by five months of age. After this age, a lameness will develop if the anconeal bone remains separated. German Shepherd Dogs, Basset Hounds and Saint Bernards have the highest incidence. It is considered a genetically transmitted disorder and affected individuals should not be bred.

What are the symptoms?
This condition can affect one or both elbows. The patient will be lame on the involved limb(s). Additionally, the elbow may appear swollen and painful, especially when the leg is extended. Most cases are seen in young dogs between six and twelve months of age.

What are the risks?
Quite commonly, without treatment the joint will become severely painful and useless. The patient will walk on three legs, or not at all if both elbows are involved. The condition worsens with age, with severe arthritic changes occuring.

What is the treatment?
Radiographs (X rays) are needed to confirm the diagnosis. Once confirmed, surgery is generally recommended. Several surgical procedures can be used and generally the anconeal process is attached with screws or removed completely. Even with surgery, the function of the elbow joint is usually compromised to some degree.

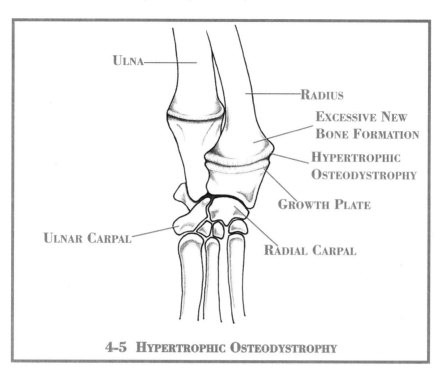

4-5 HYPERTROPHIC OSTEODYSTROPHY

HYPERTROPHIC OSTEODYSTROPHY (HOD)

This is a disease which occurs during the rapid growth phase of large dogs. (See figure 4-5.) The cause is unknown, but vitamin C metabolism may play a role. It must be noted, however, that this is not a lack of vitamin C, but possibly a metabolic problem in the way the body utilizes the vitamin.

What are the symptoms?
Affected puppies will become lame after three months of age. The long bones in the limbs will be painful and a fever may accompany the condition. One or all four legs may be involved.

What are the risks?
Discomfort and irregularly shaped bones are the most common result. The affected dog will never have normal use of the legs. Eventually complete inability to walk may develop.

What is the treatment?
There is no treatment for this disorder. Good supportive care will help comfort the patient.

EOSINOPHILIC PANOSTEITIS (EOPAN)

EOPAN is an inflammatory bone disease affecting young dogs usually between six and eighteen months of age. Large, rapidly growing breeds are the most frequently involved, especially German Shepherds. The cause is currently unknown.

What are the symptoms?

Generally an acute pain will develop over the long bones of the legs. The patient will limp on one or more limbs and a fever may be present. Sometimes the lameness will disappear only to return later in the same or a different leg. The animal tends to be in some pain when pressure is placed on the bony areas of the limb such as just below the knee or elbow.

What are the risks?

Most patients will eventually recover or "outgrow" the condition. Once the pain develops, however, it may persist for months unless a treatment is utilized. Many patients are in so much pain that it would be senseless not to commence treatment. Additionally, chronic bone inflammation may cause permanent damage to the bone surface.

What is the treatment?

Radiographs are typically utilized to confirm the diagnosis. Anti-inflammatory medications will generally allow a rapid recovery. Prednisone is the specific drug of choice and may need to be administered periodically until the patient matures.

HIP DYSPLASIA

Hip dysplasia is probably the most discussed hereditary disease in the dog. It is primarily a disorder of larger breeds and *genetics definitely plays a role*. There is no scientific evidence to prove otherwise.

Hip dysplasia actually is a term used to describe a poorly formed hip joint. The **ball and socket** of the hip are present, but they do not fit each other well. The ball (head) of the **femur** may be poorly shaped, being flattened rather than rounded. Additionally, the socket of the pelvic bone may be shallow, therefore not providing a smooth rounded surface for the ball. (See figure 4-6.)

Because the hip joint conformation is wrong, there will not be normal movement within this joint. The joint may become inflamed, with the secondary formation of bone spurs further restricting the ability to rotate. These arthritic changes progress over the life of the animal. One or both hips may be involved. *A dog with any degree of hip dysplasia, even mild, should never be bred.*

What are the symptoms?

A dog with hip dysplasia may initially appear normal; however, as the dog grows, lameness appears. Some patients have no symptoms at all. Most patients we see first presenting with noticeable signs are about eight

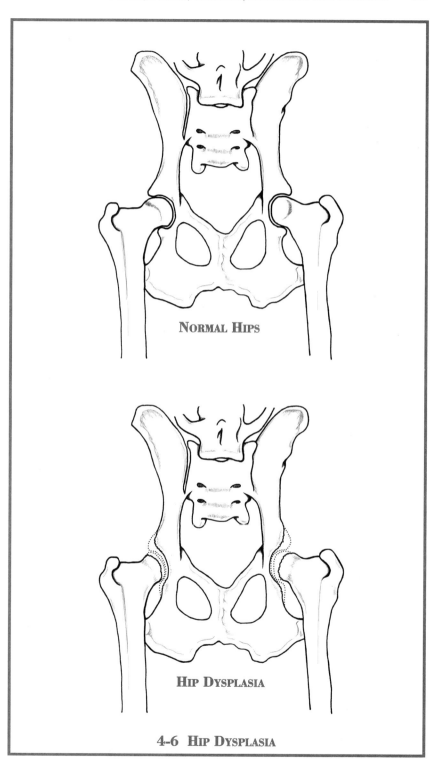

NORMAL HIPS

HIP DYSPLASIA

4-6 HIP DYSPLASIA

months of age. The patient may have difficulty getting up after lying down, avoid climbing stairways and/or be reluctant to play. It may cry from pain or walk stiff-legged in the rear when it first wakes up. After walking for several minutes it may appear normal. As the pet ages, the signs become more pronounced. Stiffness or pain in the rear limbs is the most common sign.

What is the treatment?

There is no real treatment for hip dysplasia. It is a genetic disorder of conformation. Fortunately there are several surgical procedures and medications to allow the patient to live a normal life, but the joint cannot be restored to normal. Three common surgical procedures have been utilized. A pectinomyotomy is one such procedure which involves surgically severing the pectineus muscle of the groin. This relaxes the pressure within the joint and allows easier rotation. Secondly, a synthetic ball and socket (prosthesis) can be placed in the joint to replace the malformed one. Probably the most utilized procedure is a femoral head and neck osteoectomy, which involves complete removal of the ball (femoral head) without replacement. A "false joint" will form as the muscles within the area strengthen, holding the leg in place, but allowing movement without any bone-to-bone articulation. The patient will do remarkably well. The femoral head osteoectomy is our choice of treatment for advanced cases.

More minor cases may simply be treated with anti-inflammatories such as cortisone to relieve the pain. Buffered aspirin can also be effective in patients mildly dysplastic. Nutrition and adequate vitamin C have been recommended by some as a treatment and/or preventative. Their benefits are not constant, but they appear to help some patients. Hip dysplasia is hereditary and patients afflicted should never be utilized in any breeding program.

DEGENERATIVE DISC DISEASE

See page 60.

CLEFT PALATE

This is a skeletal disorder occasionally seen in puppies of all breeds. A cleft palate results when the bones forming the roof of the mouth do not grow normally. This results in an opening in the roof of the mouth that communicates into the nasal cavity. (See figure 4-7.)

What are the symptoms?

Puppies as young as one day old will often have milk come out their noses as they nurse. They may also inhale milk into their lungs, causing a difficulty in breathing or even pneumonia. When the puppy's mouth is examined, a slit will be seen in the roof of the mouth.

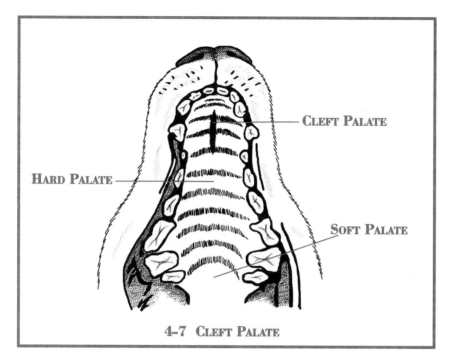

CLEFT PALATE

HARD PALATE

SOFT PALATE

4-7 CLEFT PALATE

What are the risks?

Most patients will die at an early age from pneumonia and/or malnourishment. The milk tends to enter the nasal passages and lungs rather than providing nourishment.

What is the treatment?

Mild openings in the mouth roof can be surgically corrected. More severe instances cannot. Frequently if the cleft palate cannot be surgically closed, euthanasia is advised.

OPEN FONTANELS

See Hydrocephaly in chapter 3, "The Nervous System," page 58.

LUXATED PATELLAS

The bone we know as the kneecap is also referred to as the patella. A groove in the distal femur allows the patella to glide up and down when the knee joint is bent back and forth. In so doing it guides the action of the quadricep muscle in the lower leg. The patella also provides bony protection for the knee joint. (See figure 4-8.) Occasionally because of malformation or trauma, the ridges forming the patellar groove are not prominent, creating too shallow a groove. In a patient with shallow grooves, the patella

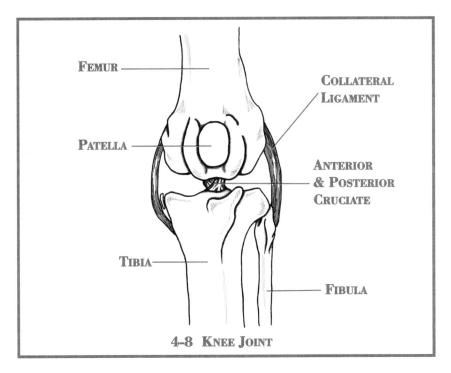

FEMUR

COLLATERAL
LIGAMENT

PATELLA

ANTERIOR
& POSTERIOR
CRUCIATE

TIBIA

FIBULA

4-8 KNEE JOINT

will luxate sideways, especially to the medial side, causing the leg to "lock up" with the foot held up off the ground. One or both knees may be involved. Smaller breeds of dogs, especially Miniature and Toy Poodles, have the highest incidence. Genetics can play a role.

What are the symptoms?
Most patients seen are middle-aged. They present with a history of an intermittent lameness on the affected rear leg(s). Patients commonly stop and cry out in pain as they are running. Their legs will be extended rearward and they are unable to flex them back into the normal position. The patella has actually flipped sideways outside of the groove and this prevents the leg from bending correctly.

What are the risks?
Uncorrected, the patellar ridges will wear, the groove will become even shallower and the patient will become progressively more lame. Arthritis will prematurely affect the joint, causing a permanently swollen knee with poor mobility.

What is the treatment?
Surgery is the treatment of choice. Surgically the patellar groove is deepened, preventing the sideways (luxating) movement of the patella. Additionally, sutures are placed to hold the patella in a more normal position.

Occasionally in pets with crooked legs (Basset Hounds), the patella may need to be surgically rotated to keep it more in line with the rest of the leg. Surgical correction generally has a good outcome and the patients lead a fairly normal life.

WOBBLER SYNDROME
See page 63.

OSTEOARTHRITIS
Osteoarthritis is generally referred to simply as arthritis. Osteoarthritis, technically speaking, is an inflammation of the bone structures of the joints. Many things, such as injury or infections, can cause arthritis; however, most cases are simply due to aging. This discussion is about osteoarthritis due to the normal aging process.

As a patient ages, the normally smooth cartilage surfaces of the joints erode and wear thin. As this erosion takes place, it is repaired by the body, causing an irregular surface to develop. These rough surfaces of the joint then cause pain and additional inflammation when the bones articulate with each other. Usually the large joints such as the shoulder, elbow, hip and ankle are the most frequently involved; however, all joints including those of the spine can be affected. The joints may become swollen. Generally some days the pain is worse than others, depending on the stress placed upon the joints. Obese patients tend to be affected the most, as the excess weight places a greater strain on these joints.

What are the symptoms?
Virtually every geriatric patient will have some degree of osteoarthritis; however, some will never show symptoms. As in humans, stiffness, pain and swelling of the joint areas are commonly noted. The pain may be chronic or intermittent, mild or severe. Osteoarthritis is progressive and the symptoms usually worsen with age.

What are the risks?
Osteoarthritis and its accompanying symptoms are not life threatening, but do progress throughout the animal's life. Many patients simply live within the limitations caused by the arthritis. Others with more severe pain may need some treatment to improve the quality of life.

What is the treatment?
In those patients experiencing pain, various anti-inflammatories have been successfully used. Buffered aspirin controls mild arthritis while more advanced cases may require usage of cortisones, phenylbutazone, or other products. Occasionally in very severe cases of osteoarthritis of the hip, a total replacement surgery can be performed, much like in humans. Over-

weight patients should be placed on a diet. Fortunately, most patients respond well to therapy, ensuring a quality life with minimal symptoms.

FRACTURES

Occasionally, due to abnormal stresses placed upon the skeletal system, fractures or breaks of the bones may occur. In a text there is no way to describe all the possible fracture types and the proper correction of such; however, these are difficult terminologies. Basically we refer to fractures not based on the name of the bone broken but rather on the characteristics of the break itself. There are four commonly seen fractures in the canine, referred to as closed, compound, epiphysial (growth plate) and greenstick (hairline). (See figure 4-9.)

Closed fractures are those in which the skin is not broken. The bone is fractured, but the overlying skin is intact. Conversely, compound fractures are breaks in which the broken bone actually protrudes through the skin, often exposed to the outside. Compound fractures are risky in that the bones are frequently contaminated with dirt so infections are common.

Epiphysial fractures are commonly seen in young, growing dogs. Bones grow from the ends. In animals less than one year of age, there are soft areas near the ends of each long bone where growth takes place. These soft areas are referred to as growth plates or epiphysial plates. (See figure 4-10.) Because these are areas of growth, they are rich in immature non-calcified cells, forming a soft spongy area of the bone. These growth plates are frequently fractured because they are the weakest part of the bone. The distal ends of the femur and humerus seem to be particularly susceptible to this fracture.

Greenstick fractures are small cracks within the bone leaving the bone basically intact, but cracked. In other words, the bone is not completely broken.

What are the symptoms and risks?

The symptoms and risks depend on the areas fractured and to what extent. Fractures involving a joint are more serious than those in other areas. A broken back may displace the spinal cord and cause complete paralysis. All fractures are serious and should be treated at once. Typically when a bone within a leg is broken, the dog will hold the entire leg off the ground. No weight is placed on the paw. With a sprain or lesser injury, it may use the leg somewhat, but walk with a limp.

What is the treatment?

As in humans, splints, pins, steel plates and screws can all be used to realign the bone and allow healing. Growing patients may heal in as little as five weeks while geriatric patients may take twelve weeks or more for

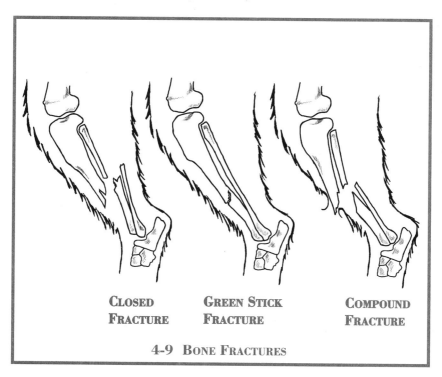

CLOSED FRACTURE   GREEN STICK FRACTURE   COMPOUND FRACTURE

4-9 BONE FRACTURES

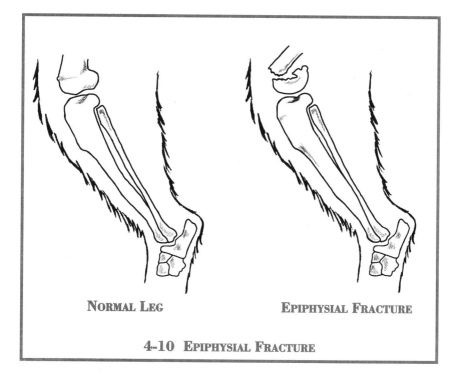

NORMAL LEG   EPIPHYSIAL FRACTURE

4-10 EPIPHYSIAL FRACTURE

the same bone to heal. Hairline fractures may only require rest, while surgical intervention will usually be needed in more severe fractures. Careful evaluation by a veterinarian will determine the proper treatment.

TUMORS OF THE BONES

Although rare, tumors of the bones do develop. Most are a malignant type called **osteosarcoma**. They are more common in geriatric patients than in younger animals.

What are the symptoms?
Usually a notable swelling will be detected over the area of the tumor. In the early stages, however, there may be no symptoms. Most tumor sites are very painful on examination. The most common areas for bone tumors in the dog seem to be the sinuses and long bones of the legs.

What are the risks?
Bone cancer is serious and life threatening. Most patients live less than one year; however, treatment may extend the life expectancy somewhat.

What is the treatment?
Treatment varies depending on the tumor location. If a limb is involved, then complete amputation may be required. Radiation and chemotherapy may also be utilized in some forms.

DISORDERS OF THE MUSCLES, LIGAMENTS AND TENDONS

Damage or malfunctioning of these organs is not as serious as injuries to the bone, but nevertheless is commonly encountered.

RUPTURED CRUCIATE LIGAMENT (KNEE JOINT)

Cruciate ligaments are found within the knee joint. There are two, called the anterior and posterior ligaments. Due to trauma, these can become torn or ruptured. In most damaging knee injuries, the anterior ligament is the one commonly ruptured. In more severe injuries, the posterior ligament will be torn as well. These two ligaments connect the femur bone to the tibia and stabilize the knee joint. (See figure 4-11.) When these become ruptured, two bones will move back and forth independently of each other, preventing the joint from functioning normally. This is referred to as a "drawer movement" because the movement is similar to the opening and closing of a drawer. (See figure 4-12.) Common causes of injury are slipping on icy or wet surfaces, automobile accidents and falling.

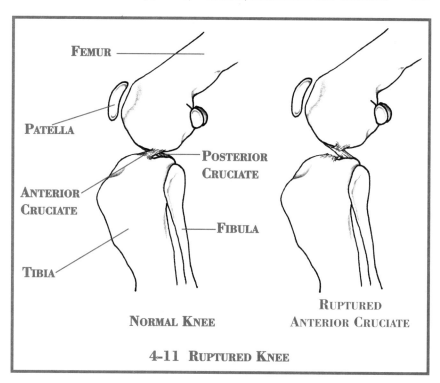

FEMUR

PATELLA

POSTERIOR
CRUCIATE

ANTERIOR
CRUCIATE

FIBULA

TIBIA

NORMAL KNEE

RUPTURED
ANTERIOR CRUCIATE

4-11 RUPTURED KNEE

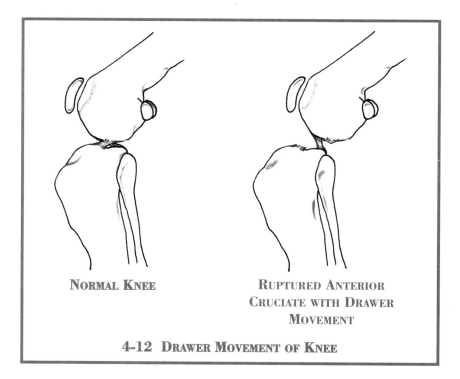

NORMAL KNEE

RUPTURED ANTERIOR
CRUCIATE WITH DRAWER
MOVEMENT

4-12 DRAWER MOVEMENT OF KNEE

What are the symptoms?

Initially the dog will limp, often severely. It may not use the leg at all, holding it off the ground. In time the knee joint will become enlarged and fluid-filled. Any patient limping on the rear leg should have a careful examination by a veterinarian for this injury.

What are the risks?

Without treatment, the patient will always limp or walk on only one rear leg. Consequently the unaffected rear limb will suffer undue stress and may also develop a ruptured cruciate ligament. In time, the affected knee will enlarge, scar and become immobile. The earlier treatment is instituted, the more likely the success.

What is the treatment?

All cases of ruptured cruciate ligaments will require surgery. Various surgical techniques are available to stabilize the knee, replacing the function of the torn ligaments. The ligaments are not repaired, but rather replaced either with synthetic material or tissue from other parts of the body. Surgery is very successful; however, the knee is generally not restored to 100 percent of its original mobility.

MASTICATORY MUSCLE MYOSITIS

This is a condition seen in dogs in which the muscles of the face become inflamed. Specifically, the muscles used for mastication (chewing) are involved. Large breeds are most commonly affected.

What are the symptoms?

Initially the muscles of the face become swollen and painful. Pain is especially noted upon opening the jaw. Eventually the condition reaches a point in which it is no longer painful. The muscles, initially swollen, now become shrunken (atrophied).

What are the risks?

In advanced cases, the patient may develop a difficulty in chewing. In some, the jaw may actually drop and hang partially open, or in others may not open fully.

What is the treatment?

Anti-inflammatories such as steroids are the best treatment. Some patients may require months of therapy. Almost all dogs will improve; however, the muscles may remain atrophied, but functional.

PERINEAL HERNIA

A perineal hernia is a situation in which the abdominal wall next to the anal opening ruptures. This allows abdominal organs such as the

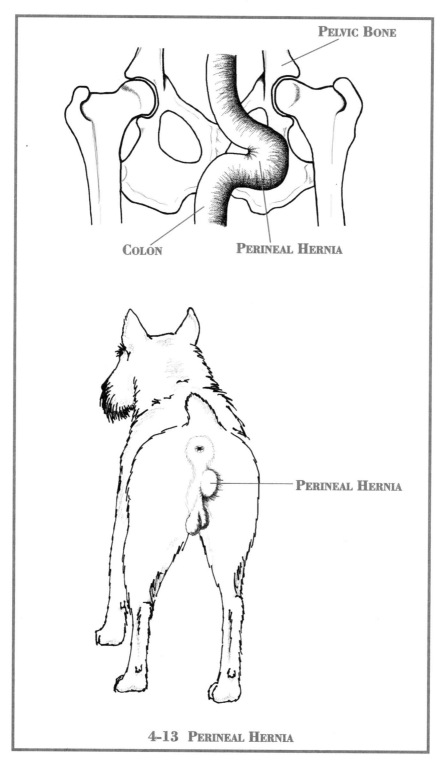

4-13 PERINEAL HERNIA

intestines and bladder to protrude outwards, confined only by the skin. Several muscles including the levator ani, coccygeus and external anal sphincter are involved at the herniation site. The hernia usually develops between the levator ani and external anal sphincter muscle. (See figure 4-13.) It is not known why these muscles become weakened; however, certain factors may be linked. Genetics plays a role, as evidenced by the fact that breeds including Boston Terriers, Collies, Boxers and Pekingese have a higher incidence than normal. Most perineal hernias involve males middle-aged and older.

What are the symptoms?
The most common symptom is a bulge of the skin next to the rectum. Commonly this bulged-out area is larger than a human fist. The bulge is created by tissues such as abdominal fat and/or intestines and bladder pushing through the hernial opening and displacing the skin. Straining to defecate, coupled with the protruding skin next to the anus, is the most common sign. Straining to defecate is due to the colon becoming deviated into the hernia, thus interfering with the passage of stool.

What are the risks?
It is not uncommon for affected patients to have difficulty passing stool. The colon and other portions of the intestines become deviated into the hernial opening, thus obstructing the flow of fecal material. If the bladder is also located within the hernia, urination may be difficult as well. An inability to defecate or urinate is always serious and should be corrected at once.

What is the treatment?
Surgical correction of the hernial opening is the best method of treatment. Usually the ruptured abdominal wall can be repaired, thus eliminating the hernia. Commonly, even with surgical correction the area remains weakened and recurrence is possible. Stool softeners are commonly utilized to help prevent straining and pressure upon the affected muscles.

CHAPTER 5

The Canine Reproductive System

INTRODUCTION

The reproductive system of the dog closely parallels that of humans. In the **female**, it is composed of the ovaries, oviducts, uterus, cervix and vagina. (See figure 5-1.) The **ovaries** are the site of production of the unfertilized eggs and many of the hormones responsible for heat cycles and the maintenance of pregnancy. From the ovaries the eggs pass into the **oviducts.** These small finger-like tubes are the site of fertilization by the sperm. From there the eggs pass into the **uterus,** which is composed of the left and right horn and uterine body. (See figure 5-2.) The developing embryos mature within the uterus, attached to its walls by the placenta which also surrounds them. (See figure 5-3.)

At birth, the fetuses pass out through the cervix, a valve-like closure that protects the uterus from contamination from the outside world, and enter the **vagina** for final exit from the body. The vagina also serves as a common opening for elimination of urine from the body. In addition, it produces the chemical substances known as *pheromones* that are attractants to male dogs during heat cycles.

In the **male**, the important structures of the reproductive system are the testicles, ductus or vas deferens, prostate gland and penis. (See figure 5-4.) Sperm production and storage occurs within the **testicles**. Upon ejaculation, the sperm is transported to the **prostate gland** by the **vas deferens**. Within the **prostate,** additional fluids are added to the sperm to nourish it and aid in its transport from the **penis** and through the uterus.

The sperm and prostatic fluids, at the level of the prostate gland, enter the common urethra and are carried from the body through the penis. The

87

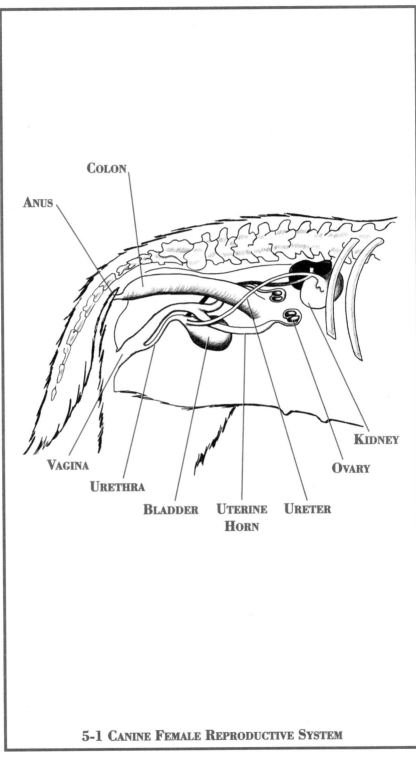

5-1 CANINE FEMALE REPRODUCTIVE SYSTEM

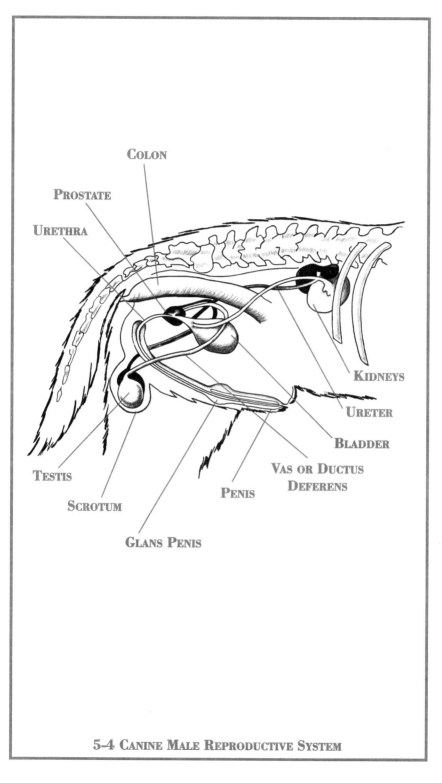

COLON

PROSTATE

URETHRA

KIDNEYS

URETER

BLADDER

VAS OR DUCTUS
DEFERENS

TESTIS

SCROTUM

PENIS

GLANS PENIS

5-4 CANINE MALE REPRODUCTIVE SYSTEM

penis of the dog has two specialized structures. The *glans penis* is a bulb-like dilation at the base of the penis which fills with blood and holds the penis within the vagina during intercourse. Within the penis is a bone that maintains the shape and direction of this organ during mating. The penis is protected from the environment as it is enclosed within the *sheath* or *prepuce*.

HEAT CYCLES

The heat cycles of the female (bitch) are caused and controlled by hormones that are produced and released by the ovaries and other glandular structures within the body. The ovaries are paired structures that increase activity when the animal passes through puberty, at the first heat cycle. This ranges between five and eighteen months of age depending on the individual and the size of the animal. In the Toy and small breeds, heat cycles occur as early as five months of age, while in the giant breeds this may not occur until the animal is fourteen to eighteen months old. Typically, these cycles will occur every six to nine months throughout the life of the animal. In the very young and very old, there may be "silent heats" with no outward signs that are detectable by the owner or sometimes even other dogs. Dogs do not undergo any form of menopause; rather, there have been rare cases of heat cycles resulting in pregnancies at fifteen years of age.

The heat or estrus cycle of the female is divided into four different stages. There is great variation in the length of these cycles among individuals of the same breeds and among various different breeds. Additionally, the same animal may have significant variations over the course of a lifetime. It is therefore impossible to talk about the cycling of bitches using exact dates or time periods.

The first stage of a heat cycle is a preparatory period referred to as **proestrus.** This follows a period in which the reproductive system was, from all outward appearances, inactive. Proestrus typically lasts five to nine days. On the first day of proestrus, the vagina becomes swollen and a bloody *discharge* is soon observed. During this stage males may show an interest in the female but she will be unreceptive to them. Internally, the *eggs leave* the surface of the ovaries and travel into the oviducts.

The next stage is referred to as **estrus** and is the active breeding phase. It will usually last from five to nine days. Bleeding from the vagina is very slight or completely absent at this point. Males will definitely be attracted to and attempt to mate with the female during this stage. In estrus, the female will allow them to mount her, resulting in *intercourse*. In the dog, a *"tie"* usually occurs in which the male and female are held together physically, with the vagina tightly enclosed around the glans penis.

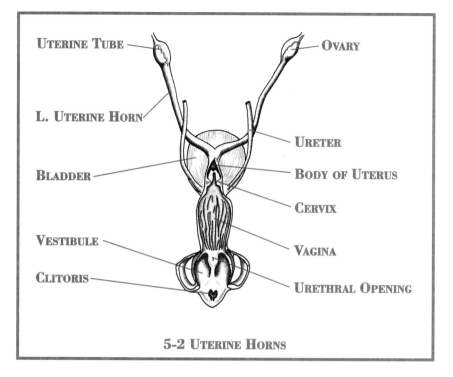

UTERINE TUBE

OVARY

L. UTERINE HORN

URETER

BLADDER

BODY OF UTERUS

CERVIX

VESTIBULE

VAGINA

CLITORIS

URETHRAL OPENING

5-2 UTERINE HORNS

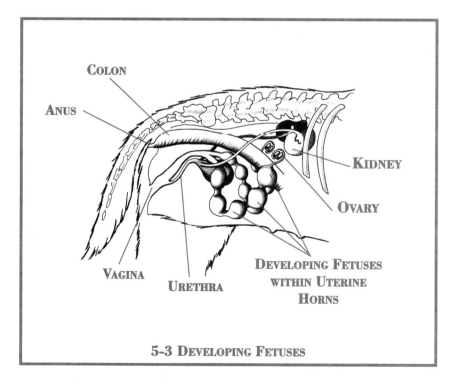

COLON

ANUS

KIDNEY

OVARY

**DEVELOPING FETUSES
WITHIN UTERINE
HORNS**

VAGINA

URETHRA

5-3 DEVELOPING FETUSES

Ejaculation will occur and sperm cells will enter the uterus and make their way to the oviduct, where their union with the egg will result in *fertilization*. A tie is not necessary for conception to take place. At this point, the union of the egg and sperm results in the formation of a fertilized egg, which is referred to as a *zygote*. This matures further, developing into an *embryo* or *fetus*.

Following estrus is the **diestrus** period. This extends from the time when the female dog is no longer receptive to the male through the end of pregnancy. In cycles in which a pregnancy did not occur, diestrus will last for a period of up to 80 days. In early diestrus, the *embryos and their placentas* attach to the wall of the uterus, from which they will derive their oxygen and nutrients.

Following diestrus is **anestrus.** This is the quiescent period between heat cycles characterized by no outward physical or behavioral signs of sexuality.

In male dogs, there is no seasonal period of increased sexual activity. Rather, they can be stimulated at any time by nearby females that are in season (heat).

DISORDERS OF THE FEMALE REPRODUCTIVE TRACT NOT ASSOCIATED WITH PREGNANCY

VAGINITIS

Vaginitis refers to an inflammation or infection of the vagina. It can be brought on or caused by problems occurring within the vagina, or be secondary to conditions elsewhere in the body. It is a fairly common disorder in dogs of all ages. It may be the result of trauma; however, this is rarely the cause.

Most cases seen in dogs are caused by the caustic and irritating effects of urine on the vaginal mucosa or lining. Since urine normally passes through the vagina with every urination and vaginitis is only seen in a very small percentage of female dogs, it should be obvious that in cases of this disorder either the urine is abnormal or its flow is in some way altered.

In cases of bladder infections (i.e., cystitis), the urine contains large numbers of bacteria. Expelled with the urine, these can easily colonize the vagina, leading to an infection and inflammation of this structure. In mature female dogs, especially in those that have been spayed, urinary incontinence can be a common problem. This is basically a chronic leaking of small quantities of urine from the bladder. When this occurs, urine may lie against the vaginal lining much of the time, leading to a "urine scald" or irritation.

Infections from bacteria, yeasts and viruses are known to occur within the vagina. The bacteria isolated from this structure are those commonly found or passed in the dog's stool. It is thought that when the animal cleans itself after urination and defecation, the licking may transfer bacteria from the anus to the vagina. As in other species, yeast infections of the vagina sometimes occur in animals that are on prolonged antibiotic therapy. It appears that these medications suppress the normal bacteria living in this structure which in some way may prevent the growth of yeast organisms.

The **herpes virus** known to infect dogs commonly infects the vaginal area. As in other animals, this is a chronic infection with occasional flare-ups of clinical signs.

Non-infectious inflammations of the vagina also occur due to the effects of shampoos, detergents, cleaning agents and other solutions. The severity of these is dependent on the properties of the causative agent.

In animals with vulvar fold abnormalities (see Chapter 2), the vaginitis may be secondary to irritations resulting from this condition.

What are the symptoms?
Dogs with vaginitis, regardless of the cause, will have similar signs. They will repeatedly attempt to clean the area through licking. They may drag the area across the carpet or grass. There will typically be a discharge, and on examination the lining will be reddened and painful. In many cases, even in spayed females, male dogs may be attracted and show an interest in breeding.

What are the risks?
Vaginitis is not life threatening. In severe cases, animals may mutilate themselves when licking or dragging the area across the ground. In cases of bacterial or yeast infections, these organisms may spread to surrounding tissues or ascend into the bladder, causing *cystitis. Canine herpes is a contagious disease* that may be spread to other dogs.

What is the treatment?
If urinary incontinence exists it can be treated medically. Once controlled, the vaginitis rapidly clears.

In cases in which the infection is secondary to cystitis, the initial problem must be treated. Primary vaginal infections can be treated either with oral or topical preparations, depending on the organism involved. In the case of canine herpes infection, there is no treatment and the animal must be isolated to prevent the spread of the disease.

VAGINAL HYPERPLASIA

This is a common disorder of young dogs, typically under two years of age. It is caused by an abnormal response of the mucosa or lining of the vagina to the hormone *estrogen*. A mass of tissue protrudes off the ventral vaginal wall just in front of the opening of the urethra. (See figure 5-5.) It is usually visible from the outside as it bulges out through the vaginal opening. Since estrogen levels within the body dramatically increase during the early stages of the heat cycle, this condition is noted at this time. After the cycle has passed, the hyperplasia may shrink or disappear and not reappear until the next heat.

What are the symptoms?

Animals with this disorder will lick at or even chew on the protruding mass. Others will show no signs other than the presence of the exposed tissue. As stated, this condition will typically be seen while the female is cycling, or occasionally in those being treated with hormonal products.

What are the risks?

Although a small percentage of dogs may mutilate the exposed tissue through licking, chewing or sitting on it, there is rarely any threat from this disease. Attempts to breed the dog may fail as the hyperplastic tissue may prevent copulation.

What is the treatment?

Spaying, or an ovariohysterectomy, eliminates this problem and is the treatment of choice. Estrogen is produced and liberated from the ovaries and their removal prevents recurrence. Within a week or two the tissue shrinks back to its normal position and size. In cases in which the surface of the protruding mass has been irritated or infected, topical creams or oral antibiotics can be used.

VAGINAL POLYPS

Vaginal polyps are fairly rare in the canine. A polyp is an extension or growth of tissue off a mucous membrane. In general, regardless of where on the body they are found, they are a form of cancer and may be either benign or malignant. In the vagina, polyps do occur, but in most cases, when carefully examined, these are actually found to be cases of vaginal hyperplasia. As stated, hyperplasia is commonly associated with heat cycles in younger dogs. Vaginal polyps, on the other hand, are typically seen in older dogs, especially over six years of age. Additionally, they are not associated with heat cycles and may even occur in spayed bitches.

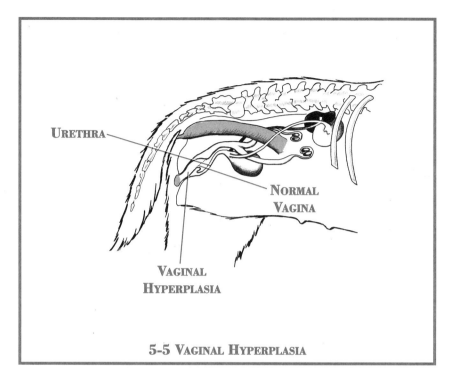

5-5 VAGINAL HYPERPLASIA

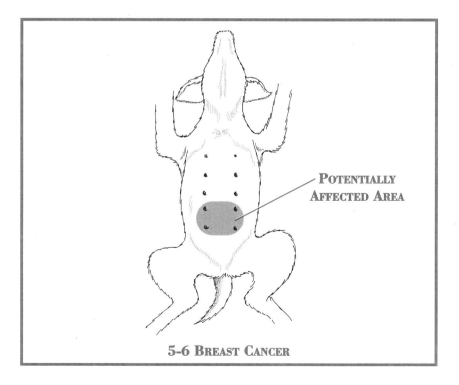

5-6 BREAST CANCER

What are the symptoms?

Vaginal polyps typically go undetected unless they show through the vaginal opening. Signs associated with these polyps result from the irritation they might cause to the patient. In these cases, the female will lick the area or may drag the vaginal area on the ground. If the mass is large, its surface may become ulcerated and bleed. Rarely do these interfere with urination.

What are the risks?

Vaginal polyps only pose a threat to the dog if they are a malignant cell type. If this is the case they can spread to other areas of the body, leading to the death of the individual. In dogs, however, most are benign growths of little concern other than the local irritation or discomfort they might cause.

What is the treatment?

Vaginal polyps are usually surgically removed when they are found. Even if they are believed to be benign, they may continue to grow, and the sooner they are removed the easier the surgery. After removal, most are sent to pathology labs for evaluation. If they are found to be malignant, additional therapy may be needed.

MASTITIS

Mastitis is an infection of the mammary glands and is usually caused by bacteria. These commonly occur in dogs during lactation but are quite rare at other times. It is possible that bacteria can gain access to the breast tissue though the bloodstream, being carried there from infections elsewhere in the body. However, it is believed that in most cases, the bacteria enter the mammary gland by migrating through the opening in the nipple during or following nursing. The organisms present are those commonly found on the skin or normally passed in the stools of the dog.

What are the symptoms?

At any one time mastitis will usually be found only in one or two of the mammary glands. The last two or three glands on either side will be the ones most frequently affected. The infected gland will initially become hard and in a few hours to a day become swollen, hot, discolored (from red to dark blue) and very painful to the touch.

The dog will have a fever and may go off food. Left untreated, the mastitis usually develops into an abscess that will rupture, draining a thick yellowish pus. In the dog, milk normally appears like a thin form of cow's milk. With mastitis, it becomes yellowish-white with obvious lumps and a foul smell. The *toxic effects of the milk soon spread to the nursing pups.* They become lethargic, discontinue nursing, develop swollen abdomens and, in some cases, die. Some females will have repeated bouts of mastitis during future pregnancies, with every instance requiring treatment.

What are the risks?

Mastitis is a risk to both the mother and the nursing puppies. The infection and resultant abscess can spread to other parts of the mother's body. Some affected glands may become scarred to the extent that future milk production or nursing from that gland is impossible. *In the puppies, it can be fatal* as they automatically consume large quantities of bacteria. At this stage of their lives, they have a very low level of resistance and what starts out as an infection of the intestinal tract (enteritis) quickly spreads throughout their bodies.

What is the treatment?

Mastitis must be treated immediately. If it is first observed in the evening, the dog should be taken to the veterinarian on an emergency basis rather than waiting for the following day. If milk and the infective discharge can still be expressed through the nipple, as much as possible should be "milked out." If an abscess has formed or the gland is impacted, it is usually necessary to lance the infected gland and drain its contents. In some cases, it is necessary to flush this area out for several days with some antibacterial solution or ointment. This cleanses the area and prevents it from healing over, which would result in the formation of another abscess. The animal is placed on a broad-spectrum antibiotic and supportive care given as needed. In problem bitches that have repeated bouts of mastitis in subsequent pregnancies, these animals may be placed on antibiotics in a preventative fashion through lactation.

The puppies are usually removed from the bitch and supplemented with canine milk replacers until the mother's milk appears normal. Antibiotics are frequently also given to the puppies.

BREAST CANCER

Breast cancer is the most commonly encountered malignant tumor of the female dog! It is responsible for the death of many dogs each year, yet it is usually avoidable.

The tumor type can be either a **"mixed mammary"** (in which many different cell types are present) or an **adenocarcinoma** (a tumor rising from glandular cells). Regardless of the type, these may spread via the lymph glands to other sites of the body.

The tumor rarely, if ever, occurs in females that have been spayed at an early age. It is thought that the tumor is stimulated or brought on by one or more of the female hormones associated with heat cycles, specifically estrogen. These hormones are produced and released by the ovaries, which are removed in a spay.

Mammary tumors are not usually seen until the animal is six or more years of age. Many dogs will have several different tumors developing within various glands simultaneously. They develop slowly but exhibit rapid periods of growth, both in size and numbers, immediately following heat cycles.

What are the symptoms?

Mammary tumors are easily felt through the skin. They are very hard, round masses with an irregular or bumpy surface. Sometimes they are close to the surface, lying just under the skin. At this location on a dog with white or very light-colored skin, the tumors can be seen and have a light yellow color. Although they can be found in any of the mammary glands, they are most frequently noted in the two rearmost ones. (See figure 5-6.)

Usually there are no clinical signs associated with mammary tumors unless they drain or spread to other parts of the body. Sometimes these tumors grow rapidly, rupture out through the skin over the mammary gland and drain a pink-tinged fluid. These are highly malignant tumors that spread to other parts of the body and therefore signs can be seen from the effects they cause on other structures. A common example of this would be when they spread to the lungs and cause a cough or difficult respiration.

What are the risks?

The vast majority of all mammary tumors are malignant and if untreated will threaten the life of the dog. They spread, generally via lymph vessels first, initially to the lungs but from there can be found in many other organs. At these sites they replace or destroy tissue that is necessary for life.

What is the treatment?

The preferred treatment is prevention by spaying. If these animals are spayed early in life, breast tumors will rarely, if ever, form. Once tumors have developed, the only treatment is surgical removal. If this is done early in the course of the disease, the cancer will probably be eliminated before it has a chance to spread to other areas of the body. At this point in time, chemotherapy is not considered to be a valuable tool in the treatment of this disease.

PYOMETRA

This disease of the uterus is caused by one of the normally occurring female hormones, *progesterone*. In some cases, excessively high levels of the hormone are produced. In others, the uterus simply becomes overly

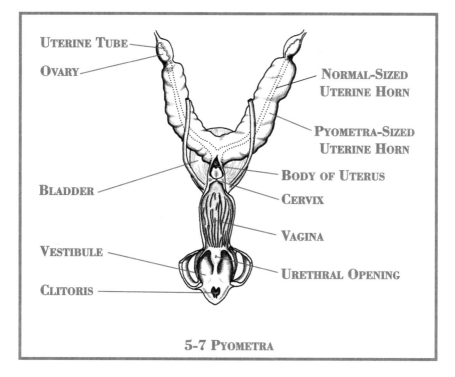

UTERINE TUBE

OVARY

NORMAL-SIZED
UTERINE HORN

PYOMETRA-SIZED
UTERINE HORN

BODY OF UTERUS

BLADDER

CERVIX

VAGINA

VESTIBULE

URETHRAL OPENING

CLITORIS

5-7 PYOMETRA

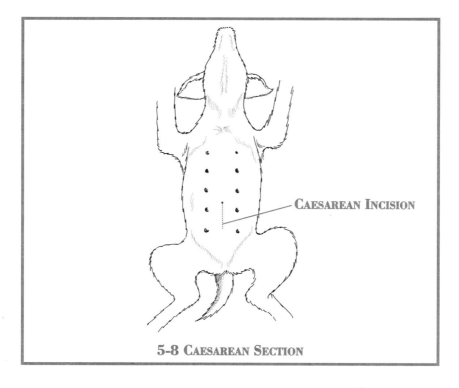

CAESAREAN INCISION

5-8 CAESAREAN SECTION

sensitive to progesterone. In either case, in response to this substance, cysts form in the lining of the uterus. Additionally, the secretory cells lining this organ are also stimulated and large quantities of fluid are released into the uterus.

All of this brings about a dramatic increase in the overall size of the uterine horns and body. (See figure 5-7.) Normally, the horns of the uterus are no larger or longer than a lead pencil. In pyometra, they become large, sac-like pouches the size of a cucumber and twelve to eighteen inches long. As the disease continues, bacteria that normally live in the vagina move through the cervix and colonize these intrauterine fluids. This results in a defensive response by the body, with millions and millions of white blood cells being shunted into the area to combat these organisms (an accumulation of large numbers of white blood cells and bacteria is what we commonly refer to as pus).

Early in the disorder the cervix remains open, allowing this accumulation of pus, fluid, bacteria and their byproducts and toxins to drain out through the vagina. With time, however, the cervix closes, trapping all of this within the uterus. At this point, the uterus continues to grow, and can easily rupture. More probably, however, the body will attempt to eliminate the accumulated material through the bloodstream. But in the case of pyometra, there is more material than the body can eliminate. Therefore, *the toxins and waste products spread out and poison the entire system.*

What are the symptoms?
Pyometra follows a heat cycle in which breeding did not occur. Typically within two to four months following the cycle, the bitch starts showing clinical signs of the disorder. The body attempts to flush the accumulated wastes and toxins with the kidney system. To do this the animal must drink huge quantities of water and therefore urinate frequently.

These are typically the signs first noticed with pyometra. Later, the owner may notice the animal licking at the vulva or a drainage occurring there. The animal will probably have a decreased appetite and due to the increasing mass in the abdomen, seem weak on the rear legs.

What are the risks?
Animals with pyometra that do not receive treatment almost always die. The uterus will continue to increase in size and will finally rupture, spilling pus, bacteria and fluid into the abdomen. This causes *peritonitis combined with toxic shock syndrome* that results in death in a few hours. Even if this doesn't occur, over time the build-up of toxins within the system will lead to kidney failure.

What is the treatment?
In female pets the treatment of choice is an ovariohysterectomy or spay. By totally removing the ovaries and uterus, the cause and the major result of

the disease is eliminated. It is important that this be done as soon as possible to prevent damage to the kidneys. Surgery is usually followed with long-term antibiotic therapy.

In valuable show/breeding animals, an attempt is often made to save the uterus for future breeding. Medical or surgical treatments can be attempted on these animals with varying rates of success. Medical therapy involves the use of prostaglandins, hormones that reverse the effects of progesterone. Surgery places tubes that are left within the uterus. These continually drain the structure until the hormonal abnormalities pass. Either of these choices is relatively expensive, not always successful and not without risk.

DISORDERS OF THE FEMALE REPRODUCTIVE TRACT ASSOCIATED WITH PREGNANCY

INFERTILITY

Failure to conceive or become pregnant following breeding is referred to as an infertility problem. This can be caused by abnormalities in either the male or the female. In dogs, it is believed that at least one out of every fifteen individuals is infertile due to a physical or physiological problem.

In the female these may be the result of infectious diseases that prevent fertilization or kill the developing fetuses (such as the bacterial disease brucellosis or the herpes virus). Hormonal abnormalities prevent normal cycling, inadequately stimulate the male or fail to maintain the fetuses within the uterus. Physiological problems can prevent the act of mating, movement of the eggs or sperm, fertilization or maintenance of the fetuses. Generally the actual cause is diagnosed where possible through physical exams, blood tests, bacterial or viral cultures, etc.

Many causes of infertility are behavioral. Today, these are just as common as those of a physical or physiological nature.

Infertility problems unique to the male will be discussed later in this chapter.

What are the symptoms?

Infertility in the female can result from many causes affecting different stages of the reproductive cycle. In some cases normal mating occurs but no signs of pregnancy are ever noted. This can be brought on by abnormalities in any part of the reproductive tract. Eggs may not form correctly or be released from the ovary; they may be prevented from entering the oviduct where fertilization should occur; sperm may be prevented from entering the oviduct; eggs that are fertilized may not attach correctly to the uterine wall; etc.

In others, the female becomes pregnant, but fails to give birth. In these examples, the puppies die inside the uterus and may be resorbed by the mother. If death occurs in the uterus *before* the embryos' skeletons have calcified (which happens between day 40 and 45 of the pregnancy), it is easy for the entire embryonic body to break down, dissolve and be carried away by the bloodstream. In those situations in which embryonic death follows calcification of the skeletons, some form of abortion or miscarriage will occur, with the fetuses or remnants of their bodies being passed through the vagina. However, in most cases where puppies are not born, fertilization did not occur and no puppies were formed.

What are the risks?
Only in rare cases is infertility dangerous to the female. Bacterial or viral organisms could affect her health, but this is uncommon. Fetal death in the uterus probably poses the greatest risk to her as the dead and decaying tissue may become trapped within the bitch's body. Many of the conditions leading to infertility are obviously fatal to the fetuses.

What is the treatment?
The diagnosis and treatment of infertility are usually difficult and expensive. They may require anything from vaginal smears, cultures and blood tests to exploratory surgery. Many are only overcome through hormonal injections and/or artificial insemination. And, as would be expected, many cases are never successfully diagnosed and therefore cannot be corrected.

BRUCELLOSIS
This is a common cause of infertility in the female. The disease is caused by the bacterium *Brucella canis*. It presents a real risk to every breeding kennel in which animals from the outside are sometimes part of the breeding program. Typically, the disease is transmitted directly between individuals during mating. However, the organism may enter the body through any membranes and individuals can become infected by licking other animals or by eating aborted or infected placentas, fetuses, etc. Once infected, dogs continue to carry the bacteria for years.

What are the symptoms?
With brucellosis, in most cases the only signs ever noted by the owners are infertility problems in their female dogs. The bitch becomes pregnant, but the embryos usually die before whelping. If fetal death occurs early in the pregnancy and resorption occurs, the owner may not realize that conception took place. If the bitch carries the puppies until the point that she was obviously pregnant but the embryos are then killed by the infection, evidence of an abortion may be noted. In those rare cases when the

puppies are carried to term and born alive, they may appear normal but usually are infected with the organism and may grow up to be carriers.

A very small percentage of infected adults will show signs ranging from fever to meningitis, but brucellosis is not known to cause fatalities in mature dogs.

What are the risks?

Bluntly stated, *brucellosis can be the end of an otherwise successful breeding kennel.* If an owner of a kennel or a single dog allows the animal to breed with another animal that has not been tested and proven clear of the disease, if either animal is infected or is a carrier, the loss can be much more than a single litter. Although the individual's newly infected dog will probably not die or even become sick, the chances of carrying a litter normally to term are very small. The animal will become infected, and either be infertile himself or cause females to become infertile. Or, the male could be a carrier for years and easily infect an entire kennel, or more than one.

Additionally, *Brucella canis* can infect humans that are exposed to dogs carrying the disease, the tissue of these dogs or any aborted products.

What is the treatment?

Although there have been a few occurrences in which animals were successfully treated for a brucellosis infection, this is very rare and very expensive. Many owners, because of the possibility of the infection spreading to people and the difficulty in treating the disease, choose to have infected animals euthanized. It is *always* recommended that these animals at least be *sterilized* and long courses of antibiotics utilized.

Dealing with brucellosis is not done through treatment but rather prevention. All animals to be used for breeding should be *tested* before being allowed to mate. Simple blood tests can be run to effectively isolate carriers.

HERPES VIRUS

Herpes virus infections can lead to infertility and death of both fetuses and newborns. This virus is typically contracted from the mother in the first few days of life, with the individual then remaining a lifelong carrier. Adult carriers rarely have any problems associated with the infection.

What are the symptoms?

Typically the only reproductive signs associated with a herpes virus infection are infertility and neonatal death. Puppies frequently die within the first few days of life. They often appear normal and seem to be thriving and then suddenly stop nursing and die. Fetal death often leads to late-term abortion but this is much less common. Puppies that live become carriers and can potentially infect their young.

What are the risks?

If infected, a female that is intended for breeding can be rendered useless. Fetal or puppy death and infertility can eliminate large numbers of potential litters. If sterilized and not used for breeding, the carrier can be an excellent pet and will probably never show any signs of the infection.

What is the treatment?

Since there is no treatment or vaccine, infected individuals should be sterilized and kept away from breeding animals. Prevention can be done through utilizing blood tests and isolating carriers. Uninfected pregnant females should be kept isolated from other dogs to prevent infection during this period. Newborn puppies should not be allowed to associate with animals other than their mother.

BEHAVIORAL INFERTILITY

Many otherwise reproductively normal dogs are infertile because of behavioral problems. Such females are fertile and cycle normally while the affected males can recognize females in heat and have normal sperm production, but these males fail to mate. Most of these cases involve animals that are either very young or have not been correctly socialized with others of their species.

In wild dogs, mating is believed to be a learned phenomenon. Younger animals watch their parents and/or participate in play behavior at an early age that simulates mating. Today, puppies are typically separated from their littermates and parents before they have had this exposure.

What are the symptoms?

Assuming that the male and female are brought together when the female is in estrus or standing heat period, mating may or may not be attempted. The female may try to prevent the male from breeding with her by sitting down, running away, becoming aggressive, etc. The male may show little or no interest, fail to mount the female correctly, be unable to get an erection, etc.

What are the risks?

Except during breeding periods, these animals live the remainder of their lives normally. They may interact with other animals quite well except in breeding situations. *These problems in no way affect their desirability as pets.* During mating, however, animals may be injured because of abnormally aggressive behavior.

What is the treatment?

Prevention of this behavior can be accomplished by allowing young dogs to play freely with each other. This is possible in kennel situations. It is always preferred that one of the pair be an experienced breeder. Additionally, when an inexperienced male is used, it is better to take the female to his residence as he must initiate mating and he will probably be more confident on his own territory.

In many situations, the breeding pair must be helped. This may mean restraining the female or assisting the male. In some cases artificial insemination is the only choice.

HYPOTHYROIDISM

Hypothyroidism is a common cause of infertility. See Chapter 7.

DYSTOCIA

Difficulty in expelling the puppies is termed **dystocia**. This can occur when the mother is totally unable to push the puppy through the birth canal or it simply takes too long. It has many causes.

The problem may relate to the fetus. When there is only one or very few puppies, they will typically be larger than normal and have difficulty getting through the birth canal. Breeds with a shortened nose such as the Pug, Boston Terrier, Pekingese, Bulldog, etc., often have problems with whelping. This is because the heads of these puppies are large and not tapered and therefore have difficulty dilating the cervix. In other cases, the alignment of a puppy in relation to the opening of the cervix may cause problems if a puppy will be an "abnormal presentation." That is, instead of pointing directly or straight through the canal, their heads may be bent backward or they might be coming out sideways. In dogs, it is not considered abnormal if the puppies come "tail or rear quarters first"; probably 40 percent of all canine births occur in this manner.

In some instances, dystocia may be caused by an abnormal structure in the mother. Her bony pelvis may be too small to allow the puppies to pass through. This can be a conformational abnormality or the result of an injury. In other cases, her uterus may fail to contract correctly (see "Uterine Inertia," below). This is common when the puppies are smaller than normal and inadequate uterine dilation fails to stimulate contractions. Behavior problems are also noted in first-time mothers. They may resist straining because of the pain, fear or simply lack of experience.

What are the risks?
Dystocia frequently leads to fetal death. Extreme pressure during prolonged periods of uterine contraction can severely damage fragile, young puppies. Additionally, this pressure or being within the birth canal for too long can impede circulation of oxygen-rich blood through the umbilical cord to the puppy. Once this has happened, if the neonate cannot breathe air while in the birth canal, it quickly suffocates.

If the puppy cannot be expelled by the mother, dystocia may also result in her death. This can occur immediately or over a period of several days because of the huge mass of decaying tissue trapped within her body.

What is the treatment?

Dystocia is always a medical emergency! Anytime that a bitch has had consistent contractions for over three hours before the first puppy or over one hour for any subsequent one, the bitch should be seen *immediately* by a veterinarian. He or she may be able to "pull" the puppy through the use of medical instruments and help the efforts of the bitch through medications such as oxytocin. In more severe situations, a caesarean section can be performed. (See figure 5-8.)

UTERINE INERTIA

A unique form of dystocia is uterine inertia. In this condition, the uterus either fails to initiate contractions or stops prematurely. This prevents the normal expulsion of the puppies.

This can have several different causes. Typically, it occurs in large or giant breeds. In these animals, the number of puppies in a litter is generally high. In any breed, as the number of fetuses within a litter increases, their individual size decreases (and vice versa). Additionally, in the large and giant breeds, their puppies are already proportionately smaller than those of the medium-sized or smaller breeds. Because of large litters of small puppies, the uterus is not as dilated as it would typically be.

One of the major factors stimulating uterine contractions is the degree of uterine dilation. Therefore in these breeds, it is easily understood why uterine inertia is more common. Some bitches have repeated problems with each pregnancy. In these it is thought to be an individual or genetic trait.

Uterine inertia can occur in any dog, especially during a prolonged and difficult whelping. In these cases, it is believed that the uterine muscles or the animal in general simply becomes exhausted.

What are the symptoms?

Classically, in cases of uterine inertia, the female simply goes out of "labor" prematurely. There will be puppies present within the uterus but she makes no further effort to expel them. Puppies already born are treated normally.

What are the risks?

If the fetuses are not born within twenty-four to thirty-six hours after the initiation of labor, they can be expected to die. If they are not discovered and are left within the mother, she will rapidly become ill and may also die. She simply cannot tolerate or deal with such a large mass of dead or dying tissue within her body.

What is the treatment?

When diagnosed, medications such as oxytocin may be useful to stimulate uterine contractions. However, if the naturally produced hormone associated with whelping, estrogen, is no longer at significant levels within the body, oxytocin usually fails to function. In these cases only a cesarean section can be performed to correct the situation. Bitches known to have problems with uterine inertia are usually x-rayed late in the pregnancy to determine the number of fetuses so that therapy can be initiated as soon as the first signs of the disorder are observed.

RETAINED PLACENTAS

While in the uterus, a fetus is enclosed in a sac-like structure called the placenta. It is attached directly to the inner wall of the uterus. Through this, the fetus receives oxygen and nutrients and expels waste. Usually, just before birth, the placenta opens and the pup is born without it. In most cases the placenta is passed soon after. In some species, retention of the placenta is a common and serious situation. However, this is usually not the case in the dog. Still, many owners are quite concerned about this. In dogs, it is uncommon for the placenta not to be passed. Even in cases where it may not pass, rarely is it of consequence. Postpartum bitches normally show a discharge from the vagina for five to fifteen days. At first this is fairly thick and green in color. Slowly, over several days, it becomes thin and turns a light brown or pink. It is believed that any placental remnants retained break down and pass in this fluid. Most veterinarians agree that the problems most owners associate with retained placentas are, in fact, associated with metritis. (See page 109.)

What are the symptoms?

When placentas are retained, the normal uterine discharge seen for several days following whelping is possibly thicker and somewhat larger in volume.

What are the risks?

Today, it is believed that there is not a high risk to the mother or puppies from placentas that fail to pass at whelping, particularly if oxytocin is given as a prophylactic measure following the completion of whelping.

What is the treatment?

Oxytocin injections can be given in the first twenty-four hours following parturition. These cause the uterus to contract and shrink rapidly, expelling any materials left behind. Little else needs to be done.

SUBINVOLUTION OF THE PLACENTAL SITES

As explained previously, it is normal for a bitch to have a vaginal discharge for several days following whelping. Initially it is a thick, green-colored liquid that slowly thins in viscosity and becomes a light brown or pink. In a few animals, however, the discharge starts out normally but turns to what appears to be pure blood. This may go on for several weeks. This is thought to be an abnormality involving the attachment sites of the placentas on the uterine wall. Normally, these revert to normal uterine tissue, but with this disorder they remain as they were during pregnancy, convolutions of blood vessels that were the transfer site of oxygen and nutrients to the placentas. Why this occurs is unknown, although it is probably caused by an abnormality in the hormone levels that are responsible for uterine physiology.

What are the symptoms?
With the exception of a bright red, bloody discharge from the vagina, these bitches and their puppies behave in a perfectly normal fashion. The blood loss, contrary to its appearance, is not significant enough to cause any problems to the mother.

What are the risks?
Assuming that the bleeding is due to subinvolution of the placental sites, there are few, if any, risks to the animal with this condition. In some cases, the occurrence or regularity of future heat cycles may be affected. It is important to eliminate from the diagnosis other possible disorders such as cancer or a clotting disorder.

What is the treatment?
In most cases, this condition resolves itself. If necessary, treatments using ergonovine or testosterone are believed to be the most effective. Many feel that injections of oxytocin in the first twenty-four hours following whelping may prevent or lessen the possibility of this disorder occurring.

UTERINE PROLAPSE

Occasionally, within the first three to four days following whelping, the uterus may evert and pass out through the vaginal opening. This is uncommon in the dog and when it does occur, it does not seem to correlate in any way with the difficulty of the birthing process.

What are the symptoms?
In cases of uterine prolapse, the animal will have a large, rough mass protruding from the vagina. The surface of this tissue can vary in color from white to pale pink to bright red. In most cases there will be very little bleeding, unless the animal has in some way damaged the tissue. Initially,

the animal will not appear ill in any way, other than to lick at the protruding mass. As the condition progresses, a fever develops, the animal goes off food, becomes lethargic and very ill.

What are the risks?

Untreated, the uterus will not revert to its normal position within the animal. Immediate problems can occur as the abnormal position of the uterus may cause a urinary obstruction preventing the bladder from emptying. This quickly leads to kidney shutdown and failure as the kidneys cannot produce urine if there is pressure resulting from the obstructed bladder.

Even if there is no problem with urination, the blood vessels going into the uterus will be compressed, thereby depriving the uterus of oxygen and nutrients. This quickly leads to tissue death. At the very best result, the prolapsed uterus might then die and separate from the body, allowing the body to in some way heal by itself. However, *this rarely if ever happens.* Rather, the mass loses its blood supply and dies, allowing the necrotic material and bacteria to flood throughout the animal's body. *If this happens and goes untreated, only death can occur.*

What is the treatment?

Initially it is sometimes possible to reposition the uterus, putting it back inside the body. This usually requires abdominal surgery. In most cases, however, it becomes necessary to spay the animal. If the animal is in good condition, these surgeries will not interfere with milk production or the development of the nursing puppies.

POSTPARTUM METRITIS

Following the birth of puppies, a uterine infection (metritis) is quite common. This is caused by bacteria gaining access to the uterus through the vagina and cervix during or following the birthing process. The organisms usually isolated are those commonly found on the skin or within the intestinal contents and feces.

What are the symptoms?

Animals with postpartum metritis are typically very sick. They have fevers, are lethargic, go off food, usually have a decrease in both the quality and quantity of milk, and typically pass a foul-smelling discharge from the vagina. The discharge may be a dark green to black and, in some cases, contain large quantities of pus.

What are the risks?

This is a serious condition. The bacteria usually pass from the uterus via the blood system and travel throughout the rest of the body. Animals have been known to die within twenty-four to forty-eight hours after the first signs were noted. Additionally, the puppies are at a severe risk as milk production is greatly reduced and frequently contaminated.

What is the treatment?
The discharge is cultured to isolate the bacteria present and to determine which medication is best. Before the results of these tests are known, the animal will be put on broad-spectrum antibiotics. Infusions of antibacterial solutions such as Betadine will be instilled into the uterus daily for at least two to three days. Severely debilitated animals may need to be placed on intravenous fluids. Another treatment frequently used prostaglandins, a relatively new treatment using those hormones (the prostaglandins) that are produced in the same area of the body where they are intended to work.

During any of the above options, the puppies may need to be removed from the bitch and fed milk replacements.

Many feel that bitches that receive oxytocin injections within the first twenty-four hours following whelping have a much lower chance of contracting metritis, because oxytocin at this time forces the uterus to contract, expelling many of the potentially toxic materials and fluids left over from the pregnancy.

MILK FEVER—ECLAMPSIA
This disease of pregnant or nursing dogs typically occurs anytime in a period that starts in the last ten days of pregnancy and runs through the first thirty days of nursing. It is the result of abnormally low calcium levels within the blood. Some believe that the calcium levels are depressed by the production of milk and the development of the fetal skeletons. Additionally, many believe that it may be further exaggerated by low calcium levels in the diet or poor absorption of this mineral in the gut. Actually, it may be caused by any or all of these and further affected by hormones and genetics. For whatever reason, during this period the blood calcium levels may drop rapidly, bringing on a life-threatening syndrome.

What are the symptoms?
Early in the syndrome, affected bitches may do little more than seem uneasy or anxious. They will fidget, often bouncing back and forth to their puppies. As this condition progresses, the animal will become more distressed, exhibiting heavy panting and moaning as if in pain. From this point the signs become more physical, with muscle twitching and staggering. The animal may walk peg-legged and there can be drooling and diarrhea. *In a few hours these signs can further degenerate to seizures, extremely rapid heart rates and death.*

What are the risks?

Most cases of eclampsia are progressive. As the puppies continue to nurse, the blood calcium levels continue to drop. Calcium is necessary for muscle and nerve function. As the levels decrease, the coordination between neural transmission and muscular activity is lost. This results in uncontrolled muscular activity ranging from mild twitching to uncontrollable convulsions.

As the condition progresses, the muscles of the heart and those responsible for breathing become involved. These muscles are obviously necessary for life and as they lose their ability to function correctly, the animal can easily die.

What is the treatment?

Treatment for milk fever (eclampsia) must be initiated as soon as possible. Although the condition is life threatening, it is easy to treat. Initially intravenous injections of calcium are given. These usually eliminate the clinical signs associated with the disease immediately. However, treatment using oral or subcutaneous injections of calcium products usually continues through the remainder of lactation. In severe cases, the puppies may be removed from the mother and fed milk replacers.

Bitches that have had a problem with eclampsia are usually treated in a preventative fashion for future litters. They will have calcium supplements added to their diet at the start of pregnancy and these will be continued through the entire nursing period.

FALSE PREGNANCY (PSEUDOCYESIS, PSEUDOPREGNANCY)

Occasionally bitches that have not been bred successfully or at all exhibit many of the physical signs and behaviors associated with pregnancy. It is caused by either an abnormal response to normal levels of hormones that circulate within the body following a heat cycle or a situation where these same hormones are present at abnormal concentrations. This occurs in all breeds, but is most common in bitches under four years of age.

What are the symptoms?

These individuals, at approximately the same amount of time following a heat cycle that would correspond with pregnancy, look and act as if they are carrying puppies. They will develop any or all of the following: abdominal distention, increased appetite, swelling of the breasts, milk production, nest making and abdominal contractions. After this "period of pregnancy," these animals may exhibit nursing behavior. They will take their toys or rags and carry them around as if they were puppies, they will lie down moving these up against their breasts and even lick and clean them as they would living puppies. In a week or less, all of these behavior patterns subside and the animal returns to normal.

What are the risks?
Most cases of false pregnancy cause few, if any, problems. In most cases, the ability of these animals to successfully breed and whelp a litter at a later date is not affected. Milk production during a false pregnancy may lead to some problem with mastitis, but this is uncommon. Additionally, some bitches may become overly aggressive during a false pregnancy and this may cause problems.

What is the treatment?
There are many different hormonal treatments that have been used on animals with false pregnancies and many of them work to some degree. However, most veterinarians and breeders prefer simply to let the condition run its course. Animals not important to a planned breeding program should be spayed. This eliminates heat cycles and therefore all false pregnancies.

DISORDERS OF THE MALE REPRODUCTIVE TRACT

CRYPTORCHID—RETAINED TESTICLE
At birth, the testicles of a puppy are still within its abdomen. As the animal develops, the testicles slowly "descend" into the scrotum. In mammals, sperm development does not occur correctly at the high temperatures found within the body. The testicles are therefore held outside of the abdomen and within the scrotum to provide a cooler environment. Frequently owners notice that the puppy they just purchased only has one or possibly no testicles within the scrotum. Although different dates are listed in some of the veterinary literature, both testicles are usually within the scrotum by the time the animal is six weeks of age and they should definitely be there by the time the puppy is eight to ten weeks of age. If one or both are not present at that location by twelve weeks of age, they probably never will be and the animal is said to be suffering from cryptorchidism or that it has "retained testicles." This is a disorder that may be passed from generation to generation.

What are the symptoms?
These animals rarely show any abnormalities because of this condition. They have normal activity levels, growth and behavior. Although fertility may be affected, they will usually show normal breeding behavior and frequently impregnate females, especially when one of the testicles has descended into the scrotum.

What are the risks?

The only risk that may be associated with cryptorchidism is that some researchers believe that these animals may have a higher incidence of other testicular diseases. Specifically, these would be cancer and torsion (see page 114–16).

What is the treatment?

Cryptorchid dogs should never be allowed to breed. This is a well-documented genetic trait, passed on to future generations. In addition, because of the potential for an increased incidence of torsion or cancer within the retained testicle, *it is strongly recommended that all of these individuals be neutered.*

ORCHITIS

Orchitis is an inflammation or infection of the testicles. Considering the position of the testicles being suspended from the body within the scrotum, it would seem likely that orchitis would be a fairly common occurrence. However, it is not. Most cases are the result of trauma, especially from bite wounds. Bacteria can easily gain access to the testicle from a bite, although these organisms can also reach the testicle from infections in the prostate gland or bladder. Although it does occur, few cases are the result of infections contracted while breeding.

What are the symptoms?

Affected animals are usually in acute pain. In an attempt to decrease the pain, they may walk bowlegged and arch their backs. One or both testicles will be swollen and possibly discolored. In the case of bite wounds, draining sores will be present. As the case progresses, the animal will develop a fever, go off food and become quite lethargic.

What are the risks?

Orchitis needs immediate treatment. It is painful and the infections can spread to other parts of the body. In some cases abscesses will form, causing severe damage to the parts involved.

What is the treatment?

Most cases respond to broad-spectrum antibiotic therapy. Where abscesses have formed, these need to be lanced and cleaned. In severe cases, it is often necessary to remove one or both testicles.

TESTICULAR TORSION

Testicular torsion describes a situation in which a testicle rotates within the scrotum and in so doing twists and pinches off the blood vessels. Just as the flow of water through a garden hose can easily be prevented by twisting, so can the passage of blood through the body's vessels. (See figure 5-9.) When this occurs, the tissues are deprived of oxygen. This condition is not as common in the dog as it is in other species, but does occur with some regularity.

What are the symptoms?

Affected animals are immediately in acute pain and have an altered gait. The animals walk bowlegged. The scrotal area becomes swollen, discolored and painful to the touch. If the involved testicle is one that is retained, there may be no change in the appearance of the scrotum; rather, the animal will show signs consistent with abdominal pain. These animals will arch their backs and exhibit pain when the abdomen is palpated.

What are the risks?

Deprived of oxygen and nutrients, the tissue within the testicle will probably die. Since there are two testicles, the animal may still be able to breed in the future. In some cases this situation can lead to the death of the animal as a fairly large amount of dead or necrotic tissue is trapped within its body.

What is the treatment?

Although it may be possible to reposition the affected testicle and thereby reestablish the blood supply, it is usually simply removed through surgery.

TESTICULAR CANCER

Tumors of the testicles are quite common in the dog. They are usually found in older animals, especially those over six years of age. The three most commonly encountered ones are **Sertoli cell tumor, interstitial cell tumor** and **seminoma**. These may or may not be malignant but are able to affect other areas of the body because of hormonal imbalances they may cause.

What are the symptoms?

In most cases there will be an enlargement of the affected testicle. It may have a hard, nodular appearance or in some cases be softer than normal, even appearing mushy. If the tumors are malignant, they may spread to other areas of the body and affect the normal function of those tissues or organs.

Many of the signs associated with testicular cancer will be those caused by abnormalities in hormone levels. Both male and female hormones are produced by the testicles, and the tumor may affect the production of either. Sertoli cell tumors are well known for their production of estrogen, the female hormone. Males with this condition develop a "feminizing syndrome." They lose much of their hair, develop a pendulent abdomen, the sheath of skin surrounding the penis sags away from the body, sperm

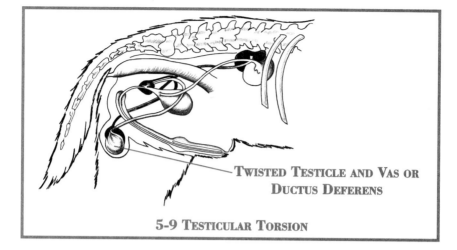

TWISTED TESTICLE AND VAS OR
DUCTUS DEFERENS

5-9 TESTICULAR TORSION

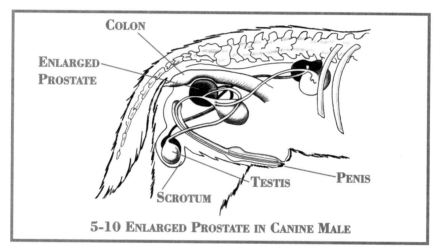

COLON

ENLARGED
PROSTATE

SCROTUM

TESTIS

PENIS

5-10 ENLARGED PROSTATE IN CANINE MALE

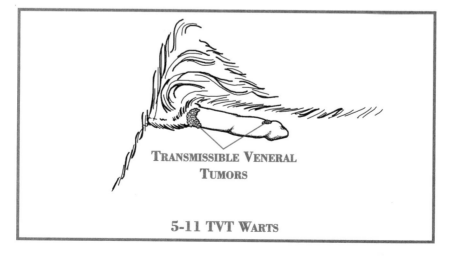

TRANSMISSIBLE VENERAL
TUMORS

5-11 TVT WARTS

production is reduced or eliminated, the animal shows no interest in breeding and the *non*cancerous testicle usually shrinks in size.

If the tumors liberate excess quantities of male hormones, the animals will typically have an increased incidence of prostate disease, hernias and tumors of the glandular tissue near the anus.

What are the risks?
As stated, testicular tumors can be malignant and in these cases they spread to other parts of the body. Additionally, hormonal imbalances frequently encountered with these tumors can cause significant physical and behavior changes.

What is the treatment?
The treatment of choice for all testicular tumors is neutering. Tissues are typically sent to pathology labs to determine the actual cell type. This helps the clinician determine the possibility of the cancer being spread to other parts of the body.

PROSTATE DISEASES

The prostate is the only accessory sex gland in the dog. Its primary function is that upon ejaculation, it adds fluid important for the life and nutrition of the sperm. For most dogs, except during breeding periods, the prostate is more of a liability, as it serves no function important to life but is a common site of disease. There are three very commonly encountered prostatic diseases.

Cystic hyperplasia of the prostate is a condition brought on by the lifelong effects of the male hormones produced by the testicles. This disease of older dogs is characterized by an *overall enlargement of the prostate*. The tissue may simply grow but in most cases the gland develops numerous internal cysts, further expanding its overall size. This is a benign growth and not cancerous.

Prostatic infections are also common. Bacteria usually enter the gland from the urinary tract. These organisms cause an inflammation and increase in the size of the gland. In many of these cases, the prostate develops numerous small internal abscesses.

The third, but *much less common*, is **cancer**. In many species, tumors of the prostate are very common, but this is not so in the dog. When they do occur in dogs, they are usually malignant changes of the glandular cells and are therefore referred to as *adenocarcinomas*.

What are the symptoms?
All of these prostatic diseases cause an overall increase in the size of the gland. The most common signs associated with this syndrome are due to this change in size.

The prostate is positioned such that it surrounds the urethra directly below the rectum. As it enlarges, it commonly places pressure on and constricts the rectum. This leads to constipation and/or straining to defecate. If the prostate is painful, and it often is in any of these disorders, defecation will also be painful, further aggravating constipation. (See figure 5-10.)

The urinary tract will also be affected. Animals may have difficulty passing their urine if the gland constricts the urethra, while others may become incontinent and be unable to hold their urine. Prostatic infections can easily spread into the bladder, causing *cystitis*. Whether from the bladder or prostate, blood and pus are commonly seen in the urine of these dogs.

Because of the pain associated with prostate disease, either from the gland itself or through the spread of infection or cancer to nearby structures, affected animals frequently walk with an abnormal gait.

What are the risks?

Prostate disease is common, very common. Many believe that over 75 percent of all dogs over the age of seven years have some form of prostatic disease. Many animals therefore exist with the problems even though they may show few outward signs. Prostatic disease can be very serious, however, as it may spread to or affect other areas and organs of the body.

The bacteria found in *infectious prostatitis* can spread throughout the body, seeding down wide areas. The *cancer* of the prostate is malignant and spreads both by local invasion to the immediately surrounding structures and also via the bloodstream throughout the body. In either case, this cancer is usually untreatable.

What is the treatment?

In the early stages of treatment, many animals with prostatic disorders will need enemas and are often placed on stool softeners. These help overcome the problems caused by the constriction of the rectum. If the urinary tract is occluded, urinary catheterization may also be necessary.

To exist and maintain itself, the prostate gland needs to be consistently supplied by the male hormone *testosterone*. Since this hormone is produced by the testicles, *the first step in treating most forms of prostatitis is neutering*. In cases of cystic hyperplasia, this in itself may be a cure. In those involving infections, antibiotic therapy without neutering is much less successful. Obviously, it would have little effect in those with cancer.

In some cases, *estrogen treatments* are also utilized. This female hormone helps to override the effects of its male counterpart. However, estrogen therapy is not without risk and is only used when absolutely necessary.

Long-term antibiotic therapy is needed in cases of infectious prostatitis. It is often difficult to get adequate concentrations of these medications into the prostate; cures therefore frequently take longer than would be expected with bacterial infections.

It is possible to surgically remove the prostate. This may have little effect on prostatic cancer as it has usually spread before a diagnosis can be made. As a part of the treatment for the other forms of prostatic disease, it is rarely used as it is very difficult and expensive.

SHEATH INFECTION—BALANOPOSTHITIS

The penis is held within a sheath of skin on the lower side of the abdomen on the dog. Commonly, this area becomes infected with bacterial organisms. These organisms may gain access to this region via the urine in cases with concurrent cystitis or prostatitis. More frequently, however, the bacteria migrate through the opening of the prepuce. This may happen when the dog licks the area in an effort to clean himself.

What are the symptoms?
Typically the only sign noted with this infection is a yellow or white discharge that chronically drips from the opening of the sheath. The animal seems unaware of the infection.

What are the risks?
There is little risk associated with balanoposthitis. It is possible that the organisms could spread up the urethra, but this is not thought to commonly occur. Neither does it appear to be a problem in breeding, nor does it lead to infecting the female. The major problem or concern is that expressed by the owner, as the chronic discharge stains carpeting and furniture.

What is the treatment?
Although usually not treated, in those cases requiring attention, oral antibiotics can be combined with prepucal flushes of antibacterial solutions, such as betadine, or antibacterial ointments. In most cases these medications are successful in eliminating the signs initially but they soon return after treatment is discontinued.

TRANSMISSIBLE VENEREAL TUMOR (TVT)

Tumors of the penis are rare but the most commonly seen is **transmissible venereal tumor (TVT).** This tumor is found in both male and female dogs and is transmitted via physical contact during mating. (See figure 5-11.) The tumor grows on the penis and vagina. During coitus, cells break off and attach themselves to the genitalia of the other animal, and then establish themselves as a new tumor. Additionally, it can also be transmitted when one animal licks an infected one and then transfers the cells of the tumor to its own reproductive organs.

What are the symptoms?

Many animals with TVT show no signs associated with the tumor. In fact, in some cases the tumor suddenly disappears, never to reappear again. This is thought to be due to an immune response on the part of the dog.

Chronic bleeding from the tumors is quite common. In some cases, the beet-red, cauliflower-like masses may get very large and in rare instances even spread via the blood or lymphatics to other parts of the body. The signs noted in most cases vary as to the size and location of the tumor.

What are the risks?

Death from TVT would be quite rare. In most cases there is only occasional bleeding from the masses. They can be a source of chronic irritation to the animal and the dog may lick or chew on them, causing some mutilation. The tumor does not spread to humans or any other species.

What is the treatment?

The tumor can be surgically removed. Chemotherapy with anti-cancer drugs is used in resistant cases or ones in which the mass has spread to other parts of the body. *To prevent future transmission, it is recommended that these animals be sterilized.* Animals with this disease or a history of carrying the tumor in their past should never be used for breeding.

PHIMOSIS

This is a condition in which the opening of the prepuce is too small. Although it is usually a defect the animal is born with, it can also be the result of injury. Typically, this is only a problem during mating. When the male gets an erection, the penis cannot pass through the prepucal opening to be exposed for breeding. In severe cases it can cause problems with urination, as urine will build up within the sheath and then slowly drip out.

What are the symptoms?

During breeding the male may make repeated and unsuccessful attempts to mate. The penis trapped in the sheath causes a large bulge under the skin. These animals frequently traumatize themselves during mating attempts, which results in blood dripping from the prepucal opening. Animals that have difficulty with urination chronically leak urine on their skin.

What are the risks?

Dogs attempting to mate, in addition to not being able to mate, can damage the penis. Those with urine leakage will suffer from urine scalding. This is an irritation from chronic exposure or contact with urine. Evidence of it will be found on the skin surrounding the prepucal opening and on the structures within the sheath.

What is the treatment?

Phimosis is easily corrected with surgery. Males that are not intended to be part of a breeding program and have no problem with urination should be neutered. In breeding males or those with difficulty voiding urine, the prepucal opening is enlarged. There is some question if dogs born with this condition should be allowed to breed.

PARAPHIMOSIS

Paraphimosis is nearly the opposite of phimosis. With this disorder, the animal is able to expose the erect penis but unable to retract it after mating. The prepucal opening is too small and will not allow the penis to slide back inside the sheath.

What are the symptoms?

These animals will stand with their penises exposed after they have had an erection. The animal will lick at the organ, which may become discolored. Blood from both the erection and normal circulation becomes trapped within the penis.

What are the risks?

Because of the lack of circulation to the penis, the tissue can easily undergo cell death if the penis is constricted in this position for more than a few hours. The exposed tissue can easily be damaged and the membranes covering its surface quickly dry out. Additionally, the urethra will be constricted, preventing urination. In hours this can lead to kidney shutdown and failure.

What is the treatment?

Anytime the penis of a dog is exposed for more than a few minutes following an erection, the animal should be treated. Initially, a lubricating jelly can be applied to the surface of the penis, allowing it to be manipulated back into the prepuce. In cases where the organ is swollen and this is not possible, surgery is required to enlarge the prepucal opening. As with phimosis, these animals probably should be neutered. Animals suffering urinary obstruction may require catheterization and fluid therapy.

MALE INFERTILITY

There is a significant percentage of male dogs that cannot successfully sire litters. It is estimated that approximately one out of every fifteen dogs is truly infertile. Additionally, many animals will have behavioral disorders that affect successful breeding. For a discussion of some of these behavioral anomalies, please see the section earlier in this chapter dealing with female reproductive problems.

As with the female dog, infertility problems in the male can be caused by infections, hormonal abnormalities or physical problems. Infections of the testicles or other parts of the reproductive tract containing organisms may affect sperm production.

Any medical problem that causes a significant fever in the animal can kill mature sperm cells present at that time. Hormonal abnormalities can also affect sperm cell production, as well as preventing the male from responding to the female. If the levels of androgens (the male hormones) are abnormally low, he may not notice that a female is in heat, or be able to get an erection or maintain sperm cell production.

Other hormones produced by other glands in the body, such as the thyroid, are also important in normal breeding activity.

There are many physical anomalies that affect a male's ability to breed. Sperm that is produced may be abnormally formed such that it cannot migrate through the uterus and oviducts correctly. In other cases, there may be abnormalities with the testicles or ductus deferens that prevent the flow of sperm to the penis. Some animals have problems with the penis that prevent its entrance into the bitch's vagina. Obviously, the list of all the possibilities that can affect fertility is almost endless.

What are the symptoms?
In most cases of infertility in the male, the animal appears to mate correctly but pregnancy fails to occur. In other, but much less common situations, the animal attempts to mount and enter the female but is unable to do so.

What are the risks?
Infertility, except when caused by bacterial or viral infections, rarely poses any threat to the dog. The vast majority of affected animals act and appear completely normal.

What is the treatment?
The diagnosis and treatment of male infertility problems are rarely simple and can be expensive. Where the infertility is caused by abnormalities such as hypothyroidism that originate elsewhere in the body, the condition is usually easier to deal with than those problems that arise within the reproductive system. A diagnosis usually comes from the results of blood tests, sperm evaluations and/or physical examination.

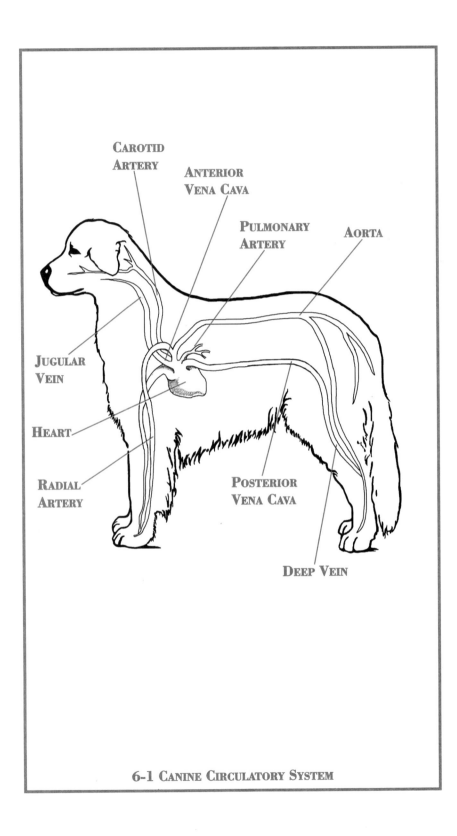

CAROTID
ARTERY

ANTERIOR
VENA CAVA

PULMONARY
ARTERY

AORTA

JUGULAR
VEIN

HEART

RADIAL
ARTERY

POSTERIOR
VENA CAVA

DEEP VEIN

6-1 CANINE CIRCULATORY SYSTEM

CHAPTER 6

The Heart, Vessels and Blood

INTRODUCTION

The canine circulatory system is much like that of humans. The heart has four chambers. The two upper chambers are the left and right atria, while the stronger, lower chambers are the right and left ventricles. (See figure 6-1.)

Blood travels from the tissues and enters the right atrium. From there it moves into the right ventricle. The right ventricle pumps blood from the body into the lungs to exchange carbon dioxide produced (by cellular metabolism) for oxygen. Blood rich in oxygen leaves the lungs through the pulmonary vein and enters the left atrium. The left atrium pumps blood to the left ventricle. The left ventricle is the most heavily muscled and therefore, strongest of the chambers. The left ventricle pumps blood to the great aorta, which supplies the body with blood and oxygen.

The chambers are separated from one another by muscle and a series of valves. The atrioventricular valve separates the right atrium and right ventricle, while the mitral valve separates the left atrium from the left ventricle. (See figure 6-2.) Each chamber and valve must function in a coordinated effort in order for the heart to pump efficiently.

Blood is composed of several different types of cells and proteins. Red blood cells give blood its color and are responsible for the transportation of both oxygen and carbon dioxide to and from the body's tissues. Another constituent of blood is the infection-fighting white blood cells. A third cell type, the platelets, circulate in the blood and are responsible for clotting. Platelets, white blood cells and red blood cells are all formed within the bone marrow. In addition to cells, the blood is made up of a protein-rich liquid portion called plasma.

HEART AND VESSEL BIRTH DEFECTS

In the fetus, blood enters from the mother through the umbilical cord. The lungs serve no function until birth, at which time the infant is exposed to breathable air. Blood in the unborn fetus therefore bypasses the lungs and flows directly from the right heart chambers to the left via a vessel called the ductus arteriosus. At birth the ductus arteriosus closes off forever, forcing blood to flow through the lungs for oxygen/carbon dioxide exchange. Similarly within the fetus, vessels bypass the liver until birth. The fetus depends on the mother's liver to provide needed functions. At birth, the vessels close and the infant's blood is then routed through the infant's liver.

PATENT DUCTUS ARTERIOSUS (PDA)

As stated, before birth, the **ductus arteriosus** allows blood to bypass the lungs. (See figure 6-3.) The lungs are not yet needed for breathing so blood simply flows from the right heart chambers to the left through the ductus arteriosus. At birth, due to pressure changes within the bloodstream, the ductus normally closes permanently, forcing blood to now enter the lung where oxygen can be exchanged.

In the case of **PDA** (patent ductus arteriosus), the vessel fails to close completely and therefore some blood continues to bypass the lungs. When this happens, even though the puppy is breathing, the proper amount of blood is not flowing to the lungs and therefore the puppy is not receiving enough oxygen to meet tissue demands. PDA can exist in all breeds; however, Poodles, German Shepherd Dogs, Cocker Spaniels, Pomeranians and Shetland Sheepdogs have the highest incidence. It is also more common in females than males.

What are the symptoms?

Initially the puppy may show no symptoms. As it grows, however, the circulatory system cannot keep up with the tissues' need for oxygen. As the puppy grows and the oxygen demands are not met, the puppy may compensate for this by becoming less active. A puppy at rest will require less oxygen than one at play. *Inactivity is one of the initial signs.* In periods of excitement these puppies may collapse as they become short of breath. The gums will appear bluish (cyanotic), reflecting the oxygen shortage. As the blood flows through the *abnormal* ductus arteriosus, a murmur (caused by turbulent blood flow) can sometimes be heard without a stethoscope. This abnormal blood flow can occasionally be felt if the chest is palpated. The signs may first be noted anywhere in the first year of life depending on the severity of the condition. Many affected puppies will not grow at a normal rate and will be smaller than their littermates.

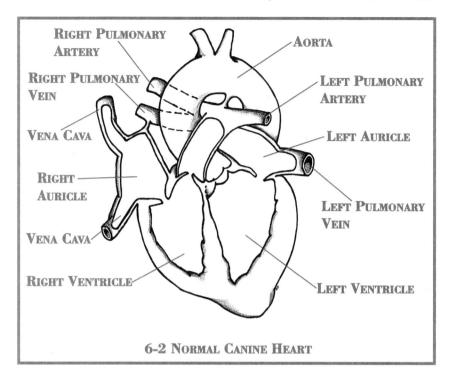

RIGHT PULMONARY ARTERY

RIGHT PULMONARY VEIN

VENA CAVA

RIGHT AURICLE

VENA CAVA

RIGHT VENTRICLE

AORTA

LEFT PULMONARY ARTERY

LEFT AURICLE

LEFT PULMONARY VEIN

LEFT VENTRICLE

6-2 NORMAL CANINE HEART

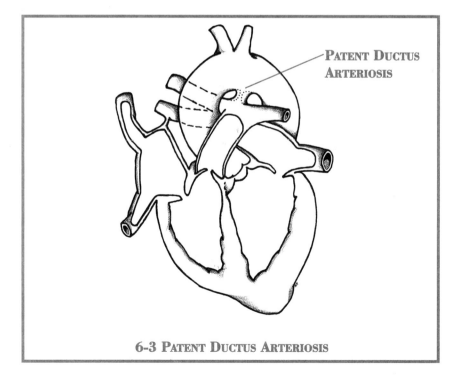

PATENT DUCTUS ARTERIOSIS

6-3 PATENT DUCTUS ARTERIOSIS

What are the risks?

Without treatment, almost all patients with PDA will live a shorter than normal life. Depending on severity, some will live only a few weeks; others survive longer.

What is the treatment?

Treatment of PDA requires surgery. The surgical procedure involves tying off the ductus arteriosus with suture material, thus routing all of the blood flow through the lungs. Surgery is quite successful and is best if done early before growth is affected.

PERSISTENT RIGHT AORTIC ARCH (PRAA)

In the unborn fetus there are blood vessels that deteriorate as the embryo grows. Occasionally, vessels in the chest cavity, called the aortic arches, will fail to disappear. The right aortic arch passes near the esophagus. (See figure 6-4.) If this blood vessel persists in the newborn, it will restrict the growth and function of the esophagus, restricting food passage to the stomach.

What are the symptoms?

Usually symptoms appear before six months of age and include stunted growth and regurgitation immediately after eating. The affected patient may also experience difficulty breathing if regurgitated food is aspirated, or if the trachea is also restricted.

What are the risks?

Without treatment, growth will be severely stunted, as the puppy will not be able to digest adequate amounts of food. Severe respiratory distress may also develop with pneumonia.

What is the treatment?

Surgery to remove the stricture caused by the persistent right aortic arch is the preferred treatment. It is important to perform surgery early in the disease, before permanent growth damage has occurred.

VENTRICULAR SEPTAL DEFECT (VSD)

In the developing embryo, the heart initially has four chambers that are not separated from one another. As the fetal heart develops, walls called septums form to divide the heart into four separate chambers. Occasionally the walls separating the heart chambers will develop incompletely, thus not properly dividing the chambers from each other.

Occasionally this congenital birth defect will be referred to as a "hole in the heart." In reality there is no hole in the heart, but rather a hole *between* the heart chambers. Most commonly this septal defect occurs between the right and left ventricles, hence the name ventricular septal defect (VSD).

What are the symptoms?

Because the left ventricle is stronger than the right, blood is forced backward against the normal flow pattern. Whenever this occurs with any cardiac disorder, an additional stress is placed on these structures, possibly leading to heart failure. Additionally, with VSD, the body tissues receive an inadequate quantity of oxygenated blood.

Patients may not have any outward signs. Occasionally, on a routine exam, veterinarians using a stethoscope hear the heart murmur associated with VSD. In severe septal defects, a decrease in stamina and retarded growth rates occur.

What are the risks?

Many patients with minor septal defects live normal lives even though a heart murmur is detectable. Occasionally the septal defect closes spontaneously as late as two years of age. Patients with large septal defects typically have a shortened life span, generally succumbing to heart failure.

What is the treatment?

In minor septal defects, treatment is generally not recommended. In severe cases, heart surgery to correct the defect can be performed.

PULMONARY STENOSIS

The pulmonary vein carries blood from the right ventricle to the lungs. Occasionally, a congenital narrowing of this vessel or its valves will impede normal blood flow. (See figure 6-5.) Without normal pressure, not enough blood can pass through the vein and enter the lungs. To compensate, the right side of the heart must pump harder. This enlarges its muscles and size. The right heart therefore becomes overworked and prone to failure.

What are the symptoms?

Most affected patients initially show no symptoms; however, a heart murmur will be present. These types of murmurs are typically noted on routine veterinary examinations with a stethoscope. Later in the syndrome, as the right side of the heart fails, it is unable to accommodate all of the blood returning from the body. This leads to edema or fluid build-up within the abdomen and limbs.

What are the risks?

In severe cases of pulmonary stenosis, the heart will be overworked. This can lead to heart failure and therefore a shorter than expected life span.

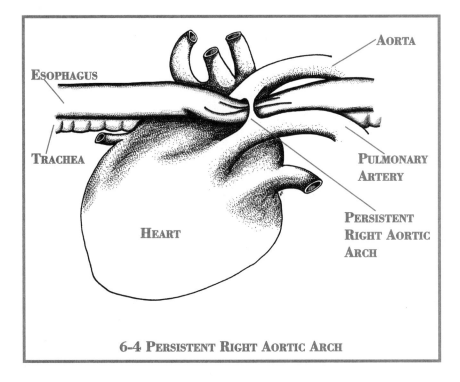

ESOPHAGUS

AORTA

TRACHEA

PULMONARY ARTERY

HEART

PERSISTENT RIGHT AORTIC ARCH

6-4 PERSISTENT RIGHT AORTIC ARCH

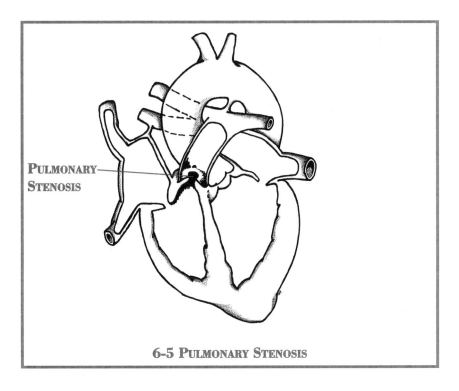

PULMONARY STENOSIS

6-5 PULMONARY STENOSIS

What is the treatment?

Minor cases are generally not treated. In severely affected patients, surgery can be performed to remove the narrowing (stenosis) and improve blood flow.

AORTIC STENOSIS

The great vessel called the aorta carries blood from the left side of the heart to all organs and tissues of the body. Occasionally a narrowing of the aorta or its valves will be present. This is a developmental congenital defect which retards normal blood flow from the aorta. (See figure 6-6.) To compensate, the left heart enlarges as it is pumping against increased resistance. The left heart becomes overworked. Larger breeds of dogs are affected more.

What are the symptoms?

Most affected patients have a low level of activity. They tire easily on exercise. Occasionally the patient may pass out due to a lack of oxygen to the tissues. A dog with aortic stenosis generally appears weak with little stamina.

What are the risks?

Aortic stenosis is serious and sudden death can occur. Patients have an overworked heart and often die from heart failure at an early age, usually under two years.

What is the treatment?

Occasionally surgery is attempted, but generally without good results. Most patients go untreated. Medications have been used, but with little success.

PORTAL CAVAL SHUNT

In the developing fetus, the fetal liver is bypassed by vessels that shunt blood around it. As long as the fetus exchanges blood with the mother, the fetal liver functions are minimal. Therefore, an extensive blood flow is not needed. A **portal caval shunt** describes a situation in which some or all of the blood vessels bypassing the liver do not degenerate prior to birth. Since some of the blood vessels maintain their embryonic patterns, the blood flows around the liver tissue and not through it.

The liver is responsible for important functions including the removal of wastes and toxins from the bloodstream; storage of materials such as glucose and fats; and the formation and storage of vitamins. Additionally, it produces various enzymes and proteins which aid in digestion. In a portal caval shunt, none of these tasks are done at an adequate level.

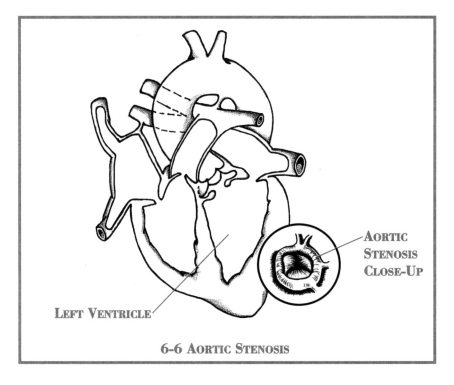

LEFT VENTRICLE

AORTIC
STENOSIS
CLOSE-UP

6-6 AORTIC STENOSIS

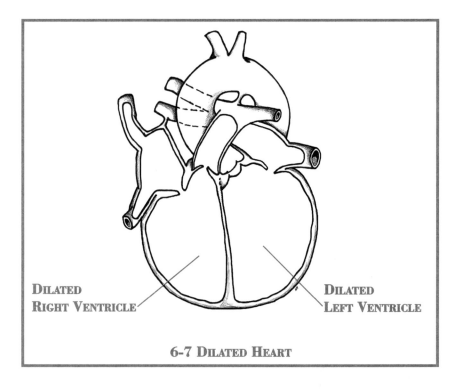

DILATED
RIGHT VENTRICLE

DILATED
LEFT VENTRICLE

6-7 DILATED HEART

What are the symptoms?

Most clinical signs relating to portal caval shunt are related to the build-up of toxins within the bloodstream. These are normal by-products of cellular metabolism, but when they exist in high concentration, they act like poisons in the body. Symptoms may develop anytime during the first six months of life. Since these poisons are building in the bloodstream, they affect other organs such as the brain. The term "hepatic encephalopathy" is used to describe neurologic signs caused by the toxic effects of metabolic waste on the brain. The build-up of metabolic toxins can cause poor appetite, dizziness, seizures, blindness, staggering, lethargy, depression and stupor.

What are the risks?

The risks are great and early death is common. As the animal grows, symptoms worsen. The increase in body size means more cells are producing metabolic by-products. These additional cells are in greater need of products formed or stored by a normal liver. Medication can help control the condition, but often it is not totally curable.

What is the treatment?

Neurological symptoms are treated with anticonvulsant drugs to prevent seizures. Generally, restricted protein diets are fed to minimize nitrogen waste build-up in the bloodstream. *Surgery, the only true cure, is required to close off the vessels bypassing the liver.*

ACQUIRED HEART DEFECTS

Acquired heart and vessel diseases are those that the patient is *not* born with, but rather develop over the course of a lifetime. As in humans, there are genetic influences that can cause early heart disease even though the individual initially had a normal heart. Besides genetics, other factors such as obesity, heartworm and infections can all lead to impaired heart function. Additionally, geriatric patients commonly develop heart disease or failure as a normal progression of aging.

CANINE DILATED CARDIOMYOPATHY

Cardiomyopathy refers to a diseased heart, specifically its muscles. Cardiomyopathy may develop secondary to infections such as parvovirus, can be drug induced, a result of cancer, etc. The majority of cardiomyopathy cases (over 95 percent), however, have no known cause. (See figure 6-7.)

The heart muscles simply fail. They weaken, losing their ability to contract with enough strength to adequately pump the blood to the body tissue. As the muscles weaken, they dilate and the heart loses its overall triangular shape and takes on the silhouette of a pumpkin. As in humans, this may occur at a young, middle or old age. In veterinary medicine, most cases are diagnosed around five years of age. Individuals of every breed can develop cardiomyopathy; however, German Shepherd Dogs, Boxers, Great Danes, Irish Wolfhounds, Irish Setters, English Springer Spaniels, Greyhounds, Doberman Pinschers and Saint Bernards have a higher incidence. *This suggests a genetic component.*

What are the symptoms?

Cardiomyopathy, being a disease of the heart muscle, can affect one or all of the four heart chambers. Because of varying degrees of severity and location of the disease within the heart, the signs can be many and varied. Usually, however, the patient will have decreased stamina and may faint, especially after exercise. Fluid may accumulate in several places: within the lungs causing coughing and/or labored breathing; within the abdomen causing an enlarged sagging gut; or within the legs causing them to have a swollen appearance and a dough-like consistency. Murmurs, an increased heart rate and abnormal heart rhythm are usually present.

What are the risks?

A diseased heart is always serious. An electrocardiogram (EKG) should be performed by a veterinarian at once. Diagnostic procedures such as an EKG, radiographs and echocardiograms will determine the severity and help plan a treatment.

What is the treatment?

Treatment is aimed at reducing the heart muscles' work and strengthening their contractions. Many drugs are available and selection is based on the patient evaluation. Commonly prescribed drugs to strengthen and control the rhythm of the heart include digitalis glycosides (digoxin, digitoxin), dopamine and hydralazine. To decrease the heart's work load, diuretics or "water pills" are utilized to reduce fluid build-up within the tissues (edema) and are often combined with restricted activity and rest.

Heart Valve Disease

The heart contains several valves, one between the upper and lower right chambers called the **right atrioventricular valve** and another valve between the two left chambers called the **left atrioventricular** or **mitral valve**. Other valves exist at the beginning of the pulmonary vein and the aorta.

The primary function of all heart valves is to prevent blood from flowing backwards once it is pumped through the valves. This maintains the flow of blood in one direction: always *forward* through the entire circulatory system. The most common heart condition of dogs is a failure of the valves to function properly. When this occurs, the blood flows backward through a valve, putting additional stress on the valves and muscles in that portion of the heart. Affected valves are usually smaller and unable to block the blood from flowing backward. This may be due to infections in a valve, heartworm infection, or simply a deterioration of the valves generally associated with aging.

The mitral valve is by far the most likely to fail. This condition is called "mitral insufficiency" or simply **"MI."** Because the left ventricle is the strongest chamber in the heart, when MI occurs blood is forced all the way back into the lungs, elevating blood pressure there. Due to the high pressure in this area, these smaller blood vessels push fluid through their walls into the lung, creating a build up of fluid in the lungs referred to as **pulmonary edema.**

What are the symptoms?
The most common sign is a dry hacking cough as the body tries to rid itself of the fluid. Initially this may be noted only at night or after exercise, but may progress to the point that coughing is noted throughout the day. The animal becomes weak and may even faint.

What are the risks?
Most patients live relatively normal lives. They simply learn not to over-exercise and to live with the cough. In more severe cases the fluid accumulates in the lungs and causes serious labored breathing. In general, all of the body's tissues fail to receive an adequate blood supply. This leads to other organ systems failing. Also in severe valvular disease, the heart muscle becomes overworked and may fail, resulting in death.

What is the treatment?
Medical therapy can be very successful in eliminating clinical signs and slowing the progression of valve disease. Medications are used to strengthen the heart and diuretics can eliminate the edema within the lungs and their tissues. Activity should be restricted and *the pet should not be overweight.* By losing weight and restricting activity, the heart's workload is lowered. Special low-salt diets can be fed. With this type of therapy, most dogs return to normal health, at least for a significant period of time.

In severe valvular disease, artificial heart valves can be placed by a veterinary surgeon. Heart surgery is expensive and should be performed by a specialist.

INFECTIOUS MYOCARDITIS

Many organisms such as viruses, bacteria and protozoa can enter the bloodstream and be carried to the heart, thereby developing an infection within the heart's muscles. An infection in the heart muscle is termed **myocarditis.** Parvovirus is probably the best-known organism to infect the heart of the dog. Lyme disease caused by *Borrelia burgdorferi* is a well-recognized bacterial cause of myocarditis. Of the protozoan organisms, *Toxoplasma gondii* has been recognized to also cause the condition.

What are the symptoms?
As in infections elsewhere in the body, a fever is generally noted. The heart rate and its rhythm often are abnormal. Pneumonia may be present, causing congestion and coughing.

What are the risks?
An infection of the heart is always serious. *The first symptom of myocarditis may be death.* Parvovirus can cause death in twenty-four hours with no other warning signs. Even after the acute stages are passed, with myocarditis there are usually lifelong abnormalities because the heart muscle is predisposed to failure or other conditions. Any animal with a fever and irregular heartbeats should be examined *at once.*

What is the treatment?
Commonly, a blood culture and other tests are utilized to identify the cause and magnitude of the infection. Electrocardiograms are also useful in diagnosis and in some cases in determining the prognosis. Viral causes are the most difficult to treat as they do not respond to antibiotics. Antibiotics are, however, extremely useful in treating bacterial myocarditis because they are carried to the site of the infection by the blood. Only a veterinary examination coupled with diagnostic tests will determine the proper treatment.

CANINE HEARTWORM DISEASE

Heartworm disease in dogs is one of the most common ailments affecting the heart. A parasite called *Dirofilaria immitis* is the causative agent and requires a mosquito to transmit the disease. *All dogs of every age are susceptible if bitten even once by a carrier mosquito.* Outdoor dogs are, however, at greater risk as their exposure to mosquitoes is more than that of the indoor dog. The life cycle of heartworm is somewhat complex and must be understood to properly utilize preventative measures. (See figure 6-8.)

The heartworm begins as an infectious parasite inside a mosquito. The larva lives in the mosquito for about two weeks, where it grows and molts into the third larval stage. This stage larva migrates into the mosquito's

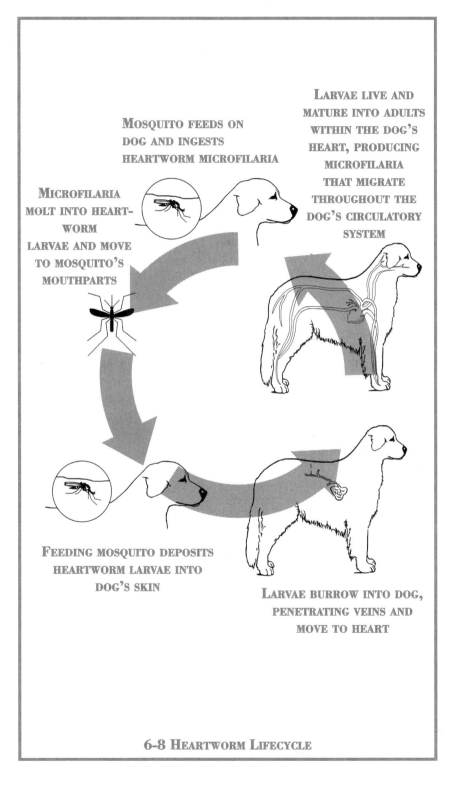

MOSQUITO FEEDS ON DOG AND INGESTS HEARTWORM MICROFILARIA

LARVAE LIVE AND MATURE INTO ADULTS WITHIN THE DOG'S HEART, PRODUCING MICROFILARIA THAT MIGRATE THROUGHOUT THE DOG'S CIRCULATORY SYSTEM

MICROFILARIA MOLT INTO HEART-WORM LARVAE AND MOVE TO MOSQUITO'S MOUTHPARTS

FEEDING MOSQUITO DEPOSITS HEARTWORM LARVAE INTO DOG'S SKIN

LARVAE BURROW INTO DOG, PENETRATING VEINS AND MOVE TO HEART

6-8 HEARTWORM LIFECYCLE

salivary glands. When the mosquito bites a canine, the worms are injected into the dog's skin. The larva remains in the dog's skin and underlying tissue for up to four months and then migrates into the bloodstream. Through the bloodstream, the **larval heartworms** are carried to the heart where they live in the blood within the chambers on the right side of the heart.

In the heart and lungs the larval worms mature into adults and may reach twelve inches in length or more. There are both male and female heartworms. The adult heartworms in the heart now produce microscopic offspring called **microfilaria.** From the time the mosquito bites the dog, it takes six months for the worms to grow into adults and produce young. The microfilaria enter the bloodstream by the thousands. When a mosquito bites the infected dog, the microfilaria enter the mosquito and molt into the infectious larvae, thus completing the life cycle. To complete the life cycle takes a minimum of six to seven months.

What are the symptoms?
Many patients exhibit few or no symptoms until the disease is in the advanced stage. In the infected dog, one first notices a decrease in activity, often accompanied by a cough. The adult worms within the right heart and lungs can cause severe lung congestion resulting in a cough.

Blood pressure will also build in the veins leading to the right heart, causing fluid to accumulate in the limbs and abdomen. Organs such as the liver can be significantly affected. In these cases jaundice (yellowing of the skin) may be noted as the liver function is compromised. As stated, most patients in the early stages have no noticeable symptoms. Many cases are diagnosed by routine heartworm blood tests performed by veterinarians on a twice-yearly basis.

What are the risks?
Left untreated, a dog with canine heartworm will eventually die from failure of the heart or other organs. The adult worms place undue stress on the heart, leading to early death. Additionally, if a worm blocks a heart valve or one of the major vessels within the lungs, death can be instantaneous, even though there have been no other signs. *All heartworm cases are serious and should be treated at once.*

What is the treatment and prevention?
Prevention is the key to eliminating a heartworm infection. Daily and monthly oral medications are both safe and effective at preventing this disease. The larval heartworms within the skin and nearby tissue are killed, preventing them from reaching the heart and maturing into adults. Preventative medication should be utilized throughout and following the mosquito seasons. There is no vaccine that prevents heartworm disease.

Additionally, routine blood tests should be performed annually to detect the disease in its early stages. Tests should be done on *all* dogs, even on those that have been on preventative medication. If a patient is identified by the blood test as having heartworm, then treatment should begin immediately.

Arsenic compounds injected intravenously are still the recommended treatment to eliminate adult worms in the heart. The arsenic is injected intravenously over a period of several days to *slowly* kill the adult heartworms. *Arsenic compounds do have side effects, so careful monitoring by a veterinarian is necessary.* Prevention is much safer and less expensive than treatment. All dogs, indoor and outdoor, should be on preventative medication every year.

ACQUIRED VESSEL DEFECTS

AUTOIMMUNE DISORDERS OF THE BLOOD

An autoimmune disorder is one in which the patient's immune system views its own cells as a foreign material or organism and attempts to destroy them. Autoimmune disorders of the blood are common in canine patients.

Autoimmune Hemolytic Anemia (AIHA)

This is an autoimmune disease in which the body attacks its own red blood cells. Red blood cells are still being provided by the bone marrow, but once released into the circulation they have a shorter than normal existence as they are constantly being attacked and destroyed by abnormal antibodies in the blood. Antibodies are normally formed by the dog's immune system when needed to destroy invading bacterial or viral signs. However, with AIHA, the dog's immune system sees its own red blood cells as foreign, and therefore produces protein molecules to destroy them.

A second constituent of AIHA is a decreased number of platelets. These tiny structures circulate within the bloodstream and function in the formation of blood cells when vessels are cut or broken. In the body over the course of a day, many small vessels break. A simple bruise is nothing more than a collection of broken vessels allowing some blood to spill into and discolor the tissue. When low platelet numbers are diagnosed, clotting does not occur correctly. AIHA patients are therefore similar to human hemophiliacs. Uncontrolled bleeding further decreases numbers of red blood cells along with the antigen response.

What are the symptoms?

A patient suffering with AIHA will have a lower than normal number of red blood cells within the blood. This is termed **anemia**. The lips, gums and eye margins will appear pale (or yellow in the later stages of the disease) and not the normal pink to red color. Commonly the patient will be tired and lethargic as there are not enough red blood cells to carry oxygen to the tissues. Fainting commonly occurs due to low oxygen levels in the brain.

As the red blood cells are being destroyed, **hemoglobin** (the oxygen carrier molecule of red blood cells) builds up to high levels within the body. The elevated level of the substance causes a yellowish color to the skin and membranes that we refer to as jaundice. The urine may also contain hemoglobin and appear dark or tea-colored. Additionally, the heart beats much more rapidly to pump the thinner blood faster through the tissue. This is an attempt to compensate for low oxygen levels.

What are the risks?
AIHA is serious and left untreated usually results in death. An animal that is anemic will try to compensate by pumping more blood. This can overload the heart, causing it to fail. If the animal is cut, it typically takes much longer for the bleeding to stop.

What is the treatment?
Most patients with AIHA will respond to steroid therapy. The steroid prednisone has been widely used to treat AIHA. Drug therapy may be required for months to years. Prednisone suppresses the immune system, helping to prevent red blood cell destruction. Blood transfusions may be required in the critically anemic patient. Thankfully, a portion of these cases may recover and no longer need therapy.

LUPUS ERYTHEMATOSIS (LE)
This is an autoimmune disease closely related to AIHA (see previous discussion). LE has the same two constituents as AIHA (i.e., anemia and low platelet count), plus two additional characteristics. LE patients also suffer from arthritis and impaired kidney function. In lupus cases, the animal's immune system also views the surfaces *within* the joints as foreign and attacks them, leading to a nonerosive arthritis. Additionally, the immune system also attacks a portion of the animal's kidney, leading to premature failure or limiting of this organ's function.

What are the symptoms?
Lupus dogs suffer from: anemia and the weakness associated with it, decreased platelet number with the resultant bleeding disorder, arthritis with joint stiffness, difficulty walking or getting up and impaired kidney function. In the early stages, impaired kidney function causes the patient to drink and urinate excessively in an attempt to compensate for the kidney's decreased ability to filter out wastes by flushing more water through the system.

What are the risks?

LE patients without treatment die from anemia, blood loss, kidney failure or some combination of these. Arthritis in these patients, although not fatal, is extremely painful.

What is the treatment?

The treatment for LE is exactly the same as AIHA, that is, steroid therapy. Prednisone is the most common product utilized. With lupus, however, patients rarely can be taken off medication as sometimes happens with AIHA. Additional therapy is also needed in LE patients to accommodate the kidney changes. This is usually done by altering the diet to decrease the involvement of the kidney through smaller, more easily metabolized protein.

VON WILLEBRAND'S DISEASE (vWD)

This is a common *inherited* bleeding disorder. Other immune disorders, such as autoimmune hemolytic anemia and lupus erythematosus, are brought on by a decrease in the number of platelets. These are tiny cells that circulate within the blood system and form the necessary lattice for blood clot formation.

With von Willebrand's, this is not the case. In addition to platelets, clot formation is the result of a long chain of chemical reactions carried out by individual molecules called "clotting factors." Each factor is numbered such that factor I leads to a reaction with factor II forming a new substance. This then reacts with factor III and so on. Von Willebrand's is a genetic disease in which factor VIII is found in deficient quantity or functions abnormally. Excessive bleeding upon injury is the result. This would be similar to hemophilia in humans. Certain breeds have a higher incidence of VWD than others. German Shepherd Dogs, Doberman Pinschers, Shetland Sheepdogs, Chesapeake Bay Retrievers, German Shorthaired Pointers, Golden Retrievers, Standard Poodles and Scottish Terriers all have a higher than normal incidence, showing that it *can be inherited*. Blood tests are available to identify VWD victims.

What are the symptoms?

Excessive bleeding is the main symptom. Bleeding generally occurs after a wound or surgery. In these cases, the blood simply does not clot in the normal time, therefore bleeding is extensive.

What are the risks?

These patients, without treatment, can bleed to death following surgery or what might normally be considered less than life-threatening injuries.

What is the treatment?

If excessive bleeding is expected for the VWD patient, a drug called desmopressin acetate (DDAVP) can be administered intranasally to increase clotting. There is no long-term treatment. *Prevention through eliminating affected individuals from any breeding program* is the goal of veterinary medicine today. Tests can be run annually to determine this and should be done on all individuals with a history of this disorder in their backgrounds.

CHAPTER 7

Hormone Disorders

INTRODUCTION

The **endocrine glands** provide chemicals called hormones. Once produced, hormones enter the bloodstream and most (other than prostaglandins) produce an effect *elsewhere* in the body.

Not all cells within the body are affected by hormones, and some cells of a particular organ may respond to a *specific* hormone. Some hormones control the release of other hormones. For example, the **pituitary gland** located at the base of the brain (see figure 7-1) produces many hormones. These hormones act on other glands such as the adrenals and cause them to release their own hormones. The pituitary gland is called *"the master gland"* as it provides more kinds of hormones than any other gland. Pituitary hormones control the hormone release for other **endocrine glands,** including the *thyroid, parathyroid, adrenal, ovaries, testicles and pancreas.*

The **pituitary gland** produces *growth hormone,* which controls growth; *prolactin,* which stimulates the mammary glands to produce milk; *thyroid-stimulating hormone (TSH),* which stimulates the thyroid gland; *luteinizing hormone (LH)* and *follicle-stimulating hormone (FSH),* both of which control heat cycles and ovulation. The pituitary gland also produces *adrenocorticotropic hormone (ACTH)* which causes the adrenal gland to produce cortisol and other hormones, and *melanocyte stimulating hormone (MSH),* which affects pigment.

The **thyroid gland**, once stimulated, produces its own hormone, *thyroxine.* The **ovaries,** once stimulated by FSH and LH from the pituitary, principally produce *progesterone and estrogens.* The **testes** provide

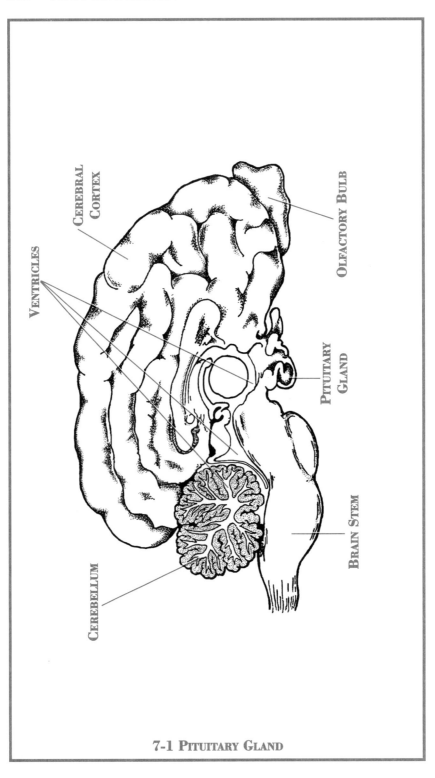

7-1 PITUITARY GLAND

testosterone. The **pancreas** produces the most well-known hormone of all: *insulin*, which regulates blood sugar. The **adrenal glands**, once stimulated by the pituitary hormone ACTH, produce naturally occurring steroids called *corticosteroids, mineralocorticoids and adrenal sex steroids*. Contrary to popular belief, steroids are *natural* to the body. We can manufacture similar steroids such as cortisones for use in pets. Frequently we hear pet owners being concerned about the side effects of steroids and certainly there are some; however, steroids are absolutely essential for life.

As one can see, hormones play a very complex role in regulating the body's functions. This chapter will discuss only those hormone conditions commonly encountered in veterinary medicine.

DISORDERS OF THE ADRENAL GLANDS

The body has two adrenal glands, one located next to each kidney. (See figure 7-2.) In the canine, adrenal glands are about the size of a pea. The **medulla,** the inner core of the glands, secretes the hormones *epinephrine (adrenaline) and norepinephrine (noradrenaline)*. These two hormones control blood pressure and heart rate. The outer shell of the adrenal glands is called the **cortex.** This secretes the *corticosteroid and sex steroid hormones*. There are two types of corticosteroids: the *mineralocorticoids* and the *glucocorticoids*. Aldosterone is a mineralocorticoid regulating the amount of sodium lost in the urine. Hydrocortisone (cortisol), a glucocorticoid hormone, helps control the metabolism of carbohydrates. The sex steroids produced by the adrenal cortex are also referred to as the sex hormones. In the male these are *androgens* and in the female they are *estrogens and progesterones*.

CUSHING'S DISEASE

Cushing's disease results when the adrenal glands overproduce steroid hormones. This may be caused by disease in either the adrenal glands, the pituitary gland (which stimulates the adrenal glands) or the hypothalamus (a section of the brain that stimulates the pituitary gland). Additionally, an artificial Cushing's syndrome can be seen if a patient is being given excessive levels of steroid medication. Tumors of the hypothalamus, pituitary or adrenal gland can cause overproduction of steroid hormones, resulting in Cushing's disease.

What are the symptoms?

The body of a patient with Cushing's disease typically will appear puffy from weight gain. Fatty deposits accumulate under the skin and within the body cavities due to uncontrolled metabolism of carbohydrates. Additionally, the skin over the abdomen and flank area will become thin and may

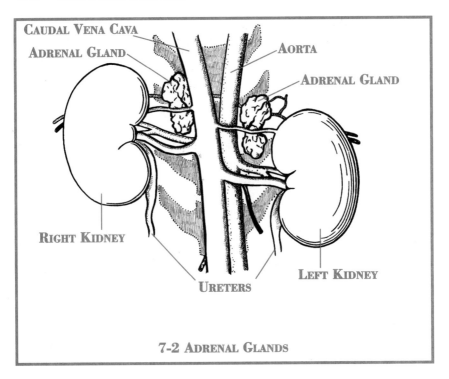

7-2 ADRENAL GLANDS

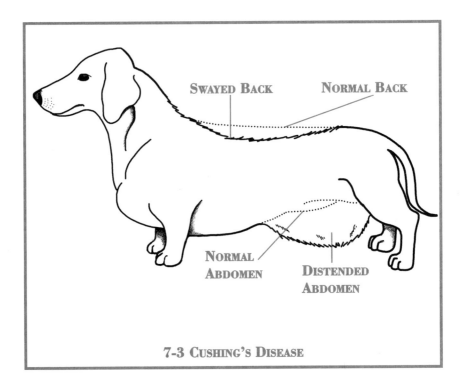

7-3 CUSHING'S DISEASE

contain small white mineral (calcium) deposits. Muscle mass and strength are lost. The patient will develop a "pot-bellied" appearance (see figure 7-3) as the abdominal muscles become weak. The legs will appear spindly and the animal may have problems getting up or jumping on furniture or into a car. Thirst and appetite will usually be excessive.

What are the risks?
Cushing's disease often results from cancer of the hypothalamus, pituitary or adrenal glands. The first two are adjacent to the brain. Any tumors in this area have potentially serious consequences. *Cushing's disease is serious and without treatment, usually fatal.*

What is the treatment?
Initially the cause must be determined. If the patient is receiving excessive steroid medication for another condition, then merely altering the dosage may correct the problem. If your pet is on steroids for a medical condition, always consult your veterinarian before increasing or decreasing the dose.

If diagnostic tests reveal a tumor, then surgery may be indicated. Drugs are also available that can destroy portions of the adrenal gland, thus reducing the hormonal output.

ADDISON'S DISEASE

Addison's disease describes a patient with *under*active adrenal glands. Occasionally due to age or damage from infections or drug therapy, the adrenal cortex will not produce enough steroid hormones.

What are the symptoms?
Weight loss, anemia, diarrhea, loss of appetite and vomiting can all be signs of Addison's disease.

What are the risks?
Fluid loss along with mineral imbalances create a serious situation. Left untreated, the patient with Addison's will experience dehydration and death.

What is the treatment?
Diagnostic blood tests to check sodium and potassium levels will help confirm a diagnosis of Addison's. Medications such as Florinef can be administered to replace the inadequate hormones. Most patients respond very well to therapy.

DISORDERS OF THE PANCREAS

The pancreas is a gray ribbon-like gland located adjacent to the stomach and anterior small intestine. (See figure 7-4.) It has two major functions.

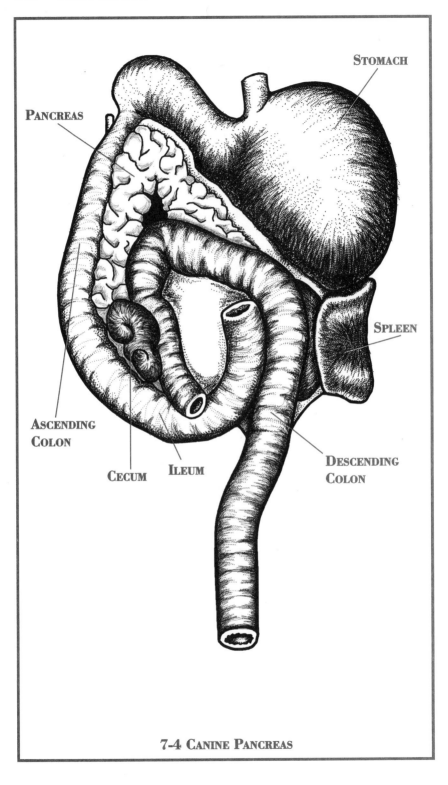

STOMACH

PANCREAS

SPLEEN

ASCENDING
COLON

CECUM ILEUM

DESCENDING
COLON

7-4 CANINE PANCREAS

It produces enzymes to aid in digestion and hormones to control blood sugar (glucose) levels.

In this chapter we are concerned with its production of **hormones, insulin and glucagon**. Its production of digestive enzymes will be discussed in Chapter 8, "The Digestive Organs." When starches and carbohydrates are eaten, they are broken down into the sugar glucose. This is absorbed through the wall of the digestive tract and passes into the bloodstream. *Insulin* allows glucose to leave the bloodstream and enter the body's tissue. It is utilized as energy for the cells. When glucose levels are high, glucagon causes it to be stored in the liver and muscles as *glycogen*.

Diabetes Mellitus (Sugar Diabetes)

Diabetes mellitus, commonly referred to simply as diabetes, is a condition in which the pancreas does not produce sufficient quantities of the hormone **insulin**. Insulin is necessary to move glucose into the cells from the bloodstream. Brain cells, as well as intestinal and red blood cells, do not need high levels of insulin for glucose transport across their walls. The body tissues need glucose for energy. However, with diabetes the glucose simply builds up in the bloodstream, causing an elevated blood sugar level. *Genetics play a role, with a higher incidence of diabetes seen in Beagles and Poodles.*

What are the symptoms?
Elevated blood sugar (glucose) can affect many systems of the body. Excess blood sugar will be lost through the kidneys, causing increased urination and thirst. Elevated blood sugar also alters the lens of the eye, leading to diabetic *cataracts*. *Weight loss* is a common symptom as the body burns muscle for energy to help compensate for the body's inability to utilize glucose. A *loss of muscle mass* combined with *inadequate energy levels* within the cells leads to generalized weakness. The most common signs of diabetes are weakness, weight loss and increased thirst and urination.

What are the risks?
The elevated blood sugar is toxic to many body systems and organs, including the blood vessels, nervous system (brain), liver, etc. *A patient with uncontrolled diabetes will not live a normal life span.* At the first indication of diabetes, a blood test should be performed by a veterinarian to determine the blood sugar level. The earlier treatment is initiated, the better.

What is the treatment?
Unlike with humans, simply controlling the diet is seldom beneficial in the canine. Similarly, oral insulin tablets are not commonly effective in pets. The treatment for a diabetic canine involves daily insulin injections.

Patients must be carefully monitored with blood and urine sugar tests to help determine the proper amount of insulin. Daily feeding must be on a regular schedule to provide a consistent supply of sugar so that insulin remains at the required level.

Most patients with diabetes can live relatively normal lives with proper care. Maintaining the diabetic pet requires dedication on the part of the owner; however, the experience is rewarding.

DISORDERS OF THE THYROID

The thyroid gland is butterfly-shaped and located near the larynx (Adam's apple) in the dog's neck. (See figure 7-5.) The thyroid gland combines the amino acid **tyrosine** with **iodine** in order to manufacture thyroid hormone. The pituitary gland near the brain exerts control over the thyroid gland. TSH from the pituitary stimulates the thyroid gland to produce its hormone, **thyroxine.** Thyroxine is the hormone that controls metabolic and activity levels. The thyroid gland also secretes another hormone, **calcitonin,** which is necessary for proper calcium metabolism.

HYPERTHYROIDISM

Hyperthyroidism is a condition in which the thyroid gland produces thyroxine in excess. Hyperthyroidism is rare in the canine, but common in the feline.

What are the symptoms?

A patient with an overactive thyroid will be anxious, hyperactive and lose weight. Trembling muscles may also be noted. *Restlessness* is the most common sign.

What are the risks?

Generally this condition is not fatal unless it continues for years. One exception would be if the cause is a tumor of the pituitary or thyroid.

What is the treatment?

If a tumor exists, then surgery to excise the tumor should be performed. In non-cancerous cases, there are oral medications which will destroy a portion of the overactive thyroid cells. Fortunately, this condition is uncommon in the canine.

HYPOTHYROIDISM

Hypothyroidism or an "underactive" thyroid gland is one of the most common endocrine disorders in the canine. In this instance, not enough thyroxine is being produced by the thyroid.

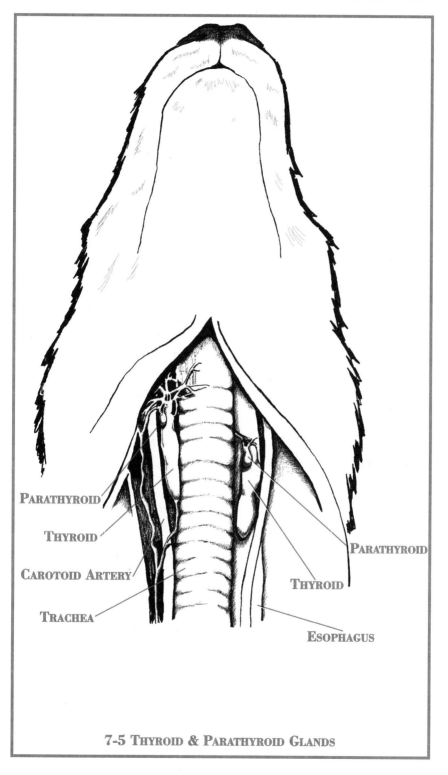

PARATHYROID

THYROID

CAROTOID ARTERY

TRACHEA

PARATHYROID

THYROID

ESOPHAGUS

7-5 THYROID & PARATHYROID GLANDS

What are the symptoms?

The hallmarks of hypothyroidism include a poor hair coat with hair loss, weight gain, lethargy and an intolerance to cold temperatures. Additionally, fertility can be decreased. These are the most common signs, although other more subtle symptoms may occur, such as altered blood pressure and cholesterol levels. Most owners notice the poor hair coat and weight gain. A blood test to measure the thyroid hormone blood levels will confirm the diagnosis.

What are the risks?

Seldom is hypothyroidism life threatening except in very severe cases. Energy levels will be poor and weight gain excessive. The associated obesity will affect other organs and a shortened life span is possible.

What is the treatment?

The treatment for hypothyroidism is easy and very successful. Oral tablets containing thyroid hormone (thyroxine) are available to supplement what the body is lacking. A single blood test will confirm the amount of hormone needed. With proper supplementation, the patient will quickly return to normal health.

DISORDERS OF THE PARATHYROID GLAND

Four pairs of parathyroid glands exist in the canine. They are located near the thyroid gland in the neck. Their function is to produce parathyroid hormone, which is necessary to control the metabolism of calcium and phosphorus. This can affect the kidneys and bone formation.

PRIMARY PARATHYROIDISM

This describes an overactive parathyroid gland producing too much parathyroid hormone, thus increasing the blood calcium levels. Calcium is selectively removed from the bones, causing them to soften.

What are the symptoms?

In most cases no visible symptoms are present; however, routine blood tests may detect a high level of blood calcium.

What are the risks?

In the long term, bones will become soft and may fracture at the slightest insult. Kidney and/or bladder stones may form as a result of the altered calcium levels.

What is the treatment?

This condition is usually caused by tumors in the parathyroid glands. Surgery to remove the growths will lower the hormone production.

CHAPTER 8

The Digestive Organs—Liver, Pancreas and Gallbladder

INTRODUCTION

For the purpose of this chapter, we will refer to the digestive system as including the **liver, pancreas and gallbladder**. Disorders of the stomach and intestines are dealt with separately in Chapter 9, "The Digestive Tract."

The liver, gallbladder and pancreas all provide substances to aid in the digestion of food, which takes place within the intestines. (See figure 8-1.)

The liver is the largest internal organ in the body (see figure 8-2) and has many functions. It is important in:

- storage of sugar
- production of proteins
- storage and production of vitamins
- formation of products necessary in normal blood
- filtering wastes from the blood
- digesting fats
- removal of certain toxins or poisons from the body

Any disorder affecting the liver may cause a variety of signs. **Bile** produced by the liver plays an important role in digestion. Bile is a waste product synthesized from the disintegration of old red blood cells. Bile's digestive function concerns fats consumed in the animal's diet. Bile produced by the liver is stored in a small "balloon-like" structure called the **gallbladder**.

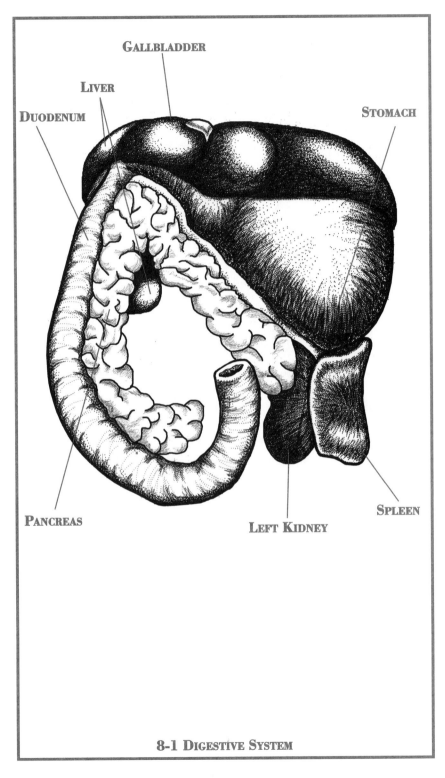

8-1 DIGESTIVE SYSTEM

The gallbladder connects to the small intestine by a tube called the **bile duct.** The bile duct carries bile to the first part of the small intestine, where it breaks down fats.

Bile acids are specific components of liver bile. Bile acids are like a detergent and they convert fat globules into water-soluble nutrients, allowing the body to absorb them through the intestinal wall into the bloodstream. In addition to bile acids, bile contains a pigment called **bilirubin.** Bilirubin is the pigment released from dead red blood cells and is responsible for the brown color of feces. If the liver becomes diseased, a frequently seen phenomenon is jaundice (icterus). Jaundice is nothing more than a build-up of pigments such as bilirubin in the bloodstream, resulting in a yellow color to the skin, gums and white of the eyes.

As described before, the gallbladder is a balloon-like structure located next to the liver (see figure 8-3) that stores and concentrates bile. Once the dog eats, the gallbladder is stimulated to carry bile to the small intestine for excretion and fat digestion.

Unlike the gallbladder, the **pancreas** is an organ that functions independently of the liver. The pancreas is a small ribbon-like structure located near and attached to the wall of the small intestine. (See figure 8-4.) The pancreas has two major functions. It produces **insulin** to aid the blood in sugar absorption (refer to Chapter 7, "Hormone Disorders"), and important enzymes to aid in the digestion of protein and fats (lipids). These enzymes travel from the pancreas to the small intestine through a small tube called the **pancreatic duct.**

The pancreas produces the protein-digesting enzymes trypsin and chymotrypsin. Other enzymes are produced, but these are the major two involved with protein digestion. Fat digestion is aided by enzymes called lipases, also produced by the pancreas. Without these enzymes, dogs would not be able to break down important dietary components.

DISORDERS OF THE LIVER

Diseases of the liver affect a wide range of the body's systems because of this organ's involvement in digestion, red blood cell metabolism, protein synthesis and other functions. Because the liver functions to filter and detoxify blood, it is very susceptible to toxins and infections. The fact that it is the largest internal organ also makes it susceptible to trauma. Because of the liver's many roles, disorders are frequently serious. Unlike other organs of the body, the liver does have some ability to regenerate and replenish damaged cells. Because of this, many disorders affect the patient temporarily, only until the liver can recover.

HEPATITIS

Hepatitis is an infection or inflammation of the liver. Organisms (bacterial *or* viral) that enter the bloodstream generally are carried to the liver and frequently cause an infection there.

CANINE HERPES VIRUS (CHV)

Canine herpes virus can be a sexually transmitted disease. The herpes virus lives in the adult female and male reproductive tracts. The virus persists in the female's vaginal secretion and the male's semen. As in many herpes infections found in other species, adult animals can live for years with no apparent signs.

Puppies are exposed through infected dams during the birthing process. As a puppy passes through the vagina, it can be exposed to the herpes-infected vaginal secretions. Additionally, the herpes virus can cross the placenta and affect fetuses prior to whelping. Nasal secretions of the carrier female can also affect puppies born unaffected. Once exposed, a puppy may die within three days with characteristic liver hemorrhage. However, many of these puppies develop into carrier adults just like their parents.

What are the symptoms?

Adult carriers typically exhibit no obvious symptoms; however, small blister-like lesions may occasionally be noted on the vaginal wall. Puppies will show signs as soon as seventy-two hours after being born. Puppies become weakened, cease nursing and cry. The feces may become soft and yellow. Respiratory signs, including a nasal discharge, may develop. Hemorrhages may develop and appear as purple blotches under the skin, especially on the stomach. The liver of the puppy becomes severely affected by the herpes virus. This limits this organ's functions, leading to diarrhea and hemorrhage.

What are the risks?

This is one of the leading causes of death in newborn puppies. Once the above signs develop, death often follows in forty-eight hours. The disease spreads rapidly through the litter as infected puppies are highly contagious. Puppies exposed after six weeks of age have a better chance of recovery. Older puppies develop the disease by coming in contact with the mother's infected, but normal-appearing, nasal secretions. We suspect many cases of herpes are wrongly diagnosed as disorders such as parvovirus and coronavirus. Autopsies of deceased puppies by a veterinary pathologist will reveal the characteristic herpes liver lesions.

What is the treatment?

Currently there is no treatment for canine herpes. All treatment is aimed at supportive care. Older puppies can be force-fed and treated with anti-diarrheal medication. The survival rate of puppies less than three weeks old is poor. It is hoped that a vaccination will be developed to protect against this disease.

INFECTIOUS CANINE HEPATITIS (ADENOVIRUS TYPE)

Commonly simply referred to as CAV-1 disease, this virus can affect dogs of all ages. The virus is shed in body secretions including saliva, urine and feces. CAV-1 is not spread in the air and the most common route of infection is by ingestion. This can occur when dogs lick and clean themselves after walking through areas containing urine or feces contaminated by the virus. Transmission from saliva can occur if dogs lick or bite each other, or drink or eat from the same source as an infected animal.

What are the symptoms?

Many affected dogs, especially adults, may be carriers and exhibit no signs. In others, especially young patients, the liver and kidneys can be damaged, resulting in seizures, bloody diarrhea and pneumonia. The seizures are the result of toxins and waste products building up within the blood that a normal liver would ordinarily remove.

What are the risks?

Infections of CAV-1 are serious. Although may patients can survive this virus, others rapidly die from severe liver impairment. In multiple-pet households and in litters, the virus can rapidly be transmitted to other animals. The virus can live outside of the dog's body and therefore contaminate the environment for several months.

What is the treatment?

There is no direct treatment for CAV-1. Antidiarrheal medications are used in those patients with diarrhea. Intravenous fluids are indicated in patients with liver and/or kidney involvement, until these dogs are on the road to recovery. Fortunately, excellent, widely used vaccines greatly reduce the frequency of this disorder. When the name "DHL" is used for vaccine in the puppy series or adult boosters, the "H" stands for hepatitis and actually refers to protection against CAV-1.

CHRONIC ACTIVE HEPATITIS

Chronic active hepatitis is a term used to describe a patient with an ongoing liver inflammation of at least several months' duration. These patients have livers that have become inflamed and therefore cannot function properly. Occasionally the cause is known, but sometimes it is not. Bedlington Terriers, West Highland White Terriers and other breeds have abnormal copper metabolism as the cause, hence the name "copper storage disease." This is a genetic condition in which abnormal levels of copper are deposited in the liver, causing a malfunction of the normal cells.

Doberman Pinschers have a higher than usual incidence of chronic hepatitis. Certain drugs used to contain seizures (Primidone, Dilantin, etc.) can be responsible for inducing hepatitis. Leptospira, a bacterium, has been identified as causing liver abnormalities. Although in the above instances the cause is known, in the majority of hepatitis patients no cause can be identified. Idiopathic hepatitis is the term used to describe a liver inflammation with no known cause.

What are the symptoms?

Symptoms vary tremendously depending on the cause and areas of the liver involved. Common signs, however, include an elevated temperature, anemia (pale gums), jaundice (yellowing of the skin, gums and eyes), diarrhea (occasionally with hemorrhage), vomiting, bloated abdomen due to fluid accumulation and liver enlargement and painful abdomen. Animals with these symptoms are usually lethargic and have little or no appetite. A liver biopsy by a veterinary surgeon is generally required to make the diagnosis of chronic active hepatitis.

What are the risks?

Because the liver is responsible for so many functions including digestion, red blood cell function and the removal of blood toxins, *all liver disorders are serious*. With treatment, many patients will live relatively normal lives. Depending on the cause, the outcome can be favorable or poor. If the liver damage is considerable, then death is the result.

What is the treatment?

If possible, the cause should be identified. In breeds suffering with a copper storage disorder, drugs such as D-penicillamine may be effective in removing excess copper. Bacterial infections can be treated with antibiotics. Patients with no known cause (idiopathic hepatitis) can be managed with drugs that help reduce the work placed on the liver.

Generally, diets containing easily digestible proteins are fed. Cottage cheese makes a good protein source for the liver patient. Excess fats are avoided. Carbohydrates are fed in large quantities. White rice is an excellent source of these carbohydrates. Commercial diets are available for patients suffering with hepatitis. The B group and other vitamins are always supplemented. Steroids such as prednisone and prednisolone can be used to fight inflammation. Other medications are available to use in specific cases of chronic acute hepatitis.

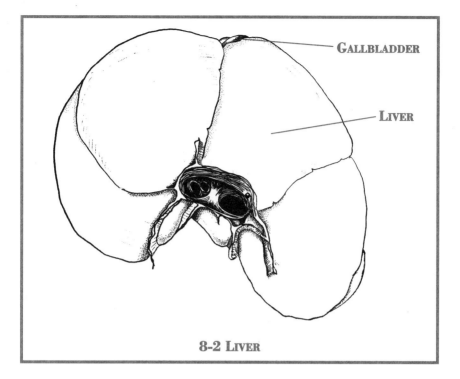

GALLBLADDER

LIVER

8-2 LIVER

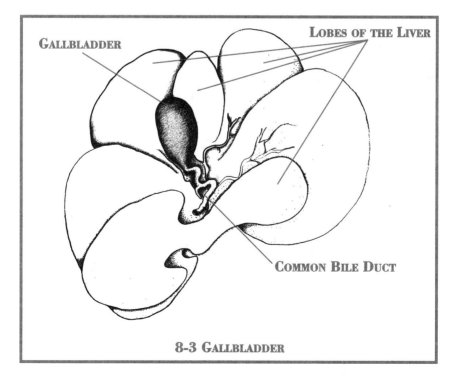

LOBES OF THE LIVER

GALLBLADDER

COMMON BILE DUCT

8-3 GALLBLADDER

LIVER TUMORS

It is not uncommon for liver cancer to develop in dogs. Tumors originating in other tissues such as the spleen and mammary glands frequently spread to the liver. Two types of tumors that do originate in liver tissue are occasionally seen in the canine. Hepatomas are growths that arise in the liver; however, they are benign and not nearly as devastating as the malignant forms called *hepatocellular adenocarcinoma*.

What are the symptoms?

Patients with liver cancer will frequently have vomiting, diarrhea and anemia. They will be lethargic and have little or no appetite. The liver is important in protein synthesis and when impaired, the entire body has lower than normal levels of these substances.

Proteins are a major constituent of the blood and when they are at lower than normal levels, fluid leaks from the vessels into surrounding tissues or body cavities. This causes swelling (edema) in the limbs and fluid accumulates in the abdomen and chest. The abdomen may appear bloated due to either the increase in size of the liver or fluid accumulation. Respiration may also be more difficult due to the fluid build-up in the chest.

What are the risks?

Benign tumors (hepatomas) are obviously much less threatening than malignant ones such as hepatocellular carcinomas. *Most malignant tumors are untreatable.* Even though surgery to remove the mass can be performed, regrowth or spread to other parts of the body is likely.

What is the treatment?

Most liver tumors require removal by surgery, and are then biopsied. Occasionally an entire liver lobe can be removed to help reduce recurrence.

DISORDERS OF THE GALLBLADDER

The gallbladder is a small balloon-like structure connected to the liver. Its primary function is to store the bile produced by liver cells. The stored bile is then released by the gallbladder and travels via the bile duct to the small intestine where it aids in the digestive process.

GALLBLADDER STONES

As in humans, occasionally a canine patient will be diagnosed with gallbladder stones. The fats making up bile can, on occasion, clump and become a solid mass referred to as a stone. The "stones" form within the gallbladder itself and can even pass down into the ducts, causing obstruction in the normal flow of bile. (See figure 8-5.)

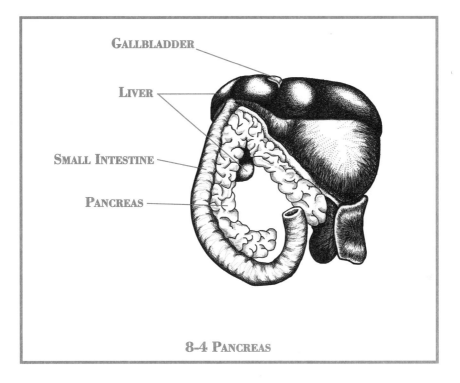

GALLBLADDER

LIVER

SMALL INTESTINE

PANCREAS

8-4 PANCREAS

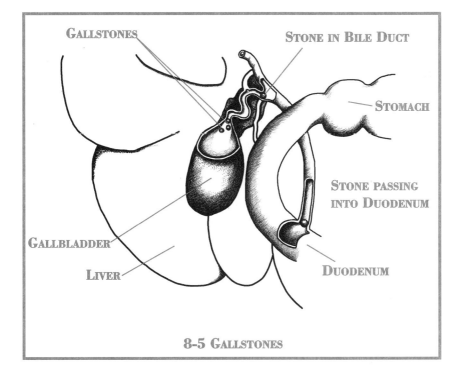

GALLSTONES

STONE IN BILE DUCT

STOMACH

STONE PASSING INTO DUODENUM

GALLBLADDER

LIVER

DUODENUM

8-5 GALLSTONES

What are the symptoms?

Most dogs with gallstones show no symptoms whatsoever as these stones simply remain in the gallbladder. However, if the stones become large or move into the bile duct and block the flow of bile from the liver or to the intestines, problems can arise. Patients with a blocked bile flow may have a loose, clay-colored stool. In severe instances, jaundice may develop, making the gums and skin appear yellow.

What are the risks?

Unless the flow of bile is interrupted, no risks are associated with gallstones. If bile flow is disrupted, then bile may flow backwards into the liver, causing a liver upset. A complete bile duct obstruction is serious and causes congestion of the organ and decreases the liver's ability to function correctly. This has the same effect as any serious hepatitis.

What is the treatment?

Surgery is required to remove the gallstones and restore the normal flow of bile. It is not known why stones initially form in dogs; however, surgical removal is very successful.

GALLBLADDER RUPTURE

Occasionally following a traumatic accident when a blow to the abdomen occurs, the gallbladder may rupture. This allows the bile to spill directly into the abdomen and not reach the intestine.

What are the symptoms?

Initially there may be no noticeable symptoms. The gallbladder contents, namely bile, are very caustic to other organs and the lining of the abdominal cavity. As bile leaks from the rupture, it comes in contact with and irritates all exposed surfaces within the abdomen. Typical signs include fever and extreme abdominal pain as *peritonitis* (inflammation of the abdominal cavity) is caused. Normal bile often contains bacteria from the liver and this aggravates the peritonitis.

What are the risks?

A ruptured gallbladder is very serious. In fact, it is *life threatening*. Peritonitis, due to bile spillage, is a progressive disorder leading to severe inflammation with adhesions forming between the various abdominal structures.

What is the treatment?

Surgery is required to repair the rupture. If the damage is severe, the majority of the gallbladder can be removed with no serious consequences. Supportive care, anti-inflammatories and antibiotics are used to treat the peritonitis.

DISORDERS OF THE PANCREAS

The pancreas is a small ribbon-like organ responsible for many functions including sugar metabolism and enzyme production to aid in the digestion of nutrients.

ACUTE PANCREATITIS

Acute pancreatitis is a term used to describe a sudden onset of cell inflammation of the pancreas. The cause of irritation is usually unknown; however, certain factors have been found to contribute to the inflammation. Middle-aged, overweight female canines have a much higher incidence of pancreatitis. Meals high in fat tend to trigger the inflammatory process. "Monday morning disease" is a term occasionally used by veterinarians to describe this condition. It seems that pets have a tendency to be overfed with high-fat or greasy meals by their owners, especially on weekends, causing the pet to develop pancreatitis by Monday.

What are the symptoms?
Pets with pancreatitis will have extremely painful abdomens. Quite commonly they "hunch up" or arch their backs, probably in response to the acute abdominal pain. Because the pancreas is important in digestion, an irritation to it may cause diarrhea, oftentimes severe. Commonly the stool appears yellow and greasy.

Vomiting may also occur. When both vomiting and diarrhea occur simultaneously, dehydration may become apparent. The body temperature may be normal or elevated.

What are the risks?
Pancreatitis is serious and painful. Most patients survive the attack, but the recovery period may take several days. Remember that the pancreas produces enzymes that digest proteins and fats. If the inflammation is severe enough, these enzymes will be released from their cells and start to digest surrounding tissues within and outside the pancreas. This can spread through large sections of the organ, as well as surrounding tissue. Many dogs have recurrent bouts of pancreatitis throughout their lives. Some dogs, even after a single incident, may develop other pancreatic disorders such as diabetes or maldigestion.

What is the treatment?
In any instance where pancreatitis is suspected, it is important to withhold food for at least twenty-four hours. This allows the enzyme-producing cells to rest and remain unstimulated. Even water should only be given sparingly or as needed to prevent dehydration. Commonly, anti-inflammatory medications are administered along with antibiotics to prevent infections.

Critical patients may need intravenous fluids until recovered. After recovery a restrictive and low-fat diet is often implemented to help with weight reduction. It is best if high-fat or fatty foods are avoided altogether, especially if a patient has recurrent bouts of pancreatitis.

MALDIGESTION (PANCREATIC EXOCRINE INSUFFICIENCY)

The pancreas plays a major role in digesting nutrients, especially proteins and fats. The pancreatic cells called exocrine cells produce the enzymes *trypsin and chymotrypsin* to break down proteins. Fat-digesting enzymes called *lipase* are also produced by the pancreas. For unknown reasons, the enzyme-producing cells of the pancreas occasionally decrease in size (atrophy) and fail to produce any or the appropriate amounts of needed enzymes. German Shepherd Dogs have a higher incidence of maldigestion, suggesting this is an inherited or genetic condition. Most patients with maldigestion develop the disorder when over one year of age.

What are the symptoms?
Patients with maldigestion show very characteristic signs. Most have a ravenous appetite, diarrhea and weight loss. Because the patients lack the pancreatic enzymes, the food they eat largely passes through the intestines unutilized. The patient in effect is starving for nutrients and compensates by eating more, while at the same time losing weight. The stool is poorly formed and often appears gray and greasy.

What are the risks?
Left untreated, a patient severely affected will starve to death despite consuming large quantities of food. There are eleven varying degrees of maldigestion depending on the quantity of enzymes the pancreas is actually capable of producing. Some patients begin with mild symptoms that progress to severe as the enzyme-producing cells increasingly fail.

What is the treatment?
Fecal testing by a veterinarian to detect the lack of pancreatic enzymes will confirm the diagnosis of pancreatic exocrine insufficiency. Once diagnosed, the treatment is aimed at replacing the enzymes that are lacking. Commercial enzyme supplements such as Viokase are available to mix in food preparations. Treatment is simply replacing the needed enzymes in the form of a food additive. Most enzyme additives are in powdered form and work by being mixed with the food. Most patients respond well to treatment and live relatively normal lives.

DIABETES MELLITUS
Please refer to Chapter 7, "Hormone Disorders."

CHAPTER 9

The Digestive Tract

INTRODUCTION

The principal components of the digestive tract are the **esophagus, stomach, small and large intestines, cecum and colon.** (See figure 9-1.) The digestive tract transports food from the mouth to the anus for elimination from the body. As food moves through the intestinal tract, it is digested or broken down into nutrients that are absorbed through the intestinal walls, then transferred to the body tissues via the bloodstream to be utilized as fuel. Each portion of the digestive tract performs specialized tasks to aid in the transfer and digestion of food.

DISORDERS OF THE ESOPHAGUS

The **esophagus** is a small hose-like tube which leads from the mouth to the stomach. As it leaves the mouth, it follows a straight path through neck and chest, passing near the heart through the diaphragm muscle and finally entering the stomach. The esophagus walls are composed of muscles which move in wave-like contractions to push food into the stomach. In the canine, it takes about five seconds for food to move from the mouth to the stomach. Surgery to the esophagus is always difficult because of its location within the chest and its poor rate of healing.

CRICOPHARYNGEAL ACHALASIA

Near the mouth at the beginning of the esophagus lies the **cricopharyngeal muscle.** This small muscular band attaches with the esophageal

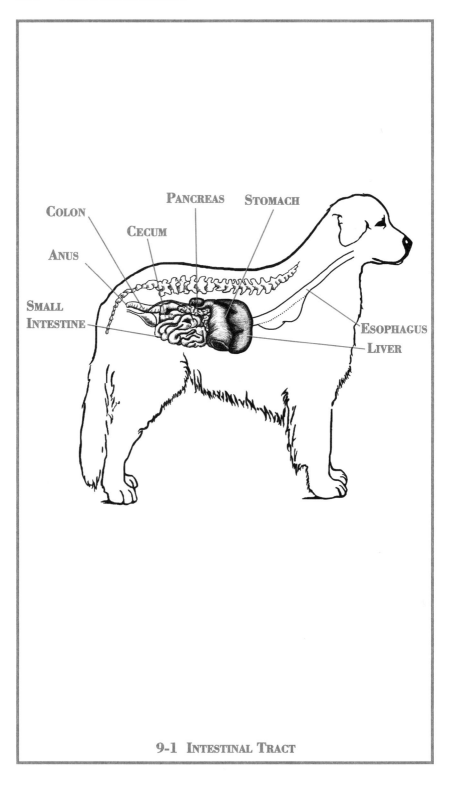

9-1 Intestinal Tract

muscles and functions to regulate the passage of food from the mouth cavity into the esophagus. (See figure 9-2.) *Cricopharyngeal achalasia is a failure of the cricopharyngeal muscle to relax.* The unrelaxed muscle closes off the opening of the esophagus, preventing food from leaving the mouth because it cannot be swallowed. The exact cause for the abnormal muscular constriction is unknown; however, it is believed to be a disorder of the nerves supplying the cricopharyngeal muscle. Most cases are congenital abnormalities and therefore appear early in life.

What are the symptoms?
A patient with cricopharyngeal achalasia will have difficulty and often a complete inability to swallow food. Food may fall from the mouth. Upon drinking water, the patient may cough as liquid may enter the trachea into the lungs.

What are the risks?
Left untreated, the patient will lose weight and possibly starve to death due to the inability to eat.

What is the treatment?
Surgery is required to sever the muscle, thus releasing the tension or constriction of the anterior esophagus. The outcome after surgery is generally good and patients live a normal life span.

CONGENITAL MEGAESOPHAGUS

Megaesophagus describes a situation in which the esophagus has lost muscle tone. Rather than appearing like a muscular hose, it dilates into a thin "bag-like" tube. (See figure 9-3.) Most cases are congenital and probably caused by a faulty nerve supply.

What are the symptoms?
The patient tends to regurgitate or vomit food shortly after eating. The diseased esophagus lacks the muscle tone to move food to the stomach. Ingested food is swallowed, but sits in the esophagus until regurgitated. Some food, particularly liquids, may pass into the stomach.

What are the risks?
Usually megaesophagus is a permanent situation. Occasionally an infection or irritation of the nerve supply may only cause temporary symptoms, but this is rare. Megaesophagus is generally a permanent condition that must be dealt with.

What is the treatment?
Congenital megaesophagus has no known cure. Patients so affected must be fed liquid diets. The food is usually placed in an elevated position so

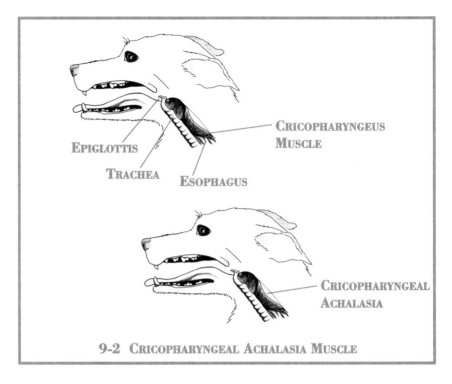

EPIGLOTTIS

TRACHEA

ESOPHAGUS

CRICOPHARYNGEUS MUSCLE

CRICOPHARYNGEAL ACHALASIA

9-2 CRICOPHARYNGEAL ACHALASIA MUSCLE

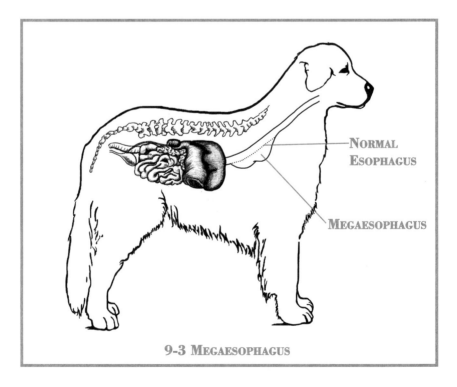

NORMAL ESOPHAGUS

MEGAESOPHAGUS

9-3 MEGAESOPHAGUS

patients eat while standing on their hind limbs. This elevated eating stance allows liquid food to travel to the stomach via gravity. With these precautions, many patients can survive and do well.

FOREIGN BODY IN THE ESOPHAGUS

The esophagus, being a tube-like structure, is capable of a certain amount of dilation to allow larger pieces of food to reach the stomach. Occasionally canines ingest objects other than normal food. A common place for this foreign material to lodge is in the esophagus near the heart, as it is here that the esophagus is unable to expand to its widest. Balls, rocks, sticks and triangular bones (pork chop) are all examples of foreign bodies which may lodge in this area.

What are the symptoms?

Typically, once the esophagus is blocked in this manner, food is regurgitated within a few minutes after eating. If the blockage is not complete, liquid foods may pass by. Chunky food generally cannot reach the stomach.

What are the risks?

A foreign body in the esophagus is always serious. Occasionally sharp objects can puncture or wear away the esophageal muscle wall, allowing food and bacteria to enter the chest cavity. *Severe, life-threatening pneumonia can develop.*

What is the treatment?

Treatment is always aimed at removing the object. This may be accomplished by anesthetizing the patient and removing the object via the mouth or pushing it into the stomach. In many instances the chest cavity and esophagus must be surgically opened and the object removed. This type of surgery poses a great risk to the patient; however, the final outcome can be excellent.

DISORDERS OF THE STOMACH

The dog's stomach is a sac-like structure designed to store large volumes of food and begin the digestive process. (See figure 9-4.) The storage of ingested food is short-term. Once eaten, most food leaves the stomach within twelve hours after entering. The esophagus carries food to the stomach, and at its base is a valve-like structure called the **cardiac sphincter**. Food exits the stomach into the first part of the small intestine, called the **duodenum.** A small muscular valve called the **pyloric sphincter** separates the stomach from the duodenum. On the interior surface of the stomach is a series of folds called **gastric folds.**

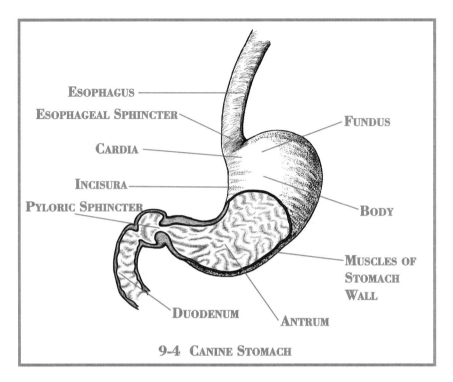

ESOPHAGUS

ESOPHAGEAL SPHINCTER

CARDIA

INCISURA

PYLORIC SPHINCTER

FUNDUS

BODY

MUSCLES OF
STOMACH
WALL

DUODENUM

ANTRUM

9-4 CANINE STOMACH

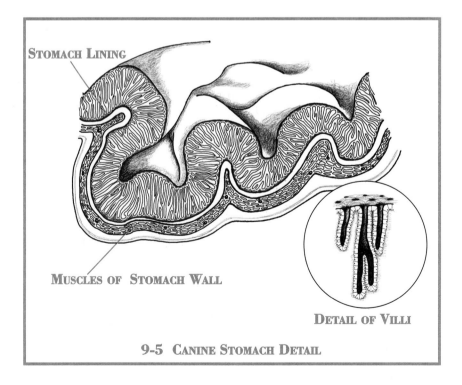

STOMACH LINING

MUSCLES OF STOMACH WALL

DETAIL OF VILLI

9-5 CANINE STOMACH DETAIL

(See figure 9-5.) These folds function to help grind and digest food. The inner stomach lining secretes acids and enzymes to break food down as the initial step in the digestive process. Once the initial stomach digestive process is complete, the partially digested food leaves the stomach through the pyloric sphincter area and then enters the duodenum.

GASTRIC ULCERS

Ulcers are small crater-like areas that develop when the inner intestinal lining is worn away. As in humans, stress or a nervous stomach can cause ulcers. This is probably due to higher than normal levels of stomach acid produced in a nervous patient. The stomach cells secrete these acids; however, excess levels can cause irritation and erosions of the stomach lining directly. Certain anti-inflammatory drugs such as aspirin, phenylbutazone, ibuprofen and cortisones can also lead to stomach ulcers, especially if used in high quantities or for long periods of time.

What are the symptoms?
Gastric ulcerations can be severe or moderate. Typical signs include vomiting (occasionally with blood) and poor appetite. If the ulcers protrude deep into the stomach tissue, severe hemorrhage may occur, leading to anemia and black tar-like stools. The stools appear dark as a result of blood becoming partially digested as it passes through the small intestines and colon.

What are the risks?
Most patients tolerate gastric ulcers very well. In fact, many ulcers heal on their own, and if they persist cause nothing more than an occasional stomach upset. Severe ulceration can lead to death caused by excessive blood loss and/or complete perforation of the stomach wall.

What is the treatment?
A careful evaluation of the pet's history is important. Any potential ulcer-causing drug should be discontinued, although other drug therapy is beneficial. Antacids such as Digel can be used to help counteract excess acid production. As in humans, various other drugs such as cimetidine (Tagamet) are available to help decrease stomach acid production. Coating agents such as Kaopectate or Pepto-Bismol are also beneficial.

GASTRIC DILATION/BLOAT (VOLVULUS COMPLEX/TORSION)

This is a true veterinary emergency. Bloat with a possible stomach twist (torsion) is one of the most dangerous intestinal disorders known in canine medicine.

The exact cause of canine bloat is unknown; however, it is believed to be brought on by abnormal stomach motility. The stomach becomes excessively dilated with gas, causing it to expand, occasionally to three to four times its normal size. As the stomach swells with gas it may "float up" on other organs and can actually rotate or twist on its axis. When the stomach twists it causes the esophagus (at the entrance) and the small intestine (at the exit) to also twist, preventing passage of gas, liquids or food. With no release of gas possible, the stomach expands further. (See figure 9-6.)

As the stomach twists, veins and arteries within stomach walls and other organs such as the spleen and liver become twisted and blood is no longer able to flow through them normally. The spleen, closely associated with the stomach, may also twist, completely obstructing the blood flow.

Not all cases of gastric dilation result in torsion. However, it is our experience that the majority do. Large breeds, especially those with deep chests, develop bloat more frequently than small breeds. Additionally, larger chest cavities and abdomens in breeds such as Labrador Retrievers, Greyhounds, Afghan Hounds, Great Danes and similar breeds seem to allow the stomach to bloat and torsion more easily.

What are the symptoms?
The initial signs are usually seen within the first few hours after eating. Generally the patient acts nervous and cannot get comfortable. Dogs may try but be unable to vomit and may have a tight bloated abdomen. (See figure 9-7.) When torsion occurs, a patient may try repeated unsuccessful attempts at vomiting. Since torsion involves the esophagus, it is not possible to bring anything up from the stomach. Along with the bloated appearance, there is excessive panting, probably due to pain and the enlarged stomach pushing the diaphragm against the chest cavity.

What are the risks?
Left untreated, virtually 100 percent of bloat patients will die. Once the stomach twists, death will result within hours. A patient that can vomit once treatment has been started has a much better chance of survival. *Treat every case of suspected bloat as a medical emergency. Do not wait!*

What is the treatment?
To be successful, veterinary treatment must begin as soon as possible. Initial treatment is aimed at relieving stomach gases and shrinking the size of the stomach. This is accomplished by passing a tube through the mouth and into the stomach. Anti-gas remedies such as Digel can be administered through the tube. This is not always possible, especially if torsion has occurred where the esophagus and stomach meet. If a tube cannot be passed through, then large needles (trocars) can be placed directly into the stomach through the left abdominal wall. Occasionally an incision can be made into the stomach through the abdomen to relieve the gas and drain stomach contents.

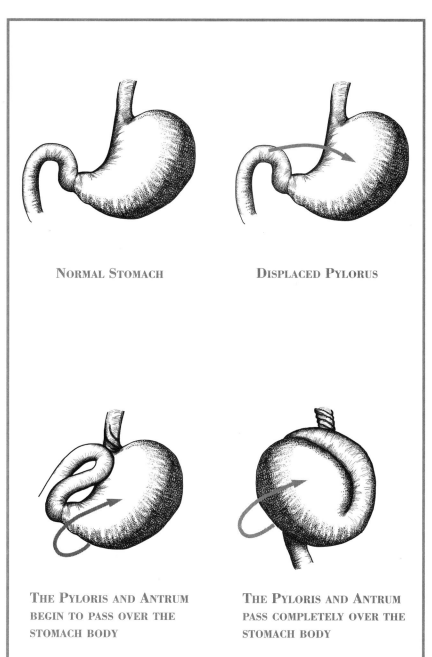

NORMAL STOMACH

DISPLACED PYLORUS

THE PYLORIS AND ANTRUM
BEGIN TO PASS OVER THE
STOMACH BODY

THE PYLORIS AND ANTRUM
PASS COMPLETELY OVER THE
STOMACH BODY

9-6 STOMACH WITH TORSION

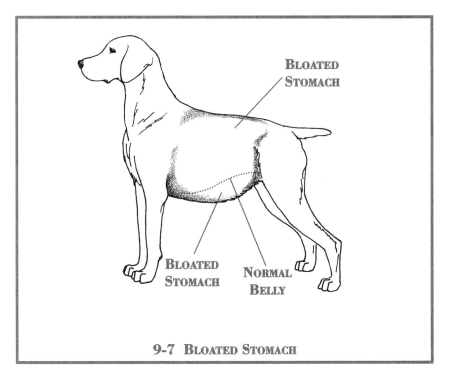

9-7 Bloated Stomach

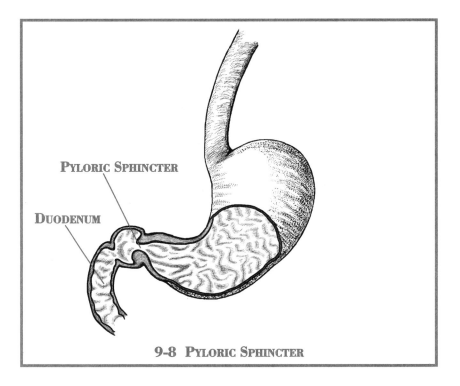

9-8 Pyloric Sphincter

Patients suspected of having torsioned generally undergo surgery at once. The abdomen is opened up and the stomach, spleen and intestines are rotated back to their original positions. The stomach is sutured in place against the ribcage to help prevent another twist from occurring. It must be pointed out that *even with prompt surgical correction, not every patient survives.* Many patients go into shock or develop infections after surgery. Careful postoperative care and monitoring are important, especially for the first seventy-two hours after surgery.

Patients that survive bloat are generally given a modified diet. Although diet has never been definitely proven to be a contributing cause, several theories show promise. It is best to avoid feeding large amounts of food at a single meal to the recovered patient. Multiple small feedings may help lessen the stomach's production of gas. Many authorities believe cereal-based diets should be avoided, as these foods tend to expand once they meet the stomach fluids. Antacids and anti-gas preparations such as Digel, or others containing simethicone, can be useful in preventing and treating bloat.

Many theories exist about bloat; however, abnormal stomach motility is still the primary suspected cause, not diet, and we, the authors, have never been able to detect trends towards bloat based on the diet. Hopefully future research will help determine the exact cause.

PYLORIC STENOSIS

Where the stomach empties into the duodenum, there is a circular valve-like muscle called the **pyloric sphincter**. (See figure 9-8.) The pyloric sphincter constricts and dilates, regulating the flow of food from the stomach into the small intestine. Occasionally, for unknown reasons, the pyloric sphincter abnormally constricts or spasms, causing a narrowing (stenosis) of the entrance into the small intestine. Small breeds, or especially nervous individuals, seem to develop this condition more frequently than others.

What are the symptoms?

Intermittent vomiting within one to two hours of eating is the most common sign. The food will appear undigested, pretty much looking just as it did when eaten. The sphincter may not always be constricting or spastic. Therefore, some meals may pass without vomiting. Additionally, liquid diets or water will pass through the narrowed sphincter easier than bulky foods. In severe cases, weight loss may develop.

What are the risks?

Many patients live normal lives with only occasional episodes of vomiting. It appears the muscular spasms are not always constant in these cases. If a patient is exhibiting severe stomach outflow restrictions from a more constant pyloric stenosis, then weight loss and even death can result.

What is the treatment?

A diagnosis is not always easy. A careful history of vomiting in relation to eating must be evaluated. Barium studies with radiographs (X rays) may reveal the narrowed stomach outflow. Once diagnosed, surgery provides the best cure. The pyloric sphincter, being a narrow muscular band, can be surgically severed, thus eliminating the constricting efforts. Additionally, the stomach outflow area can be surgically widened, allowing food to pass into the duodenum. The outcome after surgery is excellent.

FOREIGN BODIES IN THE STOMACH

Any material other than food or water found in the stomach is termed a foreign body. The authors have found items including coins, tennis balls, socks, buttons, golf balls, paper clips, Ping-Pong balls, rocks, nails, fish hooks, writing pens, soda caps and even entire beverage cans.

What are the symptoms?

A patient with a foreign body in the stomach will almost always vomit, often repeatedly and violently. If the object is small, such as a paper clip, the vomiting may only be occasional. The vomiting frequently occurs shortly after eating. The vomitus will therefore usually contain only the last meal ingested. The food will appear undigested or very similar to the way it did before being eaten. Some dogs will stop eating when there is a foreign body in their stomachs.

What are the risks?

Small foreign bodies such as coins or marbles may eventually pass completely through the stomach and intestinal tract and be eliminated from the body in the feces. Larger foreign bodies such as balls, sticks, socks, etc. may remain in the stomach for a long period of time and cause severe damage to the stomach. Left untreated, this damage can end in death.

What is the treatment?

The ingestion of small objects may require no treatment. The patient is closely monitored for vomiting until the object passes from the body in the feces. It may take one to four days for the object to pass. The presence of a foreign body can usually be confirmed with X rays and occasionally simple palpation of the stomach area. Surgery is required to remove objects that are too large to pass from the body naturally.

GASTRITIS

Gastritis describes an inflammation or infection of the stomach. As in humans, viruses and bacteria can irritate the stomach, causing gastritis.

Additionally, the ingestion of spoiled food, garbage, etc. can irritate the stomach lining.

What are the symptoms?

A patient with gastritis will generally vomit, not eat and be lethargic. Frequently the temperature is elevated above the normal 101.5 degrees. If a virus or bacteria is involved, the gastritis may eventually progress to the intestines, causing diarrhea. Infectious canine *parvovirus* is a classic example of a virus which occasionally begins as gastritis.

What are the risks?

Most instances of gastritis are not serious. However, if the vomiting becomes severe or signs persist for more than twenty-four hours, then veterinary attention should be sought.

What is the treatment?

A patient with a mild upset stomach can benefit from gastric coating or soothing preparations such as Pepto-Bismol. Generally, it is best to withhold food, but not water. Withholding food will allow the stomach to rest. Bland diets such as chicken and rice can be utilized once food is provided. Water should be given often and in small amounts, rather than allowing the animal to drink a lot at one time.

If vomiting persists, diarrhea develops or if the body temperature is excessively high (greater than 103 degrees), veterinary attention should be sought. A veterinarian will observe the patient for dehydration from fluids lost through lack of intake or in diarrhea and vomitus. Intravenous fluids can be utilized to replace lost fluids. Antibiotics are utilized to kill bacteria if necessary. Various medications are available to decrease vomiting.

TUMORS OF THE STOMACH

Although not common, stomach cancer can develop in the canine. The main type of cancer involving the stomach is a malignant tumor called an *adenocarcinoma*. This type of tumor arises from the glandular cells of the stomach lining.

What are the symptoms?

A patient with stomach cancer generally loses weight, vomits and fails to eat. The vomiting may initially be infrequent; however, over time the vomiting increases. Blood may or may not be present in the vomit.

What are the risks?

Cancer of the stomach is always serious. Even with treatment, the long-term prognosis is poor as most cases are in an advanced stage before a proper diagnosis can be confirmed. Adenocarcinomas frequently spread to other areas of the body, making treatment even more difficult.

What is the treatment?

Surgical removal of the cancerous areas is performed. Occasionally, large portions of the stomach wall are diseased and must be removed. Adenocarcinomas of the stomach may spread to other organs such as the liver and lymph nodes. To be successful, tumors at these sites must also be isolated and removed. The long-term success of treatment is generally poor.

DISORDERS OF THE SMALL INTESTINE

The small intestine is a tube-like structure which extends between the stomach and large intestine. It is the longest portion of the intestinal tract and is about two-and-a-half times the animal's total body length. An animal twenty-four inches long would have about sixty inches of small intestine.

The small intestine in the canine has three parts. (See figure 9-9.) The first portion, which attaches to the stomach, is the **duodenum.** In a forty-pound dog it is roughly ten inches long. The middle (and longest) portion is called the **jejunum.** The shortest part is the **ileum,** which connects to the large intestine.

The duodenum attaches to the stomach and is relatively short. It does, however, have very important functions. The **gallbladder** and **pancreas** connect to the duodenum by the bile and pancreatic ducts respectively. Enzymes and other secretions that are important for digestion are produced by the **liver** and pancreas and pass through these ducts and mix with the food in the duodenum.

The jejunum is the longest area of the small intestine and is rich in small finger-like projections called **villi.** Villi protrude inward into the food contents and provide a surface to absorb nutrients. Intestinal contents of the jejunum empty into the ileum and from there pass into the **colon.**

Diseases of the small intestine are usually not confined to just one area and therefore are simply discussed as small intestinal disorders.

SMALL INTESTINAL INFECTIONS (INFECTIOUS ENTERITIS)

Enteritis describes an inflammation or infection of the small intestine. In the canine, many bacteria and viruses have been implicated as a cause of enteritis. Among them are *parvovirus, coronavirus, rotavirus, salmonellosis, distemper virus* and many others. Most of these organisms affect other areas of the body as well; however, some of their principal signs are associated with the small intestine.

What are the symptoms?

Diarrhea is the most common sign associated with small intestine disease. With enteritis, the temperature is commonly elevated. However, especially with viruses, this is not always the case. A characteristic fetid odor from the feces is usually detected. Contrary to popular belief, one cannot differentiate diarrhea caused by parvovirus from other sources without sophisticated laboratory testing. They all may smell similar. The diarrhea may be green and profuse, almost like pea soup. If the intestinal wall is damaged from the infection, one may also notice blood in the stool. If the blood is from the first portions of the small intestine (duodenum), it will be digested and appear black or tar-like. If the bleeding is occurring near the colon, it may appear red.

What are the risks?

Any patient with an intestinal infection is severely ill. Depending on the cause, the recovery period may be days to weeks. Occasionally patients will die, especially if younger than six months of age. Not only young dogs can develop diseases such as parvovirus or coronavirus; *all* ages are vulnerable, though the death rate is higher in the young and geriatric. Most organisms are *highly contagious* and an outbreak may involve many animals in the household and vicinity at one time.

What is the treatment?

A mild bout of infectious enteritis may require no treatment whatsoever. The patient may have only a mild diarrhea for one or two days, then spontaneously recover. In more severe instances, the patient will need medication to stop or control diarrhea.

Supportive nutrients and fluids may need to be administered intravenously or subcutaneously until the patient recovers. Antibiotics are helpful if the cause is a *bacterium*. Antibiotics help prevent bacteria from secondarily complicating *viral* diseases such as parvovirus. Kaopectate and other intestinal coating agents are beneficial in mild cases. In some cases, medication that slows down the secretions of the intestinal tract can also be administered. The exact treatment varies by age, cause and severity. *Patients should be monitored closely.*

INTUSSUSCEPTION

Although difficult to describe, an intussusception is basically the telescoping of one intestinal segment into another. (See figure 9-10.) The cause is unknown; however, if the intestinal mobility increases (such as during an infection), the frequency of this disorder increases. A high incidence of this is seen in puppies carrying large numbers of intestinal parasites such as roundworms or hookworms. When heavily infested, the small intestine becomes *hyper*motile due to the irritation caused by the worms, thus increasing the incidence of intussusception.

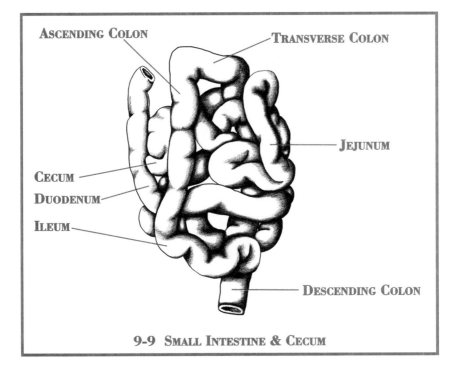

ASCENDING COLON

TRANSVERSE COLON

JEJUNUM

CECUM

DUODENUM

ILEUM

DESCENDING COLON

9-9 SMALL INTESTINE & CECUM

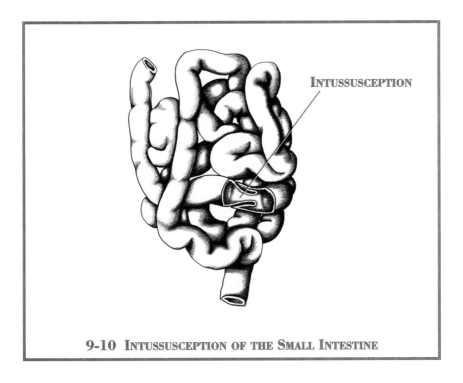

INTUSSUSCEPTION

9-10 INTUSSUSCEPTION OF THE SMALL INTESTINE

What are the symptoms?

When the small intestine telescopes into itself, movement of intestinal contents is partially or completely blocked. Commonly the patient vomits. Once the gastrointestinal tract *behind* the intussusception empties, stools are scant to none. Any fecal material that is passed is jelly-like and not well formed. The appetite will be greatly depressed.

What are the risks?

An intussusception is serious. Left untreated it will result in death. As the intestines telescope into one another, pressure restricts blood flow to the area. Portions of the intestines therefore may actually die, and toxins and bacteria may be released into the rest of the body.

What is the treatment?

To relieve the obstruction, surgery is necessary. Commonly the damaged section of the intestine is actually removed, with the fresh ends being reconnected. Infections can develop; however, especially if performed early on, surgery is quite successful.

HERNIAS AND BOWEL STRANGULATIONS

Occasionally a patient will have abnormal openings in the muscular wall of the abdomen. Abdominal contents such as sections of the intestine, masses of fat or other organs may pass through these abnormal openings. These are called hernias. They commonly occur at one or more sites.

Umbilical hernias tend to occur in young dogs and are a result of a weakness or failure of normal closure in the area where the fetal umbilical cord passed through the abdominal wall. This is the navel or "belly button." (See figure 9-11.) The other common hernia location is in the area on both sides of the abdomen where the rear legs join the body. (See figure 9-12.) This site is more commonly affected in males. As in humans, this area on both sides of the penis has openings which allow the testicles to descend from the abdomen into the scrotum shortly after birth. These natural openings through the abdominal muscles are called the **inguinal** rings. Occasionally the inguinal rings are too large or tear, allowing a larger opening, therefore permitting the hernia to occur. One or both sides may be affected.

Hernias are nothing more than abnormal openings through the muscles of the abdomen through which the abdominal contents pass. Skin still covers the area. Some umbilical hernias are more prevalent in some lines of dogs, suggesting an inherited trait. Inguinal hernias generally occur later in life. As in humans, they are commonly the result of stress or trauma on the abdominal muscles.

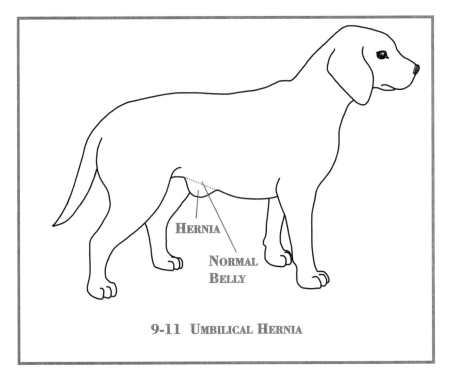

9-11 Umbilical Hernia

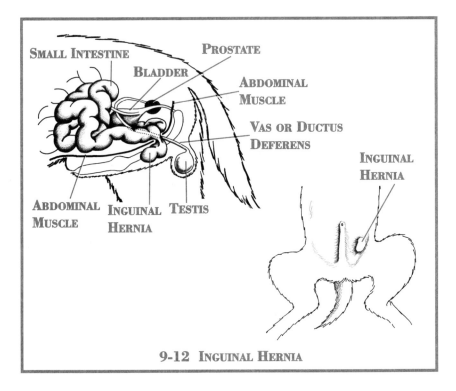

9-12 Inguinal Hernia

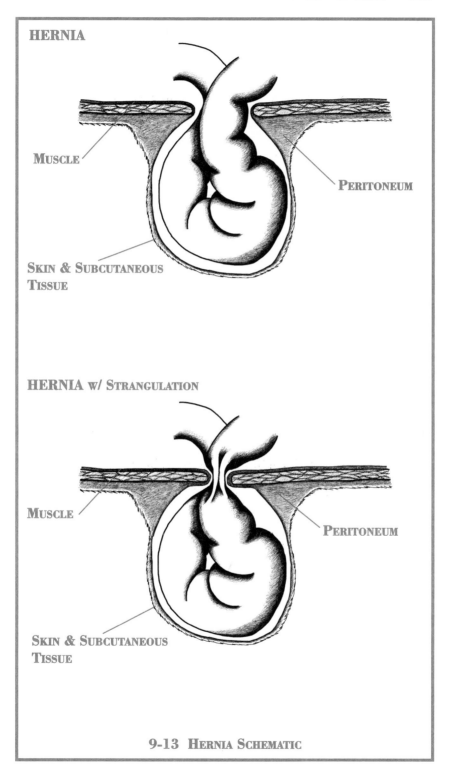

HERNIA

MUSCLE

PERITONEUM

SKIN & SUBCUTANEOUS
TISSUE

HERNIA w/ STRANGULATION

MUSCLE

PERITONEUM

SKIN & SUBCUTANEOUS
TISSUE

9-13 HERNIA SCHEMATIC

What are the symptoms?

The most commonly noted symptom is a bulge of the belly skin at the hernia site. (See figure 9-13.) This bulge is due to tissues protruding from inside the abdomen and pushing outward on the skin. In the case of umbilical hernias, the bulge will occur directly over the navel. Inguinal hernias will be noted as a bulge next to the penis. Inguinal hernias may affect one or both sides simultaneously.

What are the risks?

Hernias, being openings in the muscles, are not painful and cause no discomfort. The risk they pose is possible organ strangulation. Occasionally a piece of intestine or even the bladder may pass through the muscle opening and become constricted. The constriction can cut off the blood supply to the organ, resulting in tissue death. Left untreated this situation would lead to patient death.

Oddly enough, large hernias pose less of a risk. This is because they are less likely to strangulate the organ than a small hernia. Large hernias restrict the blood supply less than small openings, because the opening is larger. Occasionally a very young puppy (younger than six weeks of age) will have a small umbilical hernia that will heal shut or "scar in" over time. In general, a hernia in any animal over four months of age should be corrected to prevent possible organ strangulation.

What is the treatment?

As in humans, the treatment involves surgery. A veterinarian can surgically open the skin and close the abnormal opening that extends through the abdominal muscles. A full recovery is expected.

FOREIGN BODIES IN THE SMALL INTESTINE

Frequently pets eat objects other than food. Balls, corn cobs, socks, coins, strings, etc., are all examples of foreign bodies. Many objects are too large to leave the stomach and cause problems there. (See page 174.) Smaller objects such as marbles, paper clips and strings can all pass through the stomach, but may cause a blockage of the small intestine.

What are the symptoms?

Vomiting and a poor appetite are generally the initial signs. The patient will usually have a tense abdomen with few or no bowel movements. Commonly the temperature is elevated, especially if the intestine has been punctured.

What are the risks?

Strings (yarn, fishing line, etc.) present the greatest danger. Because of their length, they involve a longer section of the bowel. Movement of the

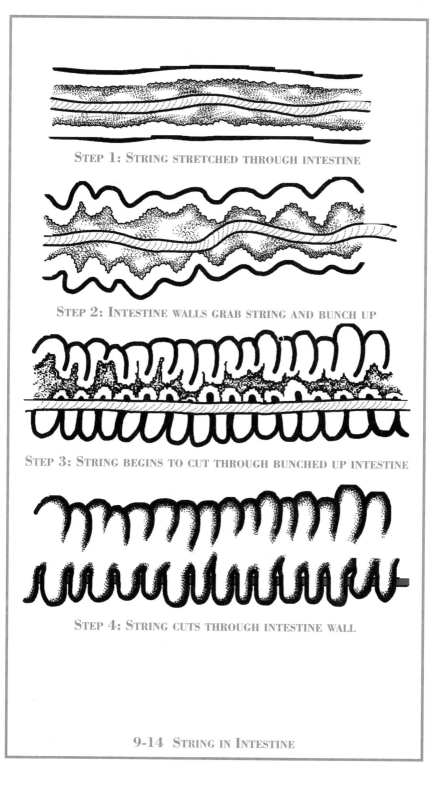

STEP 1: STRING STRETCHED THROUGH INTESTINE

STEP 2: INTESTINE WALLS GRAB STRING AND BUNCH UP

STEP 3: STRING BEGINS TO CUT THROUGH BUNCHED UP INTESTINE

STEP 4: STRING CUTS THROUGH INTESTINE WALL

9-14 STRING IN INTESTINE

small intestine causes "bunching up" on the string much like an accordion. (See figure 9-14.) With continued waves of movement across this area, the string becomes tighter and cuts through the wall of the intestine often in several places, leading to peritonitis as a result of intestinal contents leak into the abdomen.

Most intestinal foreign bodies simply get stuck in the intestine, causing a blockage that prevents food from moving through the tract. All suspected incidences of an intestinal foreign body are emergencies and should be monitored closely.

What is the treatment?

Radiographs, occasionally with barium, are utilized to confirm the diagnosis. Surgery is generally required to remove the object or material. Often the damaged section of the intestine must be removed and the unaffected end reattached. In some cases, lubricating agents such as petroleum jelly can be used to help the foreign body slide on into the colon, which is larger. From there, objects can pass on. Most patients fully recover once surgical correction is accomplished.

PROTEIN-LOSING ENTEROPATHY (INTESTINAL LYMPHANGIECTASIA)

Protein-losing enteropathy is generally abbreviated as **PLE**. Along the small intestine there is a network of small lymph vessels called **lacteals**. (See figure 9-15.) Lacteals absorb fats and proteins formed by the digestive process. From there, the absorbed fats and proteins enter the lymphatic system for distribution to the bloodstream.

Occasionally these lymphatic ducts along the intestines become blocked or fail to develop properly. The cause is generally unknown, but may be a result of chronic inflammation along the intestinal wall. The result is a failure to absorb fats and especially proteins. Proteins, even though they are eaten and digested, are not absorbed and therefore lost from the body in the feces. All breeds can be affected; however, Soft Coated Wheaten Terriers and Yorkshire Terriers have a higher incidence.

What are the symptoms?

Most patients with PLE have diarrhea. Additionally, due to protein loss in the feces, blood protein levels fall. When this happens, fluid leaves the bloodstream and accumulates in the abdominal cavity. This is termed **ascites**. A final diagnosis of PLE can only be made by a biopsy of the gut wall.

What are the risks?

Severe cases of PLE can result in death. Occasional patients fail to respond to correct therapy.

What is the treatment?

Treatment in many cases is accomplished with specialized diets. Low-fat diets are absorbed better than high-fat diets. Low-fat diets also help prevent further clogging of the lacteals, thus enabling proteins to be better absorbed through the gut, preventing their loss in the feces. Anti-inflammatory medications such as prednisone or prednisolone have proven beneficial in some patients.

PARASITIC ENTERITIS

Dogs of all ages occasionally have the small intestine's function compromised by parasites. **Roundworms, tapeworms, hookworms and whipworms** are all found within the bowels of dogs. Hookworms and whipworms are the most devastating. They attach to the intestinal wall, sucking blood from the victim and damaging the absorption surfaces of the intestine. All are found within the small intestine; however, whipworms are generally located at the very end by the *cecum and colon.*

Although all canines can become infested with parasites, the young are the most susceptible. Puppies are frequently born with or acquire parasites from their mother shortly after birth. **Roundworms** and **hookworms** are common in infants, acquired either as they pass the placenta or through the mother's milk. **Whipworms** are spread by fecal matter. **Tapeworms** generally do not transfer directly from animal to animal. Fleas, fish, snails, rodents, rabbits and other insects serve as carriers of tapeworms. Once a pet ingests a carrier, the tapeworm will complete its life cycle. Fleas serve as the principal tapeworm reservoir for the canine.

What are the symptoms?

Many patients with intestinal parasites exhibit few or no symptoms. Routine fecal exams by a veterinarian will detect the parasites or their eggs if present. Tapeworm segments occasionally are seen crawling about the anus of dogs or on fresh stool. They resemble pieces of rice. Roundworms are "spaghetti-like" and may appear in the stool. Diarrhea with or without blood, bloated abdomens and poor hair coats all indicate parasites.

What are the risks?

Mild parasite infestation causes little harm to the pet. Roundworms and tapeworms are not blood suckers and do not damage the gut wall. They survive bathing in the digesting food, competing with the pet for nutrients.

Hookworms and whipworms are more serious because in feeding, they suck blood and destroy parts of the gut wall. Severe infestations can cause blood loss leading to anemia and death. *A pet with parasites is not a healthy pet and should be treated at once.*

What is the treatment?

A fecal exam by a veterinarian will help identify parasites. Each individual patient should have a routine fecal exam at least twice yearly. Various worming medications are available to kill the identified parasites. All puppies should be routinely wormed beginning at approximately three weeks of age. Effective and safe wormers are readily available.

TUMORS OF THE SMALL INTESTINE

As with other organs within the abdomen, the small intestine can occasionally become cancerous. Being rich in glandular tissue, this area is particularly susceptible to tumors arising from those cells. These types of tumors are termed **adenocarcinomas.**

What are the symptoms?

The tumors can interrupt digestion and absorption or lead to an intestinal blockage. Additionally, they often spread to the liver or lungs, affecting the normal function of these organs. The symptoms of intestinal cancer are therefore varied, but generally include weight loss, vomiting, diarrhea and anemia.

What are the risks?

All intestinal cancers are serious and should be treated at once. Even with treatment, the long-term prognosis is typically poor.

What is the treatment?

The affected areas of the intestines are generally surgically removed and biopsied. Chemotherapy is occasionally used in conjunction with surgery. Therapy must be evaluated on an individual basis.

DISORDERS OF THE LARGE INTESTINE

The large intestine of the canine basically connects the small intestine to the anus. The large intestine is about sixteen inches in length in a forty-pound dog and is larger in diameter than the small intestine. Its primary function is to absorb water from feces as needed, thus keeping the hydration level of the body constant. Its other function is to store fecal matter awaiting passage from the body.

The large intestine has several distinct parts. (See figure 9-16.) The **cecum** is a small finger-like projection near the junction with the small intestine. Its true function is unknown. The **colon** is the longest portion of the large intestine and terminates just inside the **anus** to the final portion called the **rectum.** The terms "colon" and "large intestine" are commonly used interchangeably.

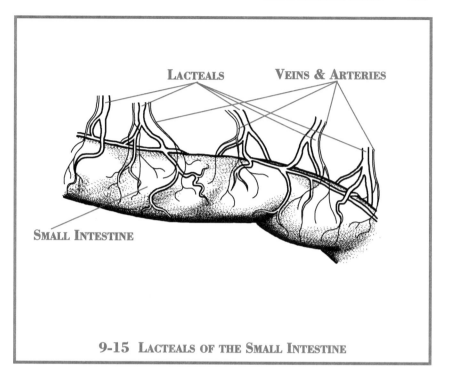

9-15 LACTEALS OF THE SMALL INTESTINE

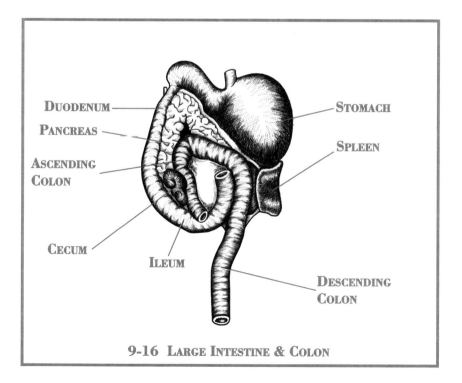

9-16 LARGE INTESTINE & COLON

Disorders of the Cecum

The cecum is a small pouch with no important function. Occasionally it can become inflamed and this is termed **typhlitis**. The most common cause of typhlitis is a whipworm infestation.

What are the symptoms?
Whipworms live in the cecum and the surrounding small and large intestines. Loose stool with flecks of blood and mucus may indicate the presence of whipworms. Abdominal pain may be present.

What are the risks?
Typhlitis is seldom a serious health risk. However, if whipworms are the cause, they should be treated.

What is the treatment?
Antibiotics are used to treat bacterial causes. If whipworms are the suspected cause, medications to control them are available.

Inversion of the Cecum

The cecum, being a pouch-like projection off the large intestine, occasionally can become inverted and rather than lying in the outer surface of the colon, actually protrudes into the intestine. This is much like pulling the thumb of a mitten into its interior.

What are the symptoms?
A cecal inversion can present as diarrhea or a total blockage of the intestinal tract. Diagnosis is difficult and frequently exploratory surgery is required for a final diagnosis.

What are the risks?
An inverted cecum obstructs the flow of feces into the colon. Severe discomfort, pain and vomiting can develop.

What is the treatment?
Generally, the cecum is surgically removed. The recovered patient has an excellent prognosis. As understood today, the cecum has no part in digestion, and removal does not impair any digestive function.

Colitis

Colitis describes an inflammation of the colon. The cause may be bacteria, stress, parasites, etc. However, there is usually no detectable reason for the inflammation.

What are the symptoms?
Most patients with colitis look and feel normal. They simply have frequent mucus and occasional flecks of blood. In severe cases vomiting may occur.

Some patients will experience severe pain when defecating because of inflammation of the colon, and may actually try and stop the defecation process, thereby resulting in constipation. There may be constipation or diarrhea, but invariably there will be an abnormal defecation process.

Some breeds are prone to developing colitis. Boxers are very susceptible, but with no known cause. Deep ulcers may develop in the colon wall, hence the name Boxer ulcerative colitis.

What are the risks?

Most patients have no serious health risk. In cases when deep ulceration of the colon develops, the situation is more serious. Additionally, some patients, especially Boxers, develop chronic colitis needing long-term treatment.

What is the treatment?

A rectal exam coupled with a biopsy of the colon wall will generally confirm a diagnosis. Fecal exams for colon parasites such as *giardia* should be performed in all cases. Bland diets such as cottage cheese and rice will help the colon rest and heal. Antibiotics will help control bacterial causes. Sulfa-containing drugs can be used long-term to control or treat chronic colitis. Azulfadine (sulfasalazine) is one such drug commonly used to control chronic colitis.

CONSTIPATION

Straining to defecate without passing the appropriate amount of stool is constipation. Generally the stool within the bowel is firm, yet has the ability to easily pass through the colon and out of the anus.

Constipation can be the result of several factors. The most common cause is eating inappropriate, non-food substances such as rocks, bones, sand, wood and other objects. Items such as chicken bones form rock-like clumps of stool within the colon. Lack of water may also cause extra-hard stools. Occasionally other causes are noted. It is possible for hernias, disc disease, injury and other conditions to cause the colon to not function properly. Long-haired breeds may develop hair mats covering the anal opening and preventing defecation. Rectal polyps and cancers, although not common, may contribute. Enlarged prostates in older male dogs may place pressure upon the colon, preventing the normal passage of feces.

What are the symptoms?

Straining with little or no defecation is a common sign of constipation. Occasionally liquid feces will pass, but the fecal mass remains retained. The patient may lick or bite at the rear end as if something is wrong. In chronic cases there may be a reluctance to eat or even vomiting.

What are the risks?

Simple constipation as a result of abnormally hard stool is usually not serious. If the inability to defecate is caused by a hernia, the rear end paralysis seen with some disc disorders, or cancer, then the risks are greater. Fortunately, 90 percent of all constipation has no detectable cause and is usually diet related.

What is the treatment?

The patient should be examined to determine the cause. Is the stool simply too hard or has the patient suffered an injury? Enemas may relieve the constipation. If a patient periodically encounters constipation, try changing foods. Avoid all-meat diets. Mineral oil and milk have laxative effects and are beneficial in some patients. Diets high in fiber are best in geriatric patients or those prone to chronic constipation. Do not worry if a patient goes one or two days without passing stool unless the dog is in great discomfort. Most cases of constipation will naturally subside in forty-eight hours. If your pet goes longer than forty-eight hours with no bowel movement, a veterinary exam is suggested.

RECTAL POLYPS

As in humans, occasional small non-cancerous growths appear in the colon, especially in the rectum area near the anus.

What are the symptoms?

Occasional straining while defecating is the most common sign. Flecks of blood may appear in the fresh stool if the polyps bleed.

What are the risks?

Rectal polyps are usually small and non-cancerous. They pose no serious health risk; however, they should be removed so as not to interfere with defecation and to prevent straining.

What is the treatment?

Rectal polyps should be removed surgically. If completely removed, they seldom regrow. Unlike in humans, rectal polyps of the canine seldom become malignant.

COLON CANCER

Colon cancer is not common in the canine. Those cases encountered are usually in geriatric patients. Unlike humans, rectal polyps seldom turn into cancer. Most tumors in the rectal area are from mucous-producing cells and are *adenocarcinomas*.

What are the symptoms?

Colon cancer will usually cause straining upon defecation and blood in the stool. Over time, as the cancer grows, the condition worsens, possibly leading to an obstruction of the large intestine. These tumors typically spread to other areas of the body with signs related to whatever other organs become affected.

What are the risks?

Cancer of the colon is always serious. Early detection and removal increases the chance for survival.

What is the treatment?

Colon tumors should be surgically excised. However, complete removal is not usually possible. Regrowth is likely.

HANGING OR DROP

ROSE

PENDULOUS

PRICK

BUTTON

SEMI-PRICK

10-1 CANINE EARS

CHAPTER 10

Disorders of the Ear

INTRODUCTION

The canine ear serves a dual purpose. Its most noted function is of course hearing. It is also extremely important as an organ of balance.

The **ear flap or pinna** is the portion of the ear that is most visible. Some dogs have ear flaps that stand erect and others have long, floppy types. (See figure 10-1.) The ear flap serves as a partial covering of the **ear canal**, while at the same time directing sound towards the **eardrum**. The flap has an inner core of cartilage to give it strength. Both outer and inner surfaces of the skin are covered by hair, although hair follicles are much less prevalent on the inner areas.

The ear canal is a long tube-like structure that travels diagonally down the side of the head, then moves horizontally into the head. (See figure 10-2.) The total length of the canal is at least two inches, even in small breeds. The canal is about as wide as a pencil. The length and size of the canal vary as to the animal's overall body size. As the ear canal passes into the head, it ends at a thin tissue called the tympanic membrane or eardrum.

This outer ear in the dog is considered to include all structures, such as the canal and ear flap, from the eardrum outward. Internally, from the eardrum comes the **middle ear,** which connects to the throat area by the **eustachian tube.** (See figure 10-3.) This tube allows air to enter the middle ear to balance the pressure against the eardrum.

Farther in from the middle ear is the inner ear. One responsibility of the inner ear is the maintenance of the dog's equilibrium or balance. This structure contains fluid-filled canals, which tell the brain the exact body

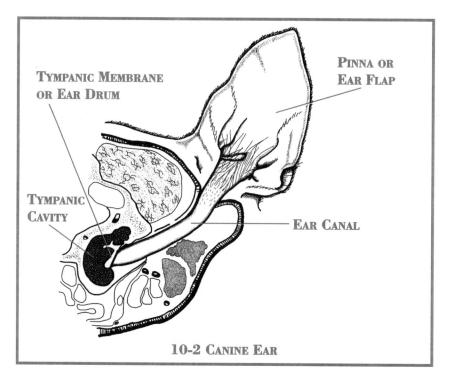

TYMPANIC MEMBRANE OR EAR DRUM

PINNA OR EAR FLAP

TYMPANIC CAVITY

EAR CANAL

10-2 CANINE EAR

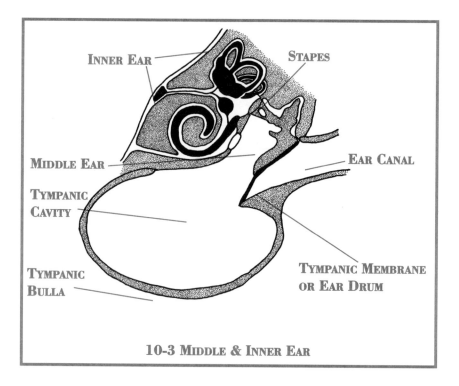

INNER EAR

STAPES

MIDDLE EAR

EAR CANAL

TYMPANIC CAVITY

TYMPANIC BULLA

TYMPANIC MEMBRANE OR EAR DRUM

10-3 MIDDLE & INNER EAR

position as the fluid shifts. If a dog's head is tilted the fluid shifts, and the brain detects the tilting.

The eardrum picks up sound waves through air vibration. The eardrum vibrates and stimulates the bones within the middle ear. The vibrating bones pass the sound vibrations to an area with tiny hairs. As the hair moves, sound waves are transformed to electrical impulses and then passed to the **inner ear** where they are transmitted by the **auditory nerve** to the brain where it is detected as sound. This is how hearing is created.

The parts of the ear, namely the ear flap, canal, eardrum and middle and inner ear, all play important roles. These structures are complex and occasionally become diseased, thus impairing their function. Disorders of the ear are frequently very painful and can affect both hearing *and* equilibrium.

Auricular Hematoma

As stated before, the ear flap (pinna) is made up of two layers of skin with an inner core of cartilage. Numerous blood vessels and nerves extend from the inner vascular areas of the head all the way to the end of the pinna. Canines, as humans, have large numbers of blood vessels and nerves that course all the way to the ear tip. Trauma to the ear flap can rupture or damage the delicate blood vessels. Trauma may be the result of a blow to the ear or a bite from another pet. Additionally, *outer* ear infections are very painful and may cause dogs to violently shake their heads or scratch their ears. This shaking and scratching can also damage the ear flap.

If a major vessel within the ear flap ruptures, large amounts of blood can leak into the space between the skin and cartilage. This pool of blood is called a **hematoma.** The flap becomes very thick and may appear swollen, as the skin and cartilage are spread apart because of the hemorrhage. (See figure 10-4.)

What are the symptoms?
The most noted symptom is a large fluid-filled cyst within the ear flap or pinna. Generally, dogs will shake their heads. The excess weight of the blood-filled flap is felt by the patient, thus causing even more head shaking. If an ear infection is also present, there may be an infectious odor coming from the ear canal as well.

What are the risks?
An auricular hematoma is not life threatening. Hematomas caused by ear infections are more serious because the underlying infection can cause hearing loss and severe discomfort. Untreated, these hematomas can become excessive in size, resulting in permanent damage to the pinna. If the dog's head is scratched or shaken hard enough, the skin over the hematoma may tear, releasing the blood. This may stimulate further bleeding.

What is the treatment?

All patients with auricular hematoma should have a careful examination to determine the cause. Was it due to trauma from another dog or the result of an ear infection? The underlying cause should be determined and treated. The blood-filled flap is usually surgically excised to remove the blood. Sutures are placed through the ear to hold the inner skin, cartilage and other skin tightly together so that the space cannot refill with blood and the structures can heal back together. It must be emphasized that all auricular hematoma patients be examined for deeper ear infections. In the authors' experience, 90 percent of all cases are caused by self-trauma resulting from an ear infection. For proper treatment of ear infections, please refer to pages 196–200.

INFECTIONS OF THE OUTER EAR (OTITIS EXTERNA)

Otitis externa describes an infection or inflammation of the external ear canal. The infection can extend from the skin circling the inside of the ear flap, to the opening of the canal and all the way to the eardrum. (See figure 10-5.) This is the most common disorder affecting the canine ear. In fact, it is probably the most common infection in the dog!

The cause of irritation may be bacteria, fungus, yeast or ear mites. Often, more than one cause can be identified in the same patient. For example, bacteria frequently invade the tissue damaged by ear mites. One or both ears may be simultaneously involved. Otitis externa can occur in any breed; however, those with floppy ears and/or hair within the ear canal have a higher incidence. This is because the ear flaps and/or hair prevent air flow from entering the canal. Without adequate air flow to dry the canal, they become dark, and moisture trapped within them makes a great environment for bacteria, yeasts and fungi to propagate. Otitis externa can also be secondary to allergies. In these patients, the wax-producing glands of the ear canal over-produce, leaving excessive material present for bacteria and yeasts to grow on.

What are the symptoms?

Otitis externa can present with a variety of symptoms and degrees. Generally the most noted sign is head shaking and/or scratching at the head with a foot. Occasionally an odor will be detected. This is from the infection causing an excess of waxy secretions and from the infection itself. If dogs are in extreme pain they may refuse to eat. In severe infections, the canal will be damaged and bloody. In the case of ear mites, which are actually very small "spider-like" bugs, the canal will be full of dried blood, which may appear similar to coffee grounds. Mites feed on the canal tissue and its secretions and can cause great damage and discomfort. Mild otitis externa may go undetected by the owner, only to be discovered upon a routine veterinary examination of the ear. In advanced cases, the ear canal becomes clogged with wax and exudate, and hearing may be impaired.

What are the risks?
All cases of otitis externa are potentially serious. *Damage may extend to the eardrum, causing permanent hearing loss.* If the drum is damaged, the infection may spread to the middle and inner ear, causing severe and permanent damage. Additionally, many animals will severely mutilate their ears when scratching themselves.

What is the treatment?
Otitis externa must be evaluated *carefully* to determine the cause. Veterinary diagnostic tests such as bacterial and fungal cultures can be performed. Microscopic examination of the draining material from within the ear may reveal ear mites.

Many ear ointments are available to kill bacteria, mites, yeast and fungi. In very severe and chronic cases surgery can be performed to "open up" and shorten the ear canal, thereby providing better drainage and drying of the sensitive tissues.

Many commercial solutions are available for routine use to help prevent infections. These washes or cleansing agents clean and dissolve ear wax and debris and dry the canals. Additionally, these preparations are slightly acidic and acid solutions discourage the reproduction of bacterial, yeast and fungal organisms. Good quality cleansing solutions, despite being acidic, are virtually sting-free. Affected pets should have their ears cleaned at least weekly with these solutions so that many infections will be avoided altogether. Breeds with excessive hair within the canal opening (Poodles, Lhasa Apsos, etc.) should have the hair clipped or plucked from the opening. This extra hair impedes proper air flow into the canal and prevents the canal from drying. Removal of this hair is a common part of routine grooming for individuals in these and many breeds.

INFECTIONS OF THE MIDDLE EAR (OTITIS MEDIA)
Otitis media describes an infection of the middle ear or the area immediately inside the eardrum. (See figure 10-6.) Generally this results from infections in the ear canal. The eardrum becomes damaged and bacteria (rarely fungi) enter the middle ear through the damaged eardrum. This infection can also arise from bacteria carried by the bloodstream or those that make their way up the throat via the eustachian tube.

What are the symptoms?
Head shaking, scratching at the head and ear area and difficulty hearing all can indicate a middle ear infection. Since major nerves supplying the facial muscles pass through the middle ear, the facial muscles can also be

AURICULAR HEMATOMA

10-4 AURICULAR HEMATOMA

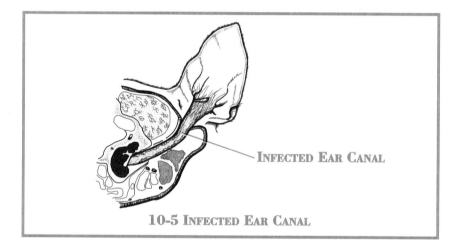

INFECTED EAR CANAL

10-5 INFECTED EAR CANAL

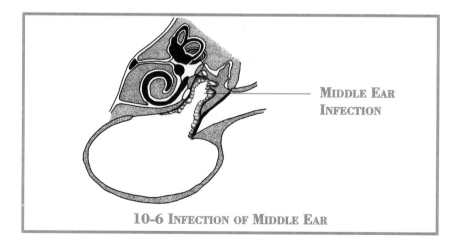

MIDDLE EAR INFECTION

10-6 INFECTION OF MIDDLE EAR

affected. If the nerves are affected, the face may droop on the affected side and the ear may hang lower than normal. Since the jaw bones of the canine extend behind the ear, pain may be felt when the dog's mouth is opened. A foul-smelling discharge may be present in the ear canal if the eardrum has ruptured. In cases of middle ear infection where the eardrum remains intact, it will appear discolored and bulging outward on examination.

What are the risks?

Because the middle ear is closely associated with major nerves and is principally responsible for hearing, *all infections are considered serious.* There is also often damage to the eardrum.

What is the treatment?

Most infections of the middle ear are bacterial in nature and may respond to oral antibiotics. Flushing the ear canal to cleanse the outer and middle ear is beneficial. Due to pain, anesthesia is generally required to flush the middle ear. A culture of the draining material will reveal the cause, which usually is bacterial; however, fungi are occasionally diagnosed. Cases not responsive to oral medications and flushing may require surgery to open and clean out the area. Medical therapy may need to be ongoing for several months until a complete cure can be achieved. For unknown reasons German Shepherd Dogs and Cocker Spaniels have a higher incidence of middle ear infections than other breeds.

INFECTIONS OF THE INNER EAR (OTITIS INTERNA)

Infections of the inner ear are not common, but are severe when encountered. Bacterial infections and cancerous growths are also known to affect the inner ear.

What are the symptoms?

The inner ear is an organ of balance. Any disruption of the inner ear can lead to loss of equilibrium, causing a head tilt. The dog tends to walk in circles toward the affected side, and frequently will fall toward the diseased ear. The inner ear also transmits sound from the middle ear to the brain. Therefore a loss of or impaired hearing may be noted with inner ear problems.

What are the risks?

Disorders of the inner ear are always serious. The inner ear is closely associated with the brain and infections or tumors of these areas may also spread to the brain. *Tumors of the inner ear are life threatening.*

What is the treatment?

Aggressive therapy is recommended to prevent damage to the surrounding areas and brain, as permanent damage frequently results. Surgery, radiographs and blood tests are often necessary to determine the exact cause. Cultures can help determine if bacterial agents are present. Tumors are removed if possible.

FOREIGN BODIES IN THE EAR CANAL

The ear canal drops downward before it enters into the head horizontally. It therefore makes a great place to collect or catch foreign material such as weeds, sticks, seeds and dirt. The most frequent foreign bodies found in the ear are bits of weeds and grasses.

What are the symptoms?

Generally the foreign materials irritate or tickle the ear canal. The patients usually shake their heads or scratch at their ears.

What are the risks?

Most foreign bodies simply irritate the canal. However, they can occasionally puncture the eardrum. They pose no real threat unless the eardrum is damaged. Once these objects are removed, the patient quickly recovers.

What is the treatment?

All foreign bodies should be removed at once. Often they are deep within the canal and can only be seen with a special ear scope (otoscope). Removal may require specialized instruments capable of reaching deep into the canal, which in some cases may require anesthesia.

HEREDITARY DEAFNESS

Inherited deafness has been reported in several canine breeds. Dalmatians are the most commonly noted; however, English Setters, Border Collies, Shetland Sheepdogs and Australian Shepherds among others have been reported with inherited deafness. The deafness tends to be linked with the white, merle or piebald coat colors.

What are the symptoms?

Most affected patients are born with some hearing capabilities, but deafness becomes apparent within a few months. The deafness is due to a degeneration of the nerves within the ear.

What are the risks?

Patients with inherited deafness do not all become deaf to the same degree. Some patients have only a partial hearing loss; in fact, it may not be noticeable to the owner.

What is the treatment?

There is no treatment for inherited deafness. Fortunately most patients cope very well with a hearing disability. Because this is inherited, affected individuals should not be used in any breeding program.

DEAFNESS AND AGING

Deafness associated with aging is common in the canine. As the patient ages, the eardrum and nerves associated with hearing deteriorate, leading to some degree of hearing deficit. Fortunately, the hearing loss progresses gradually and seldom seriously affects the pet's well-being. There is no way to predict the full extent or rapidity of the deafness. No medications are available to reverse the progression of symptoms.

Deafness associated with aging is considered a normal phenomenon. It is simply part of the normal aging process and is seen in at least 50 percent of all geriatric patients.

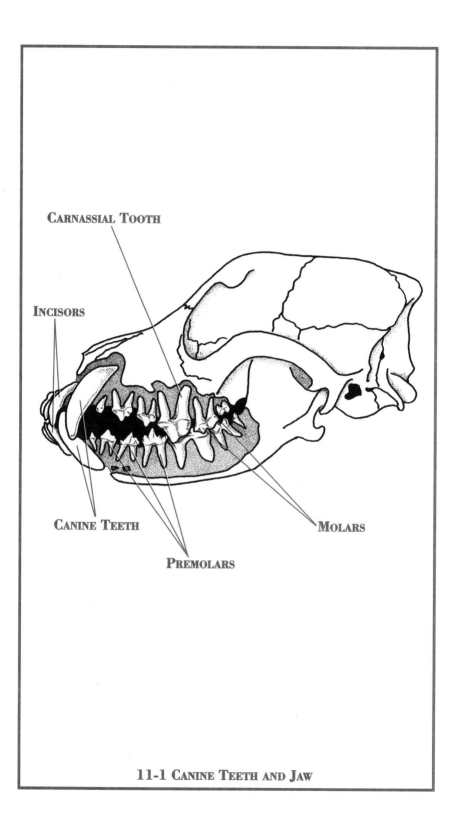

CARNASSIAL TOOTH

INCISORS

CANINE TEETH

PREMOLARS

MOLARS

11-1 CANINE TEETH AND JAW

The Mouth, Teeth, Gums and Salivary Glands

INTRODUCTION

The **mouth** is the entrance for food to enter the digestive tract, but is more than just an opening. Teeth line the upper and lower jaws and are used for tearing and shredding food. Puppies have twenty-eight teeth, while adults have forty-two. The exact number can vary slightly. (See figure 11-1.) *Saliva* produced by salivary glands is mixed with food in the mouth. Saliva acts as a lubricant and contains *ptyalin*, an enzyme which helps break down starch in the diet.

The **teeth** are living tissue and are used to break up or chew food. *Enamel*, the hardest substance in the canine body, is the outer layer of the teeth. (See figure 11-2.) *Dentine* is the next layer and the core is called the *pulp*. The pulp contains blood vessels and nerves which nourish the tooth. The root of the tooth is buried beneath the gum. Some teeth such as incisors have one root, while the others such as the upper fourth premolars have as many as three roots.

The canine has four pairs of **salivary glands**. (See figure 11-3.) The *parotid, mandibular, sublingual and zygomatic* all produce saliva. Each gland has its own duct to carry saliva from the gland to the mouth cavity.

The canine tongue is a useful and complex organ. It is used to manipulate food about the mouth, allows the animal to drink water, is the location of taste buds for the recognition of flavor and is an aid in cleaning the

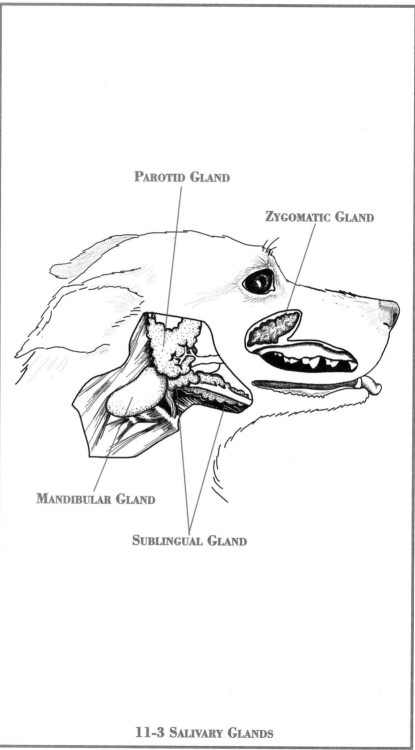

PAROTID GLAND

ZYGOMATIC GLAND

MANDIBULAR GLAND

SUBLINGUAL GLAND

11-3 Sᴀʟɪᴠᴀʀʏ Gʟᴀɴᴅs

body as well as communicating with other dogs. In drinking, water is transported from under the tongue into the mouth. Contrast this to a feline that laps water on top of the tongue. When cats drink it is relatively silent, while a canine must repeatedly thrust its tongue into the water to gulp water. Gulping is noisy. While gulping water much air can be transported along with the liquid, making hiccups a common occurrence, especially in puppies.

Canine gums vary greatly in normal coloration or pigmentation. Most breeds have pink gums. However, some breeds such as Chow Chows have deep blue-black gums. In some cases, the inner cheeks as well as the tongue are also dark-colored.

RETAINED DECIDUOUS TEETH

Usually by four weeks of age puppies get their deciduous teeth, commonly known as baby teeth. As we said, most puppies have twenty-eight deciduous teeth. Beginning around four months of age the deciduous teeth are replaced by the bigger and stronger permanent teeth. It takes an additional three to five months for the permanent teeth to replace all of the baby teeth. The adult dog averages forty-two permanent teeth. Occasionally, the permanent teeth do not erupt immediately under the deciduous teeth and therefore do not force the baby teeth out. When a dog has both an adult and baby tooth at the same site, it is referred to as a retained deciduous tooth. In the canine this usually occurs with the incisors or canine baby teeth. (See figure 11-4.)

What are the symptoms?

An extra set or double row of teeth may be noticed. With the large canine teeth it is usually the upper deciduous ones that are retained. The permanent canine teeth usually erupt in front of the deciduous canines. (See figure 11-5.)

What are the risks?

Retained baby teeth frequently cause a crowding of the teeth along the gum line. This "crowding" displaces the permanent teeth so that they are misplaced or grow at odd angles. The abnormal placement of teeth can interfere with the normal growth and development of bones in the jaw. Retained teeth may also die and abscess, causing mouth infections to develop.

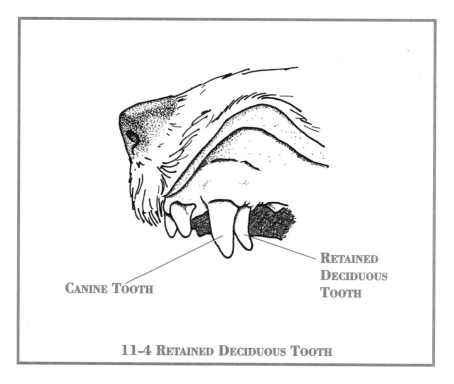

Canine Tooth

Retained
Deciduous
Tooth

11-4 Retained Deciduous Tooth

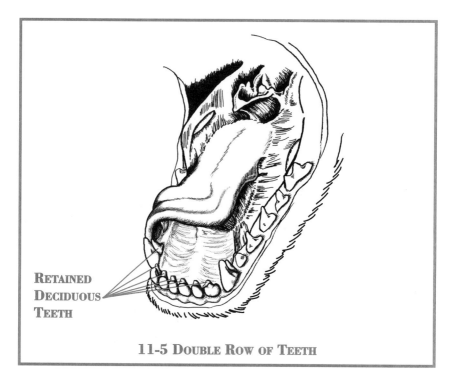

Retained
Deciduous
Teeth

11-5 Double Row of Teeth

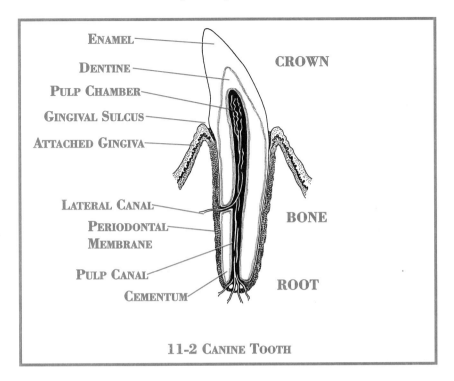

ENAMEL

DENTINE

PULP CHAMBER

GINGIVAL SULCUS

ATTACHED GINGIVA

LATERAL CANAL

PERIODONTAL
MEMBRANE

PULP CANAL

CEMENTUM

CROWN

BONE

ROOT

11-2 CANINE TOOTH

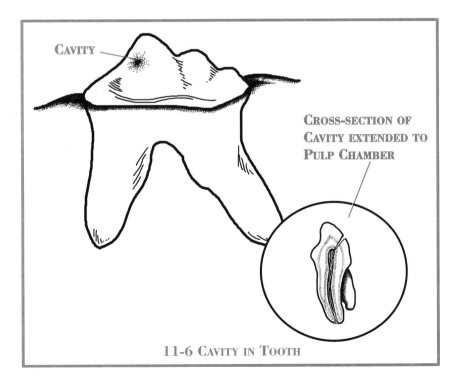

CAVITY

CROSS-SECTION OF
CAVITY EXTENDED TO
PULP CHAMBER

11-6 CAVITY IN TOOTH

What is the treatment?

Abnormally retained deciduous teeth should be extracted. This will usually require anesthesia and surgical extraction. Check a puppy's mouth weekly until about seven months of age for abnormal teeth. Consult a veterinarian for an oral examination if any retained teeth are suspected.

DENTAL CARIES—CAVITIES

A **cavity** is a corrosion through the enamel of the tooth. This demineralization or loss of tooth structure is commonly the result of bacterial or chemical action on the tooth surface.

What are the symptoms?

Cavities in teeth generally appear as dark areas on the tooth surface. A hole will usually develop and will vary in size depending on how long the cavity has been present.

What are the risks?

Probably because of low sugar diets, severe cavities tend not to occur frequently in the canine. Most canine cavities go untreated and in many cases even unnoticed. Cavities can, however, extend deeper into the pulp area (see figure 11-6) of the tooth and cause pain or even kill the tooth.

What is the treatment?

As in humans, dental caries can be repaired to stop this progression. Veterinary dental techniques have improved significantly over the past decade. Veterinarians specializing in dental care are widely available. As in humans, cavities can be drilled, cleaned and filled. Fillings are becoming more common in the canine as a repair for cavities. In the past, these teeth were simply extracted.

ABSCESSED TOOTH ROOTS

Occasionally the roots of teeth become infected. Commonly this is the result of gum disease allowing bacteria to enter the mouth and move beneath the gum line, causing an infection by the tooth roots. Any tooth can be involved. However, most frequently the incisors, canines and the upper fourth premolars are affected.

What are the symptoms?

Usually a notable swelling is visualized along the gum where the roots of the tooth are embedded. If the abscess is draining into the mouth, a foul odor may be detected in the breath. In severe root abscesses, a swelling may be noticed upon the face. Incisors simply become loose and fall out. Infected canine teeth may drain out the nasal passages and cause a larger marble-size swelling or abscess on the muzzle. Abscessation of the upper fourth premolar is common in the canine. The fourth premolar has three roots which extend up under the eye. Commonly the first indication of a root abscess is a swelling and/or drainage immediately under the eye. (See figure 11-7.)

What are the risks?

Infected teeth are serious and cause great pain to the dog. Frequently because of the pain, patients are unable to chew and will fail to eat. If they do eat, they will typically avoid chewing on the affected side. Untreated, the teeth die and are lost.

What is the treatment?

Generally *antibiotic therapy* alone will *not* clear up the infection. In some cases the infected teeth are simply extracted, thus exposing and draining the abscess. *Root canals* can be done in an effort to save the tooth. This is preferred, but more expensive. Antibiotic therapy is recommended following extraction.

FRACTURED TEETH

Because of their chewing, dogs commonly crack or break teeth. Many pets chew on hard objects such as rocks, wire and concrete. These hard substances can result in fractured teeth. (See figure 11-8.) Also, injuries such as automobile accidents can damage or break teeth.

What are the symptoms?

Cracks or missing sections of teeth are usually fairly obvious. Routine mouth examinations will help detect partial cracks. Following any injury to the head, the teeth should be carefully examined for cracks or missing sections.

What are the risks?

Tooth fractures are often not serious. Cracks that extend below the gum line or into the pulp may cause tooth death. Additionally, abscesses may result if the roots or pulp become exposed to bacteria.

What is the treatment?

If pain, abscess or tooth death occurs, then extraction of the entire tooth is recommended. In less severe cases, veterinary dentists can repair the

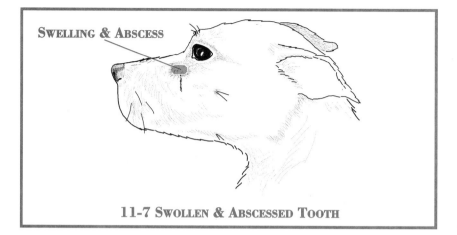

SWELLING & ABSCESS

11-7 SWOLLEN & ABSCESSED TOOTH

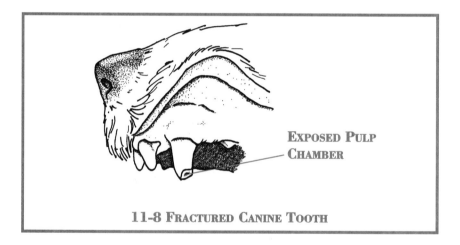

EXPOSED PULP
CHAMBER

11-8 FRACTURED CANINE TOOTH

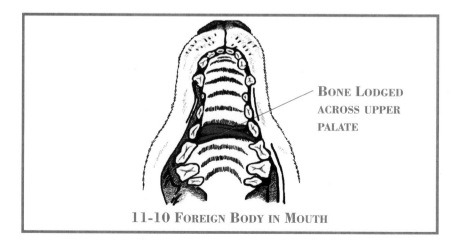

BONE LODGED
ACROSS UPPER
PALATE

11-10 FOREIGN BODY IN MOUTH

fractures or even place an artificial crown on the tooth much like in humans. Generally these specialized procedures are more for cosmetic purposes then they are a medical necessity.

MALOCCLUSION OF TEETH

Malocclusion results when the upper teeth do not align properly with the lower teeth. Normally the teeth interact in a manner that allows powerful chewing and tearing of food. If the teeth do not align in the correct fashion, this is generally the result of either abnormal jaw growth or misalignment of the teeth themselves.

What are the symptoms?

Malocclusions can sometimes only be seen on close examination. Chewing abnormalities such as food falling from the mouth may be a symptom. The *majority of malocclusion cases* seen at our hospitals *involve the length of the jaws*. If the lower jaw protrudes too far beyond the upper, the animal is said to be **undershot**. This is sometimes referred to as a "salmon jaw." (See figure 11-9.) Conversely, if the lower jaw bones are too short, the animal is said to be **overshot**. This is occasionally referred to as "parrot mouth."

What are the risks?

Normally malocclusion presents no great risk to the patient. The intake of food and chewing may be hindered somewhat. Most patients still perform these functions quite well. Tartar and plaque will build up excessively on teeth if abnormal wearing surfaces are created. Tooth wear can also be excessive if two teeth constantly grind on each other. Patients with severely undershot (parrot mouth) jaws may have difficulty picking up food and therefore large chunks are ingested easier than smaller ones.

What is the treatment?

Most patients require no treatment to correct the malocclusion. If teeth wear excessively from abnormal grinding, extractions may be necessary. Teeth should be routinely brushed and cleaned to prevent the abnormal build-up of tartar and plaque. Veterinary dental specialists can be consulted if an owner desires to alter the malocclusion. *It is wise not to breed pets with malformed jaws as there is a hereditary link* in many affected patients.

GINGIVAL HYPERPLASIA

Occasionally for unknown reasons, but probably due to constant irritation, the cells of the gums will increase in size and number, creating a

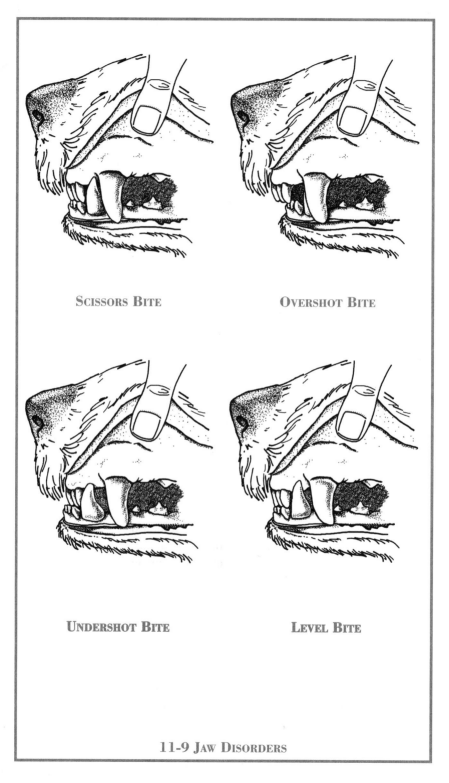

Scissors Bite

Overshot Bite

Undershot Bite

Level Bite

11-9 Jaw Disorders

cauliflower or overgrown appearance. In some cases, viruses are a possible cause of gingival hyperplasia in dogs.

What are the symptoms?

Small growths will arise from the gum tissue, usually along the tooth line. These areas of gum hypertrophy often resemble cauliflower. They may bleed from being damaged during chewing.

What are the risks?

Gingival hyperplasia is a benign growth of cells posing no serious health threat. They occasionally are damaged during chewing and may bleed and become painful.

What is the treatment?

The areas of excessive tissue growth can be surgically removed. Anesthesia is generally required. Regrowth can occur, so surgery may need to be repeated. The growth is usually biopsied and differentiated from more serious disorders such as cancer. *Gingival hyperplasia is not life threatening.*

GINGIVITIS

Gingivitis describes an inflammation or infection of the gums. As plaque and tartar build up on the teeth, the gums become loose and pull away from the teeth. Loose gums allow air and bacteria to enter the lower tissues and possibly involve the roots of the teeth.

What are the symptoms?

The gums will appear red or purplish and usually are swollen. An infectious discharge is normally noticed draining from around the teeth, giving them a "slimy" appearance. A foul breath is almost always present and gingivitis should be a primary consideration in any case of bad breath. As the gums swell and become painful, difficulty chewing or failure to eat may be noted. Bleeding ulcers may develop in advanced cases. Excessive drooling may occur.

What are the risks?

Infected gums are more serious than often thought. As bacteria invade the gums and teeth, they can also enter the bloodstream and cause infection in more critical areas such as the heart. Additionally, bacteria are constantly "showering" the larynx and trachea and being inhaled into the fragile lungs. Maintaining good oral hygiene is an important component of the overall health of a dog.

What is the treatment?

Rather than treating gingivitis, it is far better to prevent the condition by practicing good oral hygiene. All dogs should have their teeth cleaned and gums massaged by routine brushing. Excellent toothpastes and mouth-washes are now marketed specifically for pets. Used regularly, these products will greatly reduce gingivitis.

The diet can also be modified. Dry diets tend to be abrasive and help keep the teeth free of tartar and plaque. Routine examinations by a veterinarian, coupled with prophylactic cleanings, are also recommended. Once developed, gingivitis is best treated by a veterinarian using ultrasonic cleaning. Some or all of the teeth may need to be removed, depending on the severity of the gingivitis. Long-term antibiotic therapy is usually necessary to kill and control the disease-causing bacteria.

GLOSSITIS

An inflammation of the tongue is termed glossitis. Although tongue infections are rare, it is not uncommon for the tongue to become irritated or injured. Sources of irritation include burrs from weeds, porcupine quills, bee stings and burns.

What are the symptoms?

Inflammations of the tongue are very painful, at least initially. Reluctance to eat is the most common sign associated with glossitis. In the case of burrs one may notice the "slivers" or splinters protruding from the tongue's surface.

What are the risks?

The tongue tends to heal quickly even when severely damaged. Burrs and porcupine quills must be removed before healing can begin.

What is the treatment?

Many times, no treatment is necessary. Generally, removal of burrs and quills requires surgery. Antibiotics are often used to prevent this infection from spreading to other parts of the body.

TONSILLITIS

See Chapter 14, "The Lymphatic System."

CLEFT PALATE

See Chapter 4, "Bones, Joints, Muscles, Ligaments and Tendons"

TUMORS OF THE MOUTH

As with most areas of the body, the mouth tissue is susceptible to cancer. Fortunately mouth cancer is not common in the canine. The tumors may arise anywhere, including the gums, tongue, tonsils, palate and cheeks.

What are the symptoms?

Most patients with mouth cancer have foul breath. Commonly the tumor(s) bleed, sometimes profusely. As the tumor(s) grow, weight loss and a reluctance to eat will be noted. Excessive drooling is common. Upon oral examination, most tumors can be seen as growths often larger than a marble.

What are the risks?

All cases of mouth cancer are serious. Most tumors found here are malignant. Many types will spread to other areas such as the lymph nodes or lungs.

What is the treatment?

Surgery to remove the cancerous growths is required. Chemotherapy and radiation treatments can be beneficial in some instances. Malignant tumors of the mouth commonly recur or spread to other areas despite treatment.

DEPRAVED APPETITE (PICA)

PICA is a term describing a condition when a dog regularly eats objects not considered a part of the normal diet. Examples include an appetite for wood, sand, metal, stones, rubber, etc. **PICA** is not really a disorder of the mouth, but a psychological abnormality.

What are the symptoms?

The symptoms simply include a history of eating objects not designed to be ingested. To have **PICA**, a patient generally does not eat the objects just once, but rather seems to be addicted to consuming certain materials.

What are the risks?

Eating foreign objects is risky because many cannot pass through the gastrointestinal tract normally. Objects such as rocks and socks can cause a complete blockage of the intestines, requiring surgery to remove them. Additionally, they may cause damage to the mouth or abnormal wear on the teeth.

What is the treatment?

Contrary to common belief, a patient with an abnormal appetite is not lacking in vitamins, minerals or any other nutrient. **PICA** is a psychological abnormality and is more a habit than a medical problem, even though it can lead to one. There is no sure cure for **PICA**; however, providing alternative edible objects such as rawhide bones and other digestible treats will help.

FOREIGN BODIES IN THE MOUTH

Canines, because of their chewing nature, tend to get foreign bodies lodged in their mouths occasionally. Bones and sticks are the most common. Poultry and pork chop bones are also common offenders.

What are the symptoms?

Drooling and gagging are the most noted symptoms. Dogs are usually not really gagging, but rather manipulating their tongues in an attempt to remove the object. Commonly the objects are lodged across the upper palate between the teeth. (See figure 11-10.) A foul breath odor will develop if the objects remain lodged. Many of these dogs will not eat, while others go on as if nothing is wrong.

What are the risks?

If the objects are not promptly removed they may cause infections of the gums and other structures. Many patients fail to eat and lose weight.

What is the treatment?

Treatment involves identifying and removing the object. Once removed, healing is usually rapid. If a mouth infection has developed, antibiotics will be required to clear the bacteria.

DISORDERS OF THE SALIVARY GLANDS

The canine has four pairs of salivary glands, each with a different name. As previously mentioned, they are the *sublingual, mandibular, parotid and zygomatic.* Their main function is to produce saliva, which lubricates food and contains an enzyme to aid in digestion. Saliva production goes on constantly, with or without the presence of food, and is simply swallowed.

EXCESSIVE DROOLING (PTYALISM)

Excessive drooling may be the result of too much saliva production, the animal not swallowing, or of malformed lips simply letting saliva drain from the mouth. Certain drugs such as organophosphates, commonly used in flea preparations, may stimulate an overproduction of saliva. Newer and safer insecticides such as pyrethrins are not likely to cause this. Viral diseases such as rabies or distemper, inflammations such as tonsillitis, and foreign bodies may have excessive salivation as a symptom.

The most common cause of salivation is not an overproduction of saliva, but rather a malfunction of the lip folds or something that inhibits swallowing. Breeds such as the Saint Bernard, Newfoundland, Great Pyrenees, Rottweiler, Bloodhound, etc. commonly have individuals with lips that cause excessive drooling.

What are the symptoms?

Saliva will simply drip from the mouth or form long strings that hang.

What are the risks?

Drooling by itself is not harmful. The causes of drooling may have other, even fatal implications. Diseases such as rabies and distemper may be fatal. Drooling due to lip fold abnormalities can cause infections of the skin and areas that surround the mouth.

What is the treatment?

The cause of drooling must be identified. Is it overproduction, inability to swallow or simply the dog's lip fold conformation? Were organophosphate drugs recently used to treat worms or fleas? Inability to swallow correctly always has an underlying medical problem that must be identified. For abnormal lip folds a surgery can be performed to alter the lip structure and prevent further drooling.

SIALOCELE

Occasionally saliva will accumulate under the skin, causing a large cyst. The cause is unknown, but there may be a genetic predisposition, as German Shepherd Dogs and Miniature Poodles have a higher incidence than other breeds. Damage to a salivary gland or duct may cause leakage of saliva under the skin.

What are the symptoms?

The most common salivary glands involved are the sublingual glands. They or their ducts can leak and cause saliva to accumulate under the chin (see figures 11-11 and 11-12) or under the tongue.

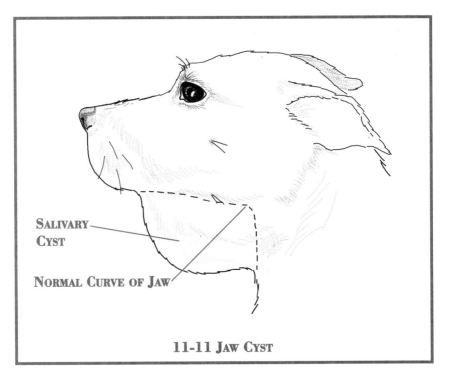

SALIVARY CYST

NORMAL CURVE OF JAW

11-11 JAW CYST

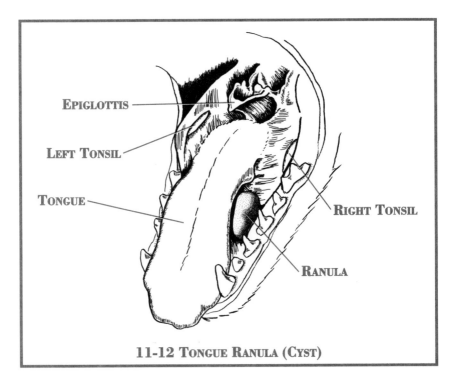

EPIGLOTTIS

LEFT TONSIL

TONGUE

RIGHT TONSIL

RANULA

11-12 TONGUE RANULA (CYST)

What are the risks?

Salivary accumulations generally are not painful and most patients have no other abnormalities.

What is the treatment?

A total cure is usually achieved by removal of the salivary gland producing the excess saliva. Specialized dye studies may need to be performed by a veterinarian to identify the involved gland. Removal of the gland has no long-term effects on the patient.

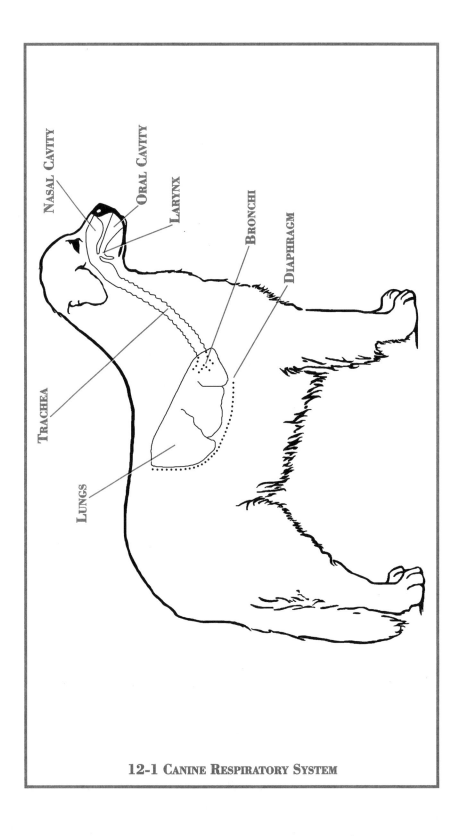

NASAL CAVITY

ORAL CAVITY

LARYNX

BRONCHI

DIAPHRAGM

TRACHEA

LUNGS

12-1 CANINE RESPIRATORY SYSTEM

C H A P T E R   1 2

Disorders of the
Respiratory System

INTRODUCTION

The respiratory system is basically composed of the **nares** or **pharynx openings** into the nose, **sinuses** within the skull, **larynx, trachea (windpipe), bronchi** (the branches of the trachea going into the lungs) and the **lungs**. (See figure 12-1.)

To the canine, the respiratory system has a dual purpose. It functions as an exchange mechanism removing carbon dioxide from the body and replacing it with oxygen. In addition, it is also a unique cooling system. Since dogs do not have sweat glands, they cannot perspire to lower their body's temperature. To cool their body they must breathe harder (pant). By breathing faster, warm air is exchanged from the body for the cooler outside air. Additionally, moisture within the respiratory system evaporates, further cooling these surfaces. Therefore, the lungs function both to exchange carbon dioxide for oxygen and to cool the body.

Breathing is relatively simple and is accomplished by the actions of the *rib muscles* (intercostals) and the movement of a great internal muscle called the *diaphragm*.

The **diaphragm** muscle separates the chest, containing the heart and lungs, from the abdomen which holds the intestines, stomach, liver, bladder, etc. As this great muscle moves toward the abdomen, it pulls fresh air and oxygen into the lungs, causing the dog to breathe in (inhale). The chest cavity surrounding the lungs is a vacuum, thus allowing the lungs to inflate easily when the dog inhales. When the muscle moves forward, it causes the lungs to compress and force air out (exhale), thus ridding the body of used air.

As dogs inhale, fresh air moves through the nose (or mouth), pharynx and larynx to the trachea. (See figure 12-2.) The **trachea** carries the air to the bronchi, which in turn supply the **lungs**. Canines have right and left lungs, just like humans. Both sides of the lungs are further divided into sections or *lobes*. At the cellular levels, the lungs are rich in air pockets called *alveoli*. (See figure 12-3.) It is here the blood makes contact with the individual cells in the lungs and oxygen is exchanged for carbon dioxide. Alveoli are supplied by a vast network of microscopic blood vessels known as capillaries; it allows the used air to follow the opposite path: passing into bronchi, into the trachea, through the larynx and pharynx, finally exiting through the nose or mouth.

In this section we will describe common disorders that affect the various components of the respiratory system.

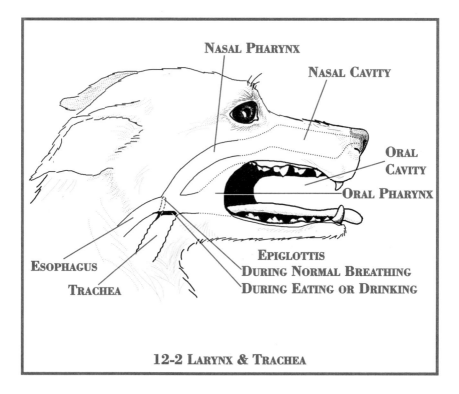

12-2 LARYNX & TRACHEA

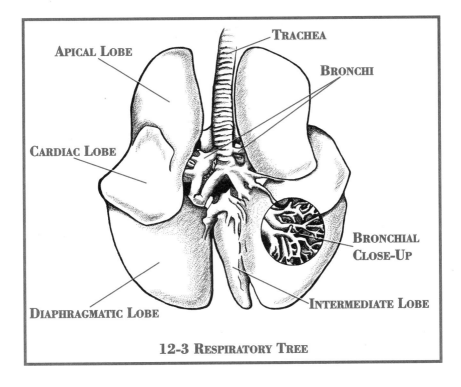

12-3 RESPIRATORY TREE

THE NOSE

The nose is the entrance into the respiratory system. Within the nose, mucous membranes form folds that clean and add moisture to incoming air. The membrane surfaces are covered by mucus produced by cells throughout the respiratory system. Dirt and debris is caught in this mucus. The respiratory surfaces are also covered by small hair-like structures called *cilia*. The cilia beat in a coordinated fashion to keep the mucus moving and also function to filter and trap dust particles. Air swirls around the series of folds. Particles such as pollen and dust are then removed by the sticky mucus and cilia, thus allowing only clean air to enter the more fragile lungs.

Cold air is also warmed by the nose and the open spaces within the head called sinuses, which form part of the nasal passages. (See figure 12-4.) Air moves into the nasal opening, then through the nose and sinuses where it is cleaned and warmed. It then passes on through the pharynx and the larynx, which is the opening into the windpipe (trachea). The nose is also an organ of smell. Any disorders affecting the nose may impede the dog's ability to smell.

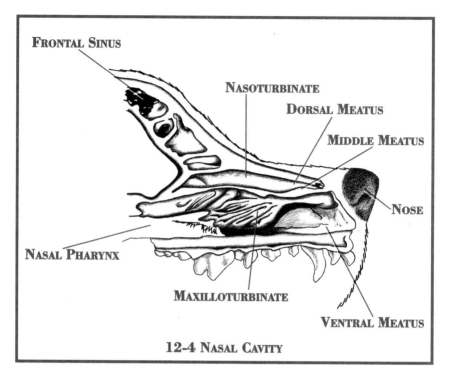

FRONTAL SINUS

NASOTURBINATE

DORSAL MEATUS

MIDDLE MEATUS

NOSE

NASAL PHARYNX

MAXILLOTURBINATE

VENTRAL MEATUS

12-4 NASAL CAVITY

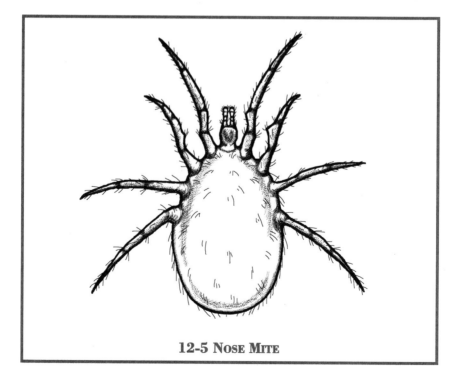

12-5 NOSE MITE

RHINITIS

Rhinitis is the term applied to an infection or inflammation of the nose. If the sinuses are also involved, it is called *sinusitis*. There are many bacteria, fungi and viruses capable of infecting the noses of canines. These infections behave very similarly to common colds in people. Bacteria such as Staphylococcus and Streptococcus, as well as viruses such as parainfluenza and adenovirus, are common nasal invaders and will cause cold-like symptoms.

What are the symptoms?

This depends somewhat on the type of infection causing the disorder. In general, one may notice excessive nasal discharge, occasionally becoming thick yellow or greenish mucus. The patient may sneeze frequently, trying to clear the nasal passages of mucus. In advanced cases, the mucus may become bloody. This patient's sense of smell is usually impaired. Despite common belief, nose temperature is not a good indicator of being sick or healthy. Normal patients may have hot, cold, dry or wet noses. *Body temperature is, however, an important indicator*. A patient with severe rhinitis may have an elevated body temperature. If this is the case, the patient generally becomes lethargic and has a poor appetite.

What are the risks?

This again depends on the exact organism(s) involved. Most cases remain confined to the nose and sinuses. In these instances the risks are minimal. If, however, the infection(s) spreads to the more delicate regions of the respiratory system such as the trachea, bronchi or lungs, then the patient may be affected more severely.

What is the treatment?

Any patient suffering from a nasal infection should rest. In addition, the dog should be isolated from other pets so as to minimize the probable spread of contagious diseases. If the symptoms persist or the patient develops a fever, go to a veterinarian at once.

In chronic cases needing treatment, a veterinarian will usually perform a culture of the nasal mucus. (See "Culture" in the Glossary.) This aids in identifying which organism(s) is responsible for the infection. Once this is performed, appropriate medications are selected. Antihistamines such as Benadryl are occasionally used to help dry and open the airways. Antibiotics such as amoxicillin, Tribrissen and Keflex are commonly used against bacterial infections. Vaporizers like those used for humans are also beneficial. Place the pet in a wire crate in a small area such as a bathroom, and vaporize the air. The moist air makes breathing easier, just as in humans.

NOSE MITES

The dog's nasal passages can occasionally be colonized by the nose mite, *Pneumonyssoides caninum*. (See figure 12-5.) These microscopic mites live inside the nose and can also move into the nasal sinuses. They are easily transferred to other dogs by sneezing and sniffing.

What are the symptoms?

The symptoms of a nose mite infection generally include sneezing, often violent. The membranes are irritated, sometimes causing the patient to have a bloody nose.

What are the risks?

There are no life-threatening risks associated with a nose mite infestation. Complications can, however, develop if bacteria enter the mucous membrane irritated by the mites.

What is the treatment?

If a nose mite infection is suspected, a diagnosis can be achieved by examining nasal mucus under a microscope. The nose mite can readily be identified. Once confirmed, the mites can be killed by organophosphorus drugs, such as dichlorvos. Although not officially approved for this use, the ivermectin compounds have proven beneficial.

NASAL FOREIGN BODY

Dogs by nature are prone to getting foreign materials lodged in nasal passages. Running with their noses to the ground makes them particularly susceptible to having objects such as sticks, weeds, pine needles, feathers, etc., enter and lodge there.

What are the symptoms?

The initial sign of an object lodged in the nose is usually sneezing. The sneeze may be mild or infrequent, or extremely violent. A large stick would cause a more severe sneezing than a pine needle. Bleeding may or may not occur. If the object is not removed, a nasal infection may develop, usually limited to that one side only. This is an important distinction from those infections brought on by other causes that affect both sides.

What is the treatment?

If possible, remove the foreign object *at once* with your fingers or tweezers. If the material is too deeply embedded, seek veterinary assistance. Sedation or anesthesia may be necessary, as many patients do not tolerate nasal examinations. Once the foreign body is removed, sneezing and bleeding usually stop and the airway heals.

THE LARYNX

The **larynx** is a circular organ composed of cartilage and muscle. It is located at the entrance to the trachea. (See figure 12-6.) Some people refer to it as the Adam's apple. The larynx houses the vocal cords, which are small muscle bands that vibrate and create sounds such as barking. Its other function is to prevent food from entering the trachea when a dog swallows. It does this by closing a small flap of muscle over the laryngeal opening. This muscular flap is called the epiglottis.

As with other areas within the respiratory system, the larynx is another location where infections develop.

LARYNGITIS

Laryngitis is the term used to describe an infection or irritation of the larynx. Many conditions caused by viruses or bacteria, such as strep throat, can also involve the dog's larynx. Excessive barking, as in a boarding kennel, can irritate this area, also leading to laryngitis.

What are the symptoms?
Generally a patient with laryngitis will have an altered voice. In the case of dogs, one may notice an altered or complete inability to bark. If the larynx swells, it can actually block air flow to the trachea and the patient can have difficulty breathing. Because laryngitis can be very painful, the patient may not eat to avoid swallowing. Frequently dogs will salivate (drool) excessively. Body temperature may rise as the infection progresses.

What are the risks?
As with humans, most cases of laryngitis are not life threatening unless the infection spreads or breathing becomes severely impaired. Mild cases may simply run their course while more advanced cases will need treatment.

What is the treatment?
If the laryngitis persists or appears severe, a veterinary examination should be performed. This may require a tranquilizer. Most patients can be examined simply with a light called a laryngoscope. A culture can be performed to help identify the organism responsible for the infection. Most viruses simply run their course in seven to ten days. Bacteria or fungi can be treated with antibiotics or antifungals. Antihistamines such as Benadryl may be beneficial in some patients.

THE TRACHEA

The **trachea** is a long hose-like tube that brings air through the neck and into the chest. (See figure 12-7.) It is also referred to as the **windpipe**.

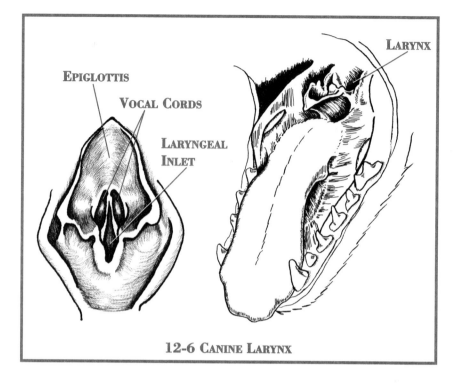

EPIGLOTTIS

VOCAL CORDS

LARYNGEAL INLET

LARYNX

12-6 CANINE LARYNX

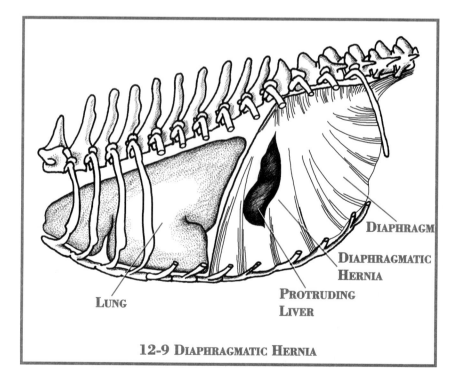

DIAPHRAGM

DIAPHRAGMATIC HERNIA

PROTRUDING LIVER

LUNG

12-9 DIAPHRAGMATIC HERNIA

Once inside the chest, it divides into two parts called the **bronchi**. One bronchus goes to the left lung, the other carries air to the right lung. The trachea contains *cartilage rings* which help keep it rigid as air moves in and out of it. Without these reinforcing cartilage rings, the trachea, because it is a tube, would simply close if the dog took a deep breath, such as during panting or heavy exercise.

TRACHEAL COLLAPSE

As mentioned earlier, the trachea is normally a rigid tube supported by tough rings made of cartilage. Occasionally the trachea will lose its rigidity and collapse while the patient is breathing. The collapsing trachea syndrome is most often seen in Toy breeds, especially Toy Poodles over the age of five years. For unknown reasons, the cartilage rings begin to weaken and the trachea no longer has proper support. (See figure 12-8.)

What are the symptoms?

The symptoms of a collapsing trachea depend on the severity of the cartilage deterioration. Usually the patient will have difficulty breathing, especially during exercise or excitement. The deeper the pet tries to inhale, the more the trachea collapses, further restricting the air flow. This pet will usually appear to tire easily, becoming short of breath. Patients with a collapsing trachea will generally cough as if trying to clear the airway. Occasionally the cough will sound like a goose honking. In very severe cases, the tongue and gums may appear blue as breathing becomes restricted.

What are the risks?

Most patients suffering with the collapsing trachea syndrome live normal, but restricted lives. Activity is generally limited as the ability to breathe deeply upon exercise is hindered. Left untreated, the restricted air flow can place undue stress on the heart and lungs as they try to compensate for the inability to breathe properly. Obese patients are at a greater risk than others.

What is the treatment?

Examination, whether by palpation with the fingers and/or with the aid of radiographs (X rays), will generally confirm the diagnosis. Depending on severity, different medications can be utilized. Usually veterinarians do prescribe drugs to help dilate the airways. Coughing may be decreased with cough suppressants such as Torbutrol.

If the patient is obese, a strict diet is generally suggested. Activity should be restricted and not encouraged. With the help of the above, this condition can be controlled but seldom cured, as nothing can restore the trachea's strength to normal levels. In very severe cases, surgery can be performed to help open the airway and provide additional strength to the trachea wall. Most cases, however, are managed medically, not surgically.

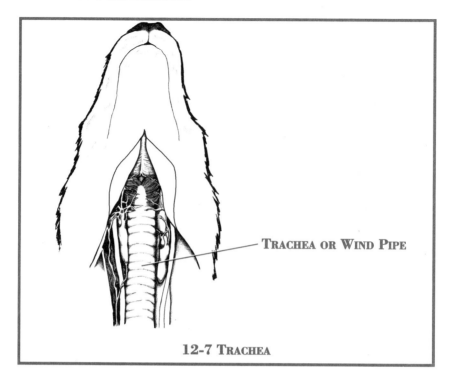

TRACHEA OR WIND PIPE

12-7 TRACHEA

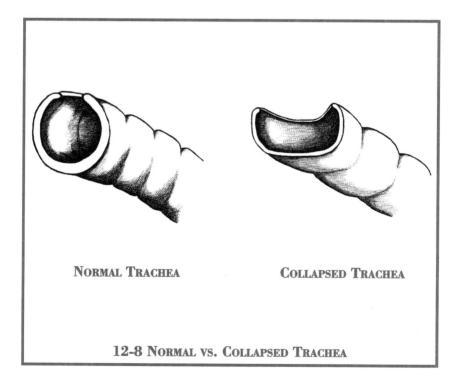

NORMAL TRACHEA   **COLLAPSED TRACHEA**

12-8 NORMAL VS. COLLAPSED TRACHEA

TRACHEOBRONCHITIS

Infections or irritations of the trachea and bronchi create a condition known as **tracheobronchitis**. In canines this ailment is common and has earned the name of "kennel cough" or "canine cough." As one might guess, coughing is the primary symptom associated with tracheobronchitis. Whether bacterial, viral or fungal, an infection within the trachea and the severity of it depends on the organism(s) involved. Adenovirus, para-influenza, Bordetella and Mycoplasma are common infectious agents involved.

What are the symptoms?

Most patients suffering from tracheobronchitis exhibit coughing. They may cough so severely that they regurgitate their food, leading the owner to believe the dog has an upset stomach, when in reality the stomach is normal. *Intestinal upsets do not begin with a cough.* Watch closely and if coughing persists until the patient vomits, the problem is in the trachea, not the stomach. The cough may also sound dry and raspy. Most patients act normal, except that they cough and occasionally gag. A fever may or may not be present.

What are the risks?

If only the trachea is involved in the infection, the risks are minimal. It must be noted, however, that many cases, especially viral, may take weeks to totally clear up.

Most cases of tracheobronchitis or kennel cough, as it is sometimes called, are extremely contagious, and easily transmitted to other dogs. Frequently the whole kennel becomes involved, therefore the name "kennel cough." Seldom life threatening, this disorder can certainly be a nuisance within the kennel. In rare instances, the infection may spread to the lungs, causing a more severe condition called **pneumonia**.

What is the treatment?

One must differentiate tracheobronchitis from **pneumonitis**, an infection within the lungs and much more serious. Occasionally a patient may have both tracheobronchitis and pneumonitis. The tracheal manipulation test will help identify tracheobronchitis. If one takes a normal dog and gently grasps or puts pressure on the trachea in the neck, the dog will not cough. If, however, there is an irritated trachea, the patient will cough upon manipulation. Practitioners refer to this as a positive tracheal manipulation reflex.

Listening to the lungs with a stethoscope will help in identifying pneumonia. Patients with tracheobronchitis are generally placed on a cough suppressant such as Torbutrol. Medications to dilate the airways may also help alleviate the symptoms. Anti-inflammatories such as prednisone are commonly used to relieve the irritations. Antibiotics are useful if the causative agent is a bacterium. Fortunately, there are safe and excellent vaccines available to prevent some of the more serious organisms causing tracheobronchitis or kennel cough. Vaccines are used to prevent infections due to adenovirus, parainfluenza and Bordetella.

THE LUNGS

The lungs are composed of millions of tiny spaces or air pockets called **alveoli.** It is here that fresh air from outside the body comes in close contact with a rich supply of small blood vessels known as **capillaries.** The blood exchanges carbon dioxide for oxygen and the red blood cells carry the oxygen to the tissues. This transfer of oxygen is absolutely essential for life. Any disease that upsets the delicate exchange of gases is potentially serious.

PNEUMONITIS

An infection or irritation of the lungs is known as **pneumonitis.** If fluid builds up within the lung tissue, it is called **pneumonia.** Pneumonia can happen after an infection or be secondary to another system failure, especially the heart. (Disorders of the heart are described in Chapter 6.) Infections of the lungs can be caused by bacteria, viruses or fungi. All can be serious.

What are the symptoms?

The most frequent and noticeable symptom of a lung infection is difficulty breathing, especially on inhalation. The breaths will be rapid and shallow. The patient has difficulty obtaining enough oxygen as the lung tissue becomes filled with fluid, thus reducing the number of functional air spaces (alveoli). The tongue, gums and lips may appear bluish or gray. This blue/gray appearance is termed *cyanosis* and is an indicator of lack of oxygen within the blood. The body temperature is usually elevated, often to over 104 degrees Fahrenheit. If the lung congestion is caused by a failing heart, the temperature may remain within normal limits (101 to 102 degrees Fahrenheit).

What are the risks?

Lung infections are always serious; however, with early diagnosis and treatment, most patients are successfully treated. In our opinion, the fungal diseases, such as blastomycosis, tend to be the most serious. Early detection and an accurate diagnosis are very important. One must rely on a veterinarian to determine if the cause is heart-related or simply a primary infection of the lungs.

What is the treatment?

If one suspects a lung disorder, a veterinarian should be contacted at once. Normally a variety of diagnostic techniques are utilized, such as chest X rays or ultrasound. If fluid is suspected, the chest can be biopsied so the material can be analyzed. This helps differentiate fungal disorders from others. If a bacterium is suspected, a culture and sensitivity test can be performed to identify the type of bacteria and help select proper antibiotics. Diuretics such as Lasix (furosemide) are occasionally administered to help clear excess fluid from the lungs.

Pneumothorax

Pneumothorax describes air within the chest cavity, but outside of the lungs.

The chest area surrounding the lungs is a vacuum, allowing the easy expansion of the lungs during inhalation. Unwanted air can enter this vacuum in two ways. A puncture wound through the chest wall and skin will allow air to be drawn into the vacuum.

Secondly, trauma to the lungs can allow air to escape into the area around them. Broken ribs can be sharp and puncture lung tissue, allowing air to leak from the lungs into the surrounding chest cavity. Whatever the mechanism, once air enters the free area of the chest, the lungs are no longer supported by the vacuum and will collapse to some degree.

What are the symptoms?

Generally pneumothorax will develop following trauma to the chest, punctures causing an opening through the chest wall or a tearing of the lung tissue itself. Bite wounds and automobile accidents are frequent causes. Unless both sides of the chest cavity are damaged, usually only the right or the left lung is collapsed.

The patient will have difficulty breathing, especially on inhalation. One will notice a rapid, shallow, difficult breathing rhythm. If the breathing is severely limited, the tongue, gums and lips may also appear blue. In severe wounds, the lungs may actually be exposed to the outside. Regardless of the degree of injury, with a pneumothorax the patient will be restless and try to lie in an upright position on the sternum. This position is known as sternal recumbency. This upright position helps the patient inflate the lungs easier.

What are the risks?

The risk associated with a pneumothorax depends largely on the extent of the trauma. A simple puncture wound from a tooth *may* cause very little concern, while more severe lacerations can be immediately life threatening.

Do not *assume* that a small puncture wound in the skin is not serious. Underlying muscles are often severely traumatized and ribs may also be broken. Additionally, chest wounds frequently are contaminated, which can result in serious lung and chest infections. Have all chest wounds, no matter how slight, examined by a veterinarian at once, as they are potentially life threatening.

What is the treatment?
The symptoms will not be alleviated until the chest wall is surgically repaired, closing the opening to the outside. Once the wound is repaired, the excess air is withdrawn from the chest cavity utilizing a needle and syringe or a special valve. Antibiotics are generally administered to combat bacterial infections.

DIAPHRAGMATIC HERNIA
The great muscle which separates the chest and lungs from the liver and other abdominal organs is called the **diaphragm**. As the diaphragm contracts and relaxes, it enlarges and compresses the chest cavity, forcing air to move in and out of the lungs. Breathing depends largely on the function of the diaphragm. Occasionally, usually following a traumatic accident, the diaphragmatic muscle will be ruptured or torn. Once an opening in the muscle occurs, abdominal contents such as the liver, stomach or intestines may herniate through the rupture, enter the chest, and put pressure upon the lungs. The diaphragm muscle is now compromised, as it cannot properly expand and contract. (See figure 12-9.)

What are the symptoms?
Signs associated with diaphragmatic hernia may occur immediately after trauma or may not be noted for weeks. Difficulty in breathing is the most common symptom. The degree depends on the extent of the damage and may vary from unnoticeable to extremely labored. In severe cases, the tongue, gums and lips may appear blue. Gastrointestinal upsets such as vomiting or not eating may also be noted when the stomach or intestines herniate through the diaphragm. They become "strangulated" or pinched off by the muscle and other organs.

What are the risks?
The risk depends on the extent of the damage. Minor damage to the diaphragm may actually go unnoticed and patients live normal lives. *Patients with a severe insult to the diaphragm will quickly perish if left unattended.*

What is the treatment?
Anytime the condition is suspected, a veterinary exam should be sought at once. X rays will often lead to immediate diagnosis. If a diaphragmatic

hernia is suspected, surgical correction is the only treatment and should be attempted as soon as the patient is stabilized.

TUMORS OF THE RESPIRATORY SYSTEM

Although not common, various types of tumors can invade the canine respiratory system. Usually these are confined to the nose and sinuses or the lungs.

POLYPS OF THE NASAL CAVITY

A benign type of cancer is occasionally seen in the nasal sinuses. These small growths are referred to as *polyps* and are not life threatening. Polyps tend to grow in the sinus and nasal cavities. As they increase in size, they form a barrier which obstructs breathing.

What are the symptoms?
Patients with nasal polyps will usually make a "wheezing" sound while breathing. This noise is caused by air swirling around the polyps when the dog inhales and exhales. If the polyps grow to a significant size, they can obstruct the air flow to the extent that the patient will breathe through the mouth, much like a human would do with a "stuffed-up" sinus.

What are the risks?
Nasal and sinus polyps are seldom life threatening. They do not spread to other areas of the body. If they become significant in size, their irritation may cause mucus to build up in the nasal passages, further restricting breathing. In addition, if the nose and sinuses lose their ability to drain properly, bacterial infections may develop. With this, the patient not only has nasal polyps, but a nasal infection (rhinitis) as well.

What is the treatment?
If one notices a "wheezing" dog, the nasal passages should be examined. Polyps near the nasal opening may be seen; however, those located deeper or within the sinuses will not be visible without the aid of specialized scopes used by veterinarians, called rhinoscopes. Similar exams are performed on humans. Mild cases or small polyps may require no treatment at all. If breathing is restricted, the polyps are generally removed by surgery. If a bacterial infection is present, antibiotics are given orally.

LUNG CANCER

Each year thousands of dogs are diagnosed with tumors in their lungs. This is usually lung cancer. Unlike humans, canines do not often have tumors that originate in the lungs. This is rare in dogs. Usually the tumors are found elsewhere in the patient's body and they have merely metastasized (spread) to the lungs.

As tumors grow, cancer cells tend to break away and float through the bloodstream. These cancer cells frequently lodge in the small vessels (**capillaries**) of the lungs and grow to form lung tumors. Eighty percent of all lung tumors of dogs are termed **adenocarcinomas**. These are malignant (life-threatening) cancer growths from abnormal glandular cells. Adenocarcinomas frequently originate from glandular tissues within the intestines, uterus or mammary glands. Cancerous cells break loose and travel by the blood to become lodged in the lungs, growing into additional tumors there. Skin and bone cancers may also spread to the lungs.

What are the symptoms?

The symptoms of lung cancer vary depending on how many tumors are present and their size. Almost universally though, these patients will have difficulty breathing. As the normal lung tissue is destroyed by growing tumors, the patient tends to have labored breathing that is rapid and shallow. Patients with lung cancer may also experience coughing, occasionally bringing up bloody mucus. In advanced cases, the patient will lose weight and eventually die. As mentioned earlier, other tissues in the dog are usually involved.

Other symptoms depend on which other organs or areas of the body are also affected.

What are the risks?

Patients with lung cancer are seriously ill. Early detection and treatment may save or extend the lives of some patients, but most lung cancers are incurable and eventually lead to death, usually within six months.

What is the treatment?

As with humans, *early detection and treatment is a must* if the patient is to survive. *Any dogs with difficulty breathing should have the chest examined.* This is generally done with a stethoscope and radiographs (X rays). X rays of the chest will frequently identify the number and sizes of the tumors. Ultrasound techniques are occasionally used.

Once the tumors have been located, they can be surgically biopsied. Biopsies are obtained by opening up the chest and removing the tumors or passing special needles through the chest wall into the tumor to obtain some of the cancer cells. The biopsied material is then examined microscopically to help determine the type of cancer. Only then can the treatment and outcome be predicted. Original tumors elsewhere in the body must be dealt with for a complete cure.

The treatment varies greatly. Small tumors may simply be surgically removed. It is possible to remove one or more lung lobes if needed. Dogs can live with lung tissue on only one side, but would have activities restricted. In more severe instances, chemotherapeutic drugs may be given. A few patients may be totally cured, but this is rare. In all likelihood, cancer in the lungs originated from tumors elsewhere in the body. *Both sites will need treatment for a cure.*

Successful treatment may slow the tumor growth, thus extending the life of the patient without ever providing a total cure. The outcome is more promising if the cancer is detected in its early stages and treatment begins immediately.

It must be noted, however, that 90 percent of all patients treated for lung cancer will die within a year. Without treatment, most die within six months. A thorough understanding between the veterinarian and the patient's owner is essential. Together they can decide the appropriate therapy and help predict the outcome.

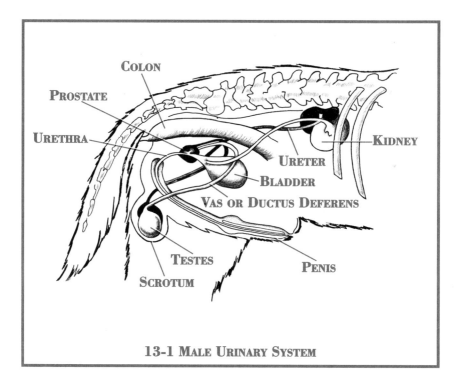

13-1 MALE URINARY SYSTEM

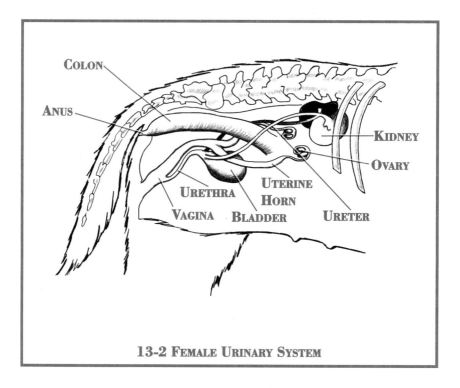

13-2 FEMALE URINARY SYSTEM

Disorders of the Urinary System

INTRODUCTION

Metabolism is the process of cells burning nutrients for fuel while building larger particles, such as proteins, from amino acids. Additionally, as the body works on a daily basis, cells undergo death and release their contents into the body. Both metabolism and cell death create waste materials such as excess nitrogen and phosphorus that would poison the body if not eliminated.

Fortunately, the urinary system is capable of detecting, filtering, removing and finally excreting toxic wastes in the blood from the body.

The urinary system includes two **kidneys** which filter waste from the blood (see figures 13-1 and 13-2) and combine it with water to form urine. From the kidneys, urine passes through small muscular tubes called **ureters** which empty into the bladder. The **bladder** is a balloon-like structure bound with muscle. It is a storage site for urine until it can be eliminated from the body. When the bladder empties, urine flows down the **urethra** to exit from the body. The male and female urinary systems are very similar. The closely associated organs of reproduction which differ are covered in Chapter 5, "The Canine Reproductive System."

DISORDERS OF THE KIDNEYS AND URETERS

The kidneys are large, bean-shaped organs, one on the right side of the body and the other on the left. Both are just under the backbone immediately behind the ribcage. (See figure 13-3.)

239

Every drop of blood circulating through the vessels of the body passes through the kidneys. Kidneys are composed of a complex network of minute blood vessels and specialized blood "filters" called **glomeruli.** The primary function of the kidneys is not really to filter blood, but rather to select certain nutrients to remain in the blood while extracting others in the formation of urine. Calcium and sodium are two substances the kidneys conserve and keep in the blood. On the other hand, very little nitrogen and phosphorus are saved, and most is passed out with the urine. Because of its high nitrogen content, urine burns grass and creates yellow spots in lawns.

Kidneys also detect the proper amount of water to leave in the blood. Excess fluid is removed from the bloodstream by the kidneys and becomes a component of urine. If a pet drinks excess amounts, then the kidneys will produce more than normal amounts of urine. The kidneys regulate the quantity of urine produced.

Nitrogen is a primary component of urine. When a dog eats, the body converts protein and other substances to sugar to be used as fuel. Proteins contain nitrogen, while sugar does not. Nitrogen then becomes a waste product of protein digestion, and nitrogen by itself is toxic to cells. Excess nitrogen is continually removed from the blood by the kidneys and excreted into the urine. Blood tests performed by veterinarians frequently monitor the blood urea nitrogen levels (BUN) to indicate kidney function. Diseased kidneys cannot remove the excess nitrogen, which then reaches elevated proportions in the bloodstream. Higher than normal nitrogen levels in the bloodstream are not a result of eating too much protein, but rather the kidneys' inability to excrete the nitrogen. Because patients with diseased kidneys have a decreased ability to excrete nitrogen, we recommend feeding these patients low-protein diets. *The lower the quantity of protein fed, the less nitrogen waste produced.* It is often erroneously believed that high-protein diets can damage the kidneys. This is not the case. Normal functioning kidneys can easily remove nitrogen produced from high-protein foods. In fact, patients with only one kidney can accomplish this task. *High-protein foods are not the cause of kidney disease in the canine.*

One generally unknown function of the kidneys is **hormone production**. A very important hormone called *erythropoietin* is produced by the kidneys and stimulates the bone marrow to produce red blood cells. Failing kidneys may produce inadequate quantities of erythropoietin hormone, resulting in abnormally low levels of red blood cells in the blood (anemia).

ACUTE RENAL DISEASE

Acute renal disease is a kidney disorder that occurs suddenly. Possible causes include bacterial infections, drug toxicities from such substances

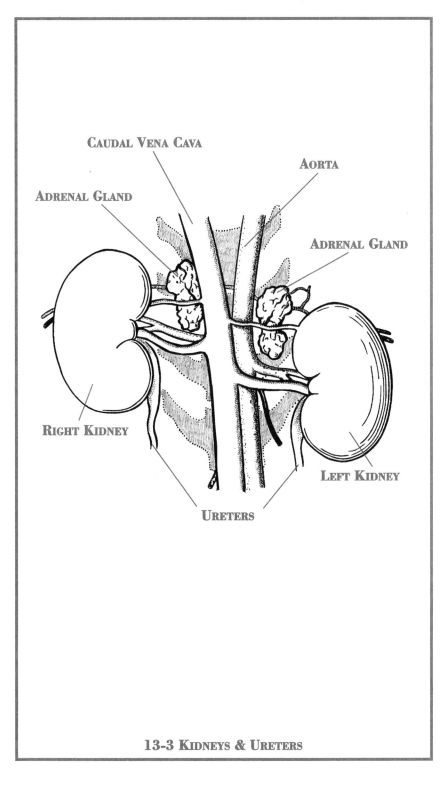

CAUDAL VENA CAVA

AORTA

ADRENAL GLAND

ADRENAL GLAND

RIGHT KIDNEY

LEFT KIDNEY

URETERS

13-3 KIDNEYS & URETERS

as gentamicin (an antibiotic), or poisons such as antifreeze that contain ethylene glycol. Regardless of the cause, the kidneys rapidly lose their ability to function correctly.

What are the symptoms?

Many symptoms of *renal disease* are caused by *toxic nitrogen levels* in the bloodstream. This is referred to as *uremia* or azotemia. Signs of uremia include mouth ulcers, vomiting, seizures, diarrhea, bleeding disorders and depression. Diseased kidneys not only cannot excrete excess nitrogen, they also cannot conserve normal amounts of water. Body fluids are lost to the urine, potentially causing dehydration. Signs of dehydration include dry or sticky gums and loss of skin elasticity. In normal patients, if one picks up the skin behind the neck it will quickly snap back to normal. In dehydrated patients the skin will remain elevated and "tent-like."

What are the risks?

Any kidney disorder should be considered serious. Since most cases of acute renal disease have known causes, treatment is usually successful.

What is the treatment?

Proper treatment is decided once the cause is identified. Intravenous fluids may be necessary to flush out the kidneys and supply needed fluids for the body. Any kidney-harming drug should be discontinued. If bacteria are suspected, then the appropriate antibiotic will usually eliminate the infection. It is very important to begin treatment early to prevent permanent damage to the delicate kidney tissues.

CHRONIC RENAL DISEASE

Chronic renal disease often has no identifiable cause. It is generally related to aging and is simply a deterioration and loss of filtration area within the kidney. These areas are called **glomeruli.** When a significant portion of the glomeruli die or are injured, there may not be enough to remove normal wastes from the bloodstream and therefore toxic levels of these substances develop in the body. These kidneys can no longer conserve water, so abnormally large amounts of urine are produced and water is lost from the body.

What are the symptoms?

Unlike acute renal disease, the signs of chronic renal disease develop slowly over time. Due to the inability of the kidneys to conserve water, one will frequently notice an increased urination, both in frequency and volume. To compensate and in an attempt to keep the body hydrated the patient will consume larger quantities of water.

In the early stages of the disease, the nitrogen levels may or may not be elevated in the bloodstream. *The kidneys can lose over 75 percent of their normal function before they are no longer capable of detoxifying the body.* If nitrogen is elevated in the blood (uremia/azotemia), then mouth ulcers may develop in addition to weight loss, poor appetite, bleeding disorders and possible seizures. The early warning signs are increased thirst and urination followed by symptoms of uremia. In severe cases, due to a lack of the hormone erythropoietin there may be a decreased production of red blood cells, thereby creating anemia.

What are the risks?
Many older patients have some degree of kidney failure. Mildly affected patients will live relatively normal lives. They compensate for their loss of kidney function by drinking excess quantities of water to flush their system. More severely affected patients will not be able to cope with the loss of kidney function and may die from renal failure. Renal failure is the number one cause of "death from natural causes" in the canine. Unlike humans, the canine heart generally outperforms the kidneys of the individual animal.

What is the treatment?
Most cases of chronic renal disease and failure are not reversible. The kidneys have simply worn out. If the early signs of disease are recognized before kidneys actually fail (i.e., increased thirst and urination), there are treatments to help slow down this degenerative process. Low-protein diets will reduce the intake of nitrogen and therefore decrease the work load of the kidneys. Commercially prepared diets are available from veterinarians. Hill's K/D and U/D are examples of diets low in protein manufactured just for these patients. As we have noted, diets high in protein do not cause kidney problems or disease. This is often inferred because low-protein diets are utilized in the management of renal disease.

INHERITED RENAL DISEASE

Inherited kidney disorders frequently affect patients five years of age and younger. Unlike chronic renal diseases of older patients, the cause is not a degeneration of kidney tissue, but rather a failure of the kidneys to develop and mature normally. Inherited kidney disorders have been well documented, especially in the following breeds: Rottweilers, Samoyeds, Beagles, Lhasa Apsos, Miniature Schnauzers, Shih Tzus, German Shepherd Dogs, Doberman Pinschers, Chow Chows, Cairn Terriers, Basenjis, Chinese Shar Peis, Standard Poodles, Welsh Corgis, Norwegian Elkhounds, Soft Coated Wheaten Terriers and Bulldogs. Individuals from any breed may be involved; however, the above listed breeds are the most commonly diagnosed.

What are the symptoms?

The symptoms are the same for patients suffering from chronic renal disease (see pages 242–43); however, the age of onset is much younger. Patients who have renal disease from birth typically fail to grow to a normal size. In some cases their growth is markedly stunted.

What are the risks?

Patients with inherited renal disease fail to thrive and live shorter life spans. Many die before one year of age.

What is the treatment?

There is no cure for inherited renal disease. The treatment is the same for patients with chronic renal disease (pages 242–43). Low-protein diets are fed to help decrease the work of the failing kidneys. *Patients with a history of inherited renal disease should never be utilized in a breeding program.* A careful evaluation of the history of the parents and grandparents should be evaluated. *Animals with a history of producing offspring with inherited renal disease should not be bred again.*

DISORDERS OF THE BLADDER AND URETHRA

The **bladder** is a balloon-like structure surrounded by layers of muscle. Each kidney has one *ureter* which deposits urine into the bladder. A twenty-five-pound dog has a bladder capable of storing about four ounces of urine. Urine storage is the primary function of the bladder. From the bladder, urine exits the body through the *urethra*. The urethral opening is at the end of male penis and within the vaginal area of the female. (See figures 13-4 and 13-5.) Contrary to popular belief, urine is not dirty or contaminated. In fact, normal urine is sterile until it exits the body. The bladder, even though it is basically a storage unit for sterile urine, does commonly become diseased.

BLADDER ATONY

Bladder atony describes a situation in which the bladder has lost its nervous control. This can be caused by injuries to the nerves supplying the bladder. Lesions of the spinal cord in the area where these nerves originate are a common cause. In other cases these nerves may degenerate and fail to function. Bladder infections can also lead to this organ's decreased muscle tone.

What are the symptoms?

The main symptom is difficulty in urination or a loss of bladder control. Frequently the bladder is extremely full, yet the patient does not urinate. Because of a failing nerve supply, the patient does not have the ability to control the muscles lining its wall and expel the urine, or in other cases to relax the muscles forming the valve at the base of the bladder in order to allow urine to flow into the urethra.

What are the risks?
Patients with loss of proper bladder muscle tone fail to urinate properly. If permanent damage or nerve degeneration has occurred, the condition is usually irreversible. Bladder infections then frequently occur because the bladder cannot empty properly, thus excessively retaining urine, which allows bacteria to easily grow if they gain entrance into the bladder from the urethra.

What is the treatment?
Catheters are placed up through the urethra and into the bladder to drain the urine. Permanent catheterization may be necessary in patients that fail to recover normal bladder tone. Various drugs to help affect the urethral and bladder muscles are utilized and occasionally work. Such drugs may include phenoxybenzamine and bethanechol. The response to treatment varies greatly and is dependent on the exact cause and extent of the damage.

URINARY INCONTINENCE
Incontinence describes an inability to retain urine within the bladder. The bladder can no longer function as a storage organ, as urine simply passes through it into the urethra and out of the body. Patients with urinary incontinence involuntarily leak urine from their bodies.

The causes of urinary incontinence may include infections of the bladder or congenital abnormalities; however, the overwhelming majority involve hormone imbalances. The principal hormone involved in bladder control is *estrogen*. Estrogen hormones prevalent in the female are necessary for the normal function of the muscles located at the base of the bladder where it empties into the urethra. *These muscles cannot constrict and block off the urethra openings without estrogens.* The majority of estrogen hormone is produced by the ovaries. The adrenal glands also produce a minor, but much lesser amount. In the male, the hormone testosterone is necessary for the urethral muscles to function properly. Testosterone is predominantly produced by the testicles.

As a pet ages, production of the sex hormones estrogen and testosterone begins diminishing. Hormonal urinary incontinence is more prevalent in geriatric patients than in younger animals. As might be expected, spayed females and castrated males have the highest incidence of urinary incontinence. This is because in the process of spaying the female, the ovaries are removed to prevent heat cycles. In castrating (neutering) the male, the testicles are removed. Removing the ovaries and testicles greatly reduces the sex hormone levels within the body. This does not imply that all spayed females or castrated males will develop incontinence. In fact, *less than 5 percent will ever be affected*. It appears that the amount of sex hormones produced by the adrenal glands is generally more than adequate for normal bladder and urethra function.

What are the symptoms?

In common hormonal incontinence, the patient appears very healthy, but leaks urine. Typically they are unaware of the urine leakage. While the patient sleeps, a puddle of urine may form in the bedding area.

What are the risks?

Infection from incontinence is the most common risk as bacteria may spread up the ureters to the kidneys. Hormonal deficiencies pose no real threat to the patient except that skin irritations may develop about the genital area due to constant urine leakage.

What is the treatment?

Various drugs have been used very successfully to increase the muscle tone lost from hormonal incontinence. Diethylstilbestrol (DES) is widely used in incontinent females as a replacement for estrogen. Phenylpropanolamine or ephedrine can also be used in females, either alone or in conjunction with DES. In the male, testosterone injections are frequently effective. Phenylpropanolamine or ephedrine can also be used in the male, with or without testosterone. Antibiotics are commonly used if an infection is suspected.

URINARY CALCULI (URINARY STONES)

In the canine, small sand-like crystals can occasionally form within the urine. The crystals may clump together and form calculi or stones. In contrast to humans, this rarely occurs in the dog's kidney. In dogs, crystal and stone formations principally occur in the bladder. The crystals may be small and similar to sand or clump into larger aggregates called stones and be as large as several inches in diameter. (See figure 13-6.)

The cause of urinary calculi formation is unknown. Some patients simply seem more prone to form calculi than others. Many dissolved salts exist in the urine of a dog. It is these salts that join together to form stones.

It is generally believed that excess salts in the diet are not the cause of stone formation. However, the way the body metabolizes salts and other products may play a role. Complex laboratory analysis of urinary stones has identified several different types in the canine, including struvite (the most common), calcium oxalate (the second most common), urate, silicate, cystine and mixed types. All are stones comprised of various elements and may include magnesium, calcium, phosphate and ammonia. The most

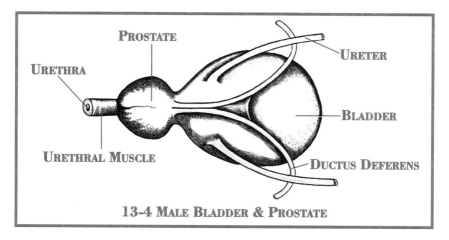

13-4 MALE BLADDER & PROSTATE

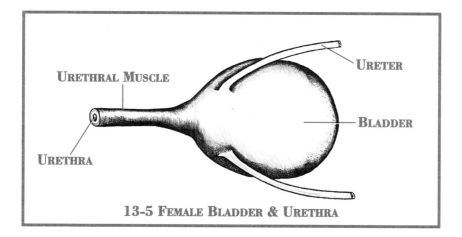

13-5 FEMALE BLADDER & URETHRA

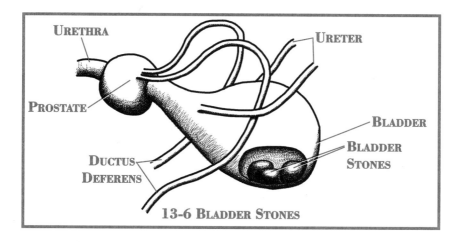

13-6 BLADDER STONES

common stone, struvite, is a mixture of magnesium and ammonium phosphate. Some types of stones form more quickly in *acid urine* (pH less than 7.0) while others prefer more *alkaline urine* (higher pH). Acid urine discourages the formation of struvite and urate crystals, but favors calcium oxalate crystal formation.

Certain breeds are prone to specific types of stones. The stones typically found in Dalmatians are commonly the urate variety. Cystine crystals most commonly involve male dogs of the following breeds: Dachshunds, Basset Hounds, Yorkshire Terriers, Irish Setters, Chihuahuas and Bulldogs. The breed, the acidity of urine and the diet can *all* help *predict* the stone type, but only a laboratory analysis of the stone can conclusively *identify* its type.

What are the symptoms?

Urinary calculi present with similar signs despite their differences in composition. Stones in the bladder will irritate the inner bladder lining, causing painful urinations. The bladder wall may bleed, producing noticeable amounts of blood in the urine. Stones, particularly if large, will occupy a significant space within the bladder, limiting the amount of urine the bladder can retain. Therefore the patient may urinate small quantities more frequently than normal. Bladder infections (cystitis) may develop as a result of bladder and urethra damage caused by the crystals and/or stones. The common signs are: frequent urination that is often painful, blood in the urine, involuntary dripping and a painful abdomen.

What are the risks?

Urinary stones are always serious. The worst instance involves cases where small stones become lodged within the urethra, obstructing normal urination. *A patient unable to urinate will normally die within forty-eight hours.* Difficulty in urination is always an emergency.

What is the treatment?

Treatment varies with each individual. Surgery is often necessary to remove stones formed within the bladder and/or urethra. In some cases, special commercially prepared diets can be used. These diets can dissolve the stones while they are in the bladder. After or during removal, preventative medications are available that alter the urine pH. Some products *lower the pH*, which makes the urine more *acid*. This will discourage the formation of stones such as struvite and urate crystals. Other medications *raise the urine pH*, making the urine more *alkaline*. This discourages stones such as calcium oxalate from developing. Diets low in elements such as magnesium have been utilized to help reduce struvite crystal formation. A careful analysis of each patient and stone type is necessary to determine the proper treatment.

CYSTITIS—INFECTION OF THE BLADDER

Cystitis describes an inflamed bladder. This is usually caused by bacteria that have entered the bladder from the outside, usually through the urethra, thereby resulting in an infection. Female dogs have a shorter and wider urethra than males and therefore bacteria have easier access to the female bladder. This probably contributes to the fact that most bladder infections are found in females.

What are the symptoms?
Frequent urination is the most common sign associated with bladder infections. The bladder becomes painful when irritated and therefore the patient urinates more in an attempt to keep the bladder empty. The act of urination may be painful and cause a burning sensation. Therefore the patient starts to urinate, but quits only to try again a short time later. Occasional accidents of urination may happen in unwanted areas of the house. If a severe irritation has developed from the bacteria, blood may appear in the urine.

What is the risk?
Normally the urine and the organ it passes through are sterile or free from bacteria. If bacteria have entered the bladder, it is possible for infections to not only affect that area, but the kidneys as well. Kidney infections are rare, but very serious. *Suspected cases of cystitis should be treated at once.*

What is the treatment?
Bladder infections are generally caused by bacteria. A urine culture will reveal the type of bacteria. Excellent antibiotics are now available to treat many bacteria affecting the bladder. Occasionally, drugs are given in addition to antibiotics to help lower the pH (acidity) of the urine. This is done because bacteria tend not to thrive in acid urine.

URETHRITIS

Urethritis is simply an irritation of the urethra. As in humans, many of these are bacterial in origin. Commonly infections of the urethra accompany bladder infections (cystitis).

What are the symptoms?
The act of urination may create a burning sensation and cause the patient to stop urinating once the process has begun. A thick yellow discharge may be noted at the urethral opening.

What are the risks?
Urethral infections are seldom serious. They should, however, be promptly treated to prevent the bacteria from entering the bladder and causing an infection there.

What is the treatment?

Infections of the urethra generally respond well to antibiotics. A culture of the urine and/or urethral discharge will reveal the type of bacteria. This is especially important in breeding animals to decrease the likelihood of transmitting the infection sexually. *Bacteria such as Brucellosis canis can be severe* and very difficult to treat. (See Chapter 5, pages 102–03)

CHAPTER 14

The Lymphatic System

INTRODUCTION

The lymphatic system filters and removes debris from the body. It is important in *providing body immunity* against diseases, as it can produce cells to fight infections.

The lymphatic system is composed of small circular glands called **lymph nodes.** The lymph nodes are connected to each other by a series of vessels called **lymphatics**. The lymphatics make up a large network of vessels throughout the body. The liquid they carry is referred to as **lymph.** They filter out cellular waste products and foreign material. This is then carried to the lymph nodes and on to the chest of the animal where the material enters the bloodstream for excretion from the body. The large organ called the **spleen** located in the abdomen is also connected to the lymphatics. (See figure 14-1.)

The lymph nodes are glandular structures that produce disease-fighting white blood cells called **lymphocytes**. Lymphocytes circulate in the bloodstream to aid the immune response in various diseases. Other cells in the lymph nodes, called "B" cells, secrete small disease-fighting proteins called **antibodies**. Antibodies bind with foreign particles called **antigens** and help inactivate them. The lymph glands also act as filters to remove potentially dangerous infectious particles from the bloodstream. In summary, the lymphatic system is extremely important in giving the body immunity against diseases.

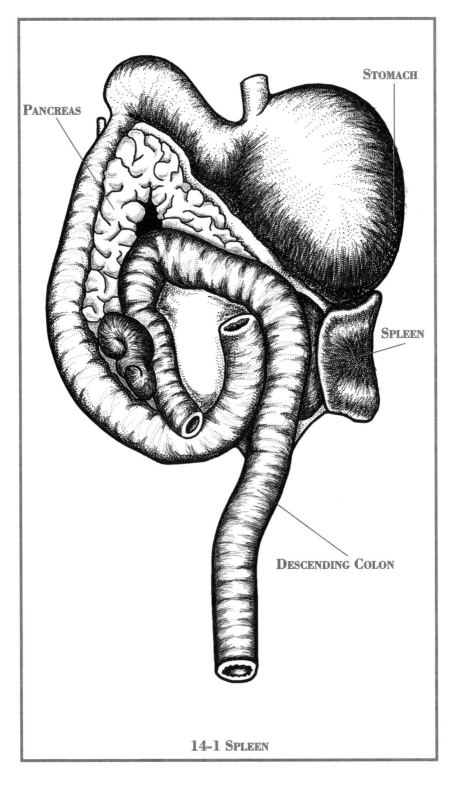

PANCREAS

STOMACH

SPLEEN

DESCENDING COLON

14-1 SPLEEN

LYMPHOMA (LYMPHOSARCOMA)

Lymphosarcoma is a form of cancer affecting the canine lymph nodes. It is one of the most common cancers affecting young animals.

What are the symptoms?

The most noted sign is a generalized swelling of the lymph nodes. Commonly the submandibular, prescapular, inguinal and popliteal lymph nodes will enlarge to the size of a hen's egg. (See figure 14-2.) Normally these glands are marble-sized and not easily felt. Weight loss will be evident in the latter stages of the disease.

What are the risks?

Lymphoma is serious and life threatening, as is any malignant cancer. Because the lymph nodes are all interconnected by the lymphatics, many lymph nodes commonly become cancerous before a diagnosis can be made. Early detection and treatment can, however, prolong the life of some patients.

What is the treatment?

Normally a biopsy of one or more lymph nodes will confirm the diagnosis of lymphosarcoma. Various chemotherapeutic agents can be administered to fight the cancer. Anti-inflammatory medications such as prednisone are frequently used in conjunction with stronger chemotherapeutic agents. With treatment, some patients can survive a year or more.

At this point in veterinary medicine, we are rarely able to truly cure these patients. Therapy is aimed at upgrading the quality of life for several months to a year.

LYMPHADENITIS

Lymphadenitis describes lymph nodes enlarged from infection or inflammation. These nodes are therefore affected by a non-cancerous condition. Usually the lymph node and the area adjacent to the infection become enlarged and inflamed. For instance, if a dog has a sore throat from an infection with Streptococcus bacteria, then commonly the lymph node closest to the infection will be enlarged. In the case of a sore throat, the submandibular lymph nodes or tonsils may enlarge (see figure 14-3) because lymphatics from the throat area drain into these lymph nodes.

What are the symptoms?

Enlargement of one or more lymph nodes is the most common sign. Usually, with an infection, an elevated temperature is also present. Other signs depend on the area involved. For instance, a dog with a sore throat may also cough, drool, swallow repeatedly and be reluctant to eat. Some of these signs would be caused by the enlarged lymph nodes interfering with

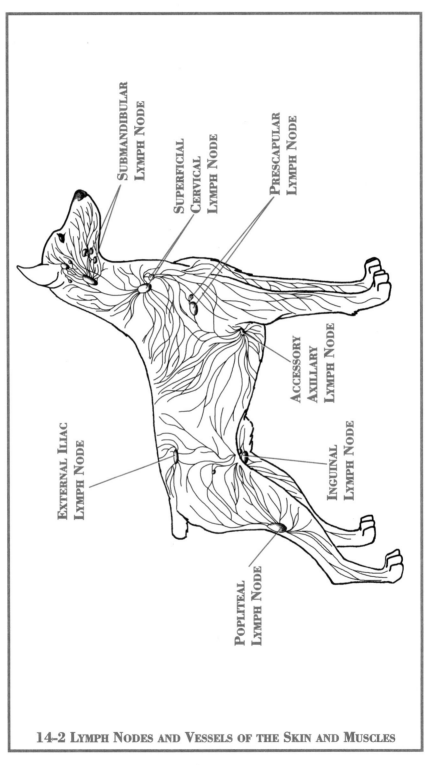

14-2 Lymph Nodes and Vessels of the Skin and Muscles

Submandibular Lymph Node

Superficial Cervical Lymph Node

Prescapular Lymph Node

Accessory Axillary Lymph Node

External Iliac Lymph Node

Inguinal Lymph Node

Popliteal Lymph Node

swallowing. If, due to an infection in the foot, the enlarged lymph node is in the rear limb, limping may be prevalent because the nodes will be painful and muscle movement increases the discomfort.

What are the risks?
Lymphadenitis is usually not serious, assuming the infection is diagnosed and curable. In most cases, once the infection is cleared, the enlarged lymph nodes will return to normal size.

What is the treatment?
Initially the cause of the enlarged lymph node must be determined. If a bacterial infection is present, antibiotics will help fight the disease. If a stick is lodged in the throat, then the foreign body must be removed. As one can see, it is very important to first determine the cause, then select the proper treatment.

TONSILLITIS

Tonsillitis describes an inflammation of the tonsils. Generally the tonsils are considered part of the lymphatic system. Canines have two tonsils located on the sides of the oral cavity at the rear. They are each found within a fold of tissue referred to as a **tonsilar crypt**. When enlarged, they fold out of the crypt and are easily visible with the naked eye. (See figure 14-4.) What are the symptoms?

As with other throat and mouth irritations, many patients will be reluctant to eat and will drool excessively because swallowing is painful. Other dogs with the same condition will swallow repeatedly. The tonsils will appear enlarged and reddened.

What are the risks?
As in humans, tonsillitis is seldom serious; however, it can be chronic and annoying.

What is the treatment?
The cause of the enlarged tonsils should be determined. Streptococcus or other bacteria frequently infect the area. Foreign objects such as sticks lodged in the throat can cause inflammation of the tonsils. Antibiotics are effective if bacteria are the cause. *Only in severe chronic tonsillitis of unknown origin should the tonsils be removed.* The canine tonsils are lymphoid tissue and therefore important in fighting diseases and when possible *should be left intact.*

LYMPH NODE HYPERPLASIA

Occasionally the lymph nodes enlarge in size for no apparent reason. When biopsied the tissues appear normal. They are simply larger than normal. This increase in size is called **hyperplasia**.

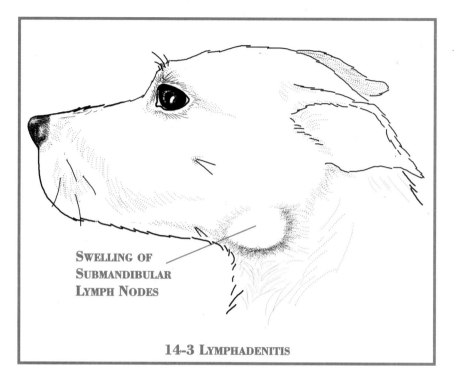

SWELLING OF
SUBMANDIBULAR
LYMPH NODES

14-3 LYMPHADENITIS

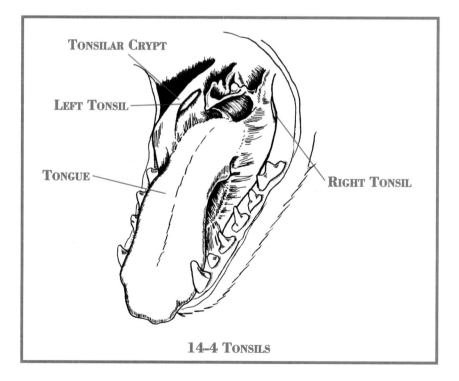

TONSILAR CRYPT

LEFT TONSIL

TONGUE

RIGHT TONSIL

14-4 TONSILS

What are the symptoms?

Enlargment of lymph nodes with no apparent signs of illness is the most recognized sign. The animal will not have a fever and usually these lymph nodes are not painful even if reddened.

What are the risks?

Lymph node hyperplasia poses no risk to the patient. Occasionally a more serious condition called lymphosarcoma (see page 253) can initially appear similar to lymph node hyperplasia.

What is the treatment?

A biopsy of the enlarged lymph nodes will provide an accurate diagnosis and differentiate lymph node hyperplasia from the more serious lymphosarcoma. In lymph node hyperplasia, anti-inflammatory medications such as prednisone may help the lymph node return to a more normal size.

INADEQUATE IMMUNE SYSTEM

The immune system is primarily responsible for fighting diseases. Some patients have a better capability of mounting an immune response to a disease than others. Individuals that easily become ill are thought to have "weak" immune systems. Patients with a great ability to remain healthy have strong immune systems.

The cause of an inadequate or weak immune system generally cannot be determined. For unknown reasons, the lymph nodes may have a decreased ability to produce adequate quantities of antibodies and/or the disease-fighting cells called **lymphocytes**. Certain dogs in some breeds have a reduced ability to fight some or all infectious diseases. Rottweilers and Chinese Shar Peis are noted examples of breeds with immune systems that unsuccessfully fight parvovirus. A certain percentage of these same dogs do not respond to parvovirus vaccines to develop protective immunity. *Genetics certainly plays a role in the immune response.* Certain drugs, most notably steroids, are known to decrease the immune system's ability to fight infections.

What are the symptoms?

No *set* of symptoms describes a patient with a weak immune system. Historical response to diseases provides the best clue. Patients that are frequently sick or become more ill than normal from a particular disease are suspected of having weak immune systems.

What are the risks?

Patients with inadequate immune systems are more susceptible to infections, including deadly diseases such as distemper and parvovirus. The death rates from infections will be higher in individuals with weak immune systems.

What is the treatment?

No exact treatment is known to bolster the immune system. Good nutrition will certainly help, but is not a cure. Certain drugs have been experimentally capable of helping the immune system. It must be noted that certain individuals within every breed have weak immune systems. It has, however, been well demonstrated that certain breeds and lines within those breeds have a greater percentage of patients with deficient immune systems than would be considered normal. *Genetics definitely plays an* important *role in immunity capabilities.*

CHAPTER 15

Common Canine Infectious Diseases

INTRODUCTION

Infectious diseases typically affect more than one organ system in the body. Because of this, we have devoted a separate chapter to discussing infectious diseases rather than including them in several different sections throughout the book.

There are literally hundreds of bacteria, viruses and fungi that can be pathogens in the canine. This chapter will deal mainly with those that are found in most areas of the country and pose a particular health risk to large numbers of pets. This chapter will cover Canine Distemper, Hepatitis, Adenovirus Cough, Leptospirosis, Coronavirus, Rotavirus, Parvovirus, Parainfluenza, Bordetella, Lyme and Rabies.

CANINE DISTEMPER VIRUS

Canine distemper is a paramyxovirus which appears very similar to the paramyxovirus causing human measles. This virus in the canine can affect a wide range of organs including the skin, brain, eyes and intestinal and respiratory tracts. The virus is transmitted both through the air and body secretions such as urine. Dogs of any age can be affected; however, most are puppies under six months of age.

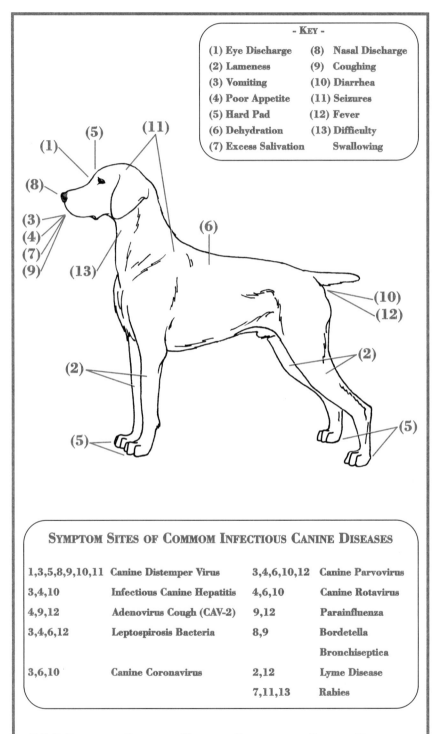

- KEY -

(1) Eye Discharge
(2) Lameness
(3) Vomiting
(4) Poor Appetite
(5) Hard Pad
(6) Dehydration
(7) Excess Salivation
(8) Nasal Discharge
(9) Coughing
(10) Diarrhea
(11) Seizures
(12) Fever
(13) Difficulty
  Swallowing

SYMPTOM SITES OF COMMOM INFECTIOUS CANINE DISEASES

1,3,5,8,9,10,11	Canine Distemper Virus	3,4,6,10,12	Canine Parvovirus
3,4,10	Infectious Canine Hepatitis	4,6,10	Canine Rotavirus
4,9,12	Adenovirus Cough (CAV-2)	9,12	Parainfluenza
3,4,6,12	Leptospirosis Bacteria	8,9	Bordetella Bronchiseptica
3,6,10	Canine Coronavirus	2,12	Lyme Disease
		7,11,13	Rabies

15-1 SYMPTOM SITES OF COMMON INFECTIOUS CANINE DISEASES

What are the symptoms?
Distemper virus can affect many systems of the body. The most common signs are nasal and eye discharge, coughing, diarrhea, vomiting and seizures. Mildly affected patients may only cough and be misdiagnosed as "Kennel Cough." Patients that recover may have severe tooth enamel damage. The nose and foot pads of the young dog may become thickened, hence the nickname "hard-pad disease."

What are the risks?
Distemper is serious and can spread rapidly through a kennel, especially if unvaccinated individuals are present. Not all patients will die, but a significant number may.

Dogs of every age are susceptible; however, the very young and old have the highest death rates. Death rates may be as high as 75 percent. It is erroneously believed by some that all older dogs have a natural immunity. Although some may have immunity, many do not. Patients that recover from distemper may suffer permanent damage to vision as well as the nervous system. Puppies that recover can have severely mottled teeth due to abnormalities of the developing enamel.

What is the treatment?
There is no specific treatment for canine distemper. Therapy is largely supportive. Intravenous fluids are administered to prevent dehydration. Anti-seizure medications can be used if neurologic signs develop.

Excellent vaccines have been developed to prevent distemper. The vaccines have been widely used for many years and have made significant strides in reducing the frequency of this disease. In the past, vaccines composed of the human measles virus were occasionally utilized as a preventative. Using measles vaccines is a *seldom* practiced procedure today. Excellent vaccines with minimal side effects are available for puppies and dogs of every age. It must be emphasized that many older dogs do not develop a lifelong immunity to distemper. The vaccinations should be given yearly throughout a dog's entire life.

INFECTIOUS CANINE HEPATITIS

Canine hepatitis is cause by canine adenovirus type 1 (CAV-1). The virus is found worldwide and is spread by body fluids including nasal discharge and urine. *Recovered patients can shed the virus for up to nine months in the urine.* Its primary mode of transmission is by direct contact. Contaminated runs, cages, dishes, hands, boots, etc., can all be sources of transmission.

What are the symptoms?
Initially the virus affects the tonsils and larynx, causing a sore throat, coughing and occasionally pneumonia. As the virus enters the bloodstream

it can affect the eyes, liver and kidneys. The clear portion of the eyes, called the cornea, may appear cloudy or bluish. This is due to fluid accumulations (edema) within the cell layers that form the cornea. The name "hepatitis blue eye" has been used to describe eyes so affected. As the liver and kidneys fail, one may notice seizures, increased thirst, vomiting and/or diarrhea.

What are the risks?

Unvaccinated dogs of all ages are at risk; however, the disease is most prevalent in patients under one year. *Death can result as soon as two hours after the initial signs.* Death can be so sudden it may appear as if the patient were poisoned.

What is the treatment?

There is no specific treatment for infectious canine hepatitis. Intravenous fluids and supportive care are indicated. Excellent vaccines are available to immunize puppies as well as adults. The vaccines may contain adenovirus type 1 or type 2. Adenovirus type 2 (CAV-2) is a cause of canine cough. Because the viruses are similar, vaccines against one also protect against the other. Modern vaccines contain either CAV-1 or CAV-2, but not both. However, they protect against both hepatitis and cough.

ADENOVIRUS COUGH—CAV-2

Canine adenovirus type 2 is the cause of adenovirus cough. Occasionally this is referred to as "kennel cough," but this isn't really correct. Several viruses and bacteria can cause a dog to cough. CAV-2 is only one. In reality, kennel cough merely describes a coughing dog and the term has nothing to do with the cause. CAV-2 is primarily spread through the air and can affect dogs and puppies of all ages.

What are the symptoms?

A patient with CAV-2 will have coughing as the most common sign. Occasionally a fever will be present. In some instances, bacteria may invade the areas damaged by the adenovirus and also may invade the lungs, causing pneumonia.

What are the risks?

Adenovirus type 2 will seldom cause death in the normal patient. It does, however, wear down the immune system and allow bacteria to secondarily invade the area. Bacterial pneumonia may result and even cause death. Of particular mention is that CAV-2 is *very contagious* and frequently will affect the majority of dogs in the same household or immediate area. This fact probably led to the term "kennel cough" because the majority of the dogs in an entire kennel may exhibit coughing during the same period of time.

What is the treatment?
Most patients will recover in one to two weeks with no treatment whatsoever. The disease is allowed to run its course. Often infected patients are placed on antibiotics to keep bacteria from entering the irritated areas and possibly causing a secondary pneumonia. Although this is more a nuisance disease than a killer, it is so widespread that effective vaccinations have been developed to prevent it.

CAV-2 is closely related to the hepatitis-causing canine adenovirus type 1 (CAV-1) and the vaccines against one will cross-protect against the other. Any modern vaccine containing either CAV-1 or CAV-2 will protect against both the cough and hepatitis forms of adenovirus.

LEPTOSPIROSIS BACTERIA
There are several types of Leptospira bacteria affecting the canine; however, only two types are commonly encountered. Leptospira icterohaemorrhagiae and Leptospira canicola are the two most affecting canines in the United States.

Lepto bacteria affect many organs, but the most pronounced effect is on the kidneys. The bacteria pass in the urine and can easily affect other canines in close contact. Urine-contaminated water sources are a common cause of transmission. *Infected canines can also serve as a source of infection for humans.*

What are the symptoms?
Clinical signs may include fever, poor appetite, vomiting, dehydration and death. As the kidneys fail, there may be an inability to form urine, causing death. Many patients can be infected and appear healthy for years while still serving as carriers to other susceptible pets.

What are the risks?
Death from kidney failure is always a possibility when affected by lepto bacteria. In the breeding females, abortions and early infant death can also be attributed to lepto.

What is the treatment?
Some patients may respond to antibiotic therapy, but many never completely recover. Fortunately, excellent vaccines are available to prevent leptospirosis in the canine. Because dogs can serve as sources of infections for humans, it is essential that pets be vaccinated. This is necessary not only for the patient's protection, but for humans as well. Humans, especially children, should avoid contact with unvaccinated house pets.

CANINE CORONAVIRUS

Since the early 1970s coronavirus has been of prime concern to the dog owner. The virus is spread by contaminated foul material and affects canines of all ages; however, the highest mortality occurs in infants.

What are the symptoms?

Diarrhea is the most common sign associated with coronavirus infection. The diarrhea may vary from mild to severe and may contain blood. Many patients also vomit usually prior to developing diarrhea.

What are the risks?

Most patients infected with canine coronavirus will develop diarrhea for a period of seven to ten days, then recover. Death is possible, but is more likely to occur in puppies under six months of age.

What is the treatment?

Diarrhea and/or vomiting commonly cause dehydration, so therapy is aimed at maintaining adequate fluid levels. Fluids fed intravenously may be needed. Excellent and safe vaccines have been developed to prevent this disease. Coronavirus vaccines are recommended in most parts of the country. *Pets of all ages*, not just the young, *should be vaccinated.*

CANINE PARVOVIRUS

Parvovirus is probably the most famous canine disease next to rabies. In the 1970s parvovirus swept the country, killing literally thousands of dogs. Today strains still exist and death from parvovirus is not uncommon. It appears that the virus continually mutates and new variations appear worldwide.

What are the symptoms?

Vomiting, diarrhea and death are all common in patients with parvovirus. Entire litters may be involved. It is important to note that the virus may directly attack delicate tissue such as the heart muscle and can cause death with no vomiting or diarrhea noted. The diarrhea is usually severe— projectile and bloody.

What are the risks?

Parvovirus is one of the most contagious and fatal diseases known to the canine world. Puppies under six months of age may have a mortality rate of 80 percent or higher from certain strains. It must be noted that although parvovirus is generally thought of as a puppy disease, it does cause death in dogs of every age.

What is the treatment?

There is no direct treatment for parvovirus. It is important to prevent dehydration. The use of intravenous fluids is common, as well as antibiotics to prevent secondary bacterial infections. Extreme hygiene is important to keep patients dry, clean and warm until the disease can run its course. Excellent multi-strain vaccines have been developed to prevent parvovirus. It must be noted that protection gained from vaccines is not 100 percent against every strain and mutant form. Strict vaccination procedures are recommended for canines of every age to help reduce the incidence of death attributed to parvovirus.

CANINE ROTAVIRUS

Rotavirus has been identified as a cause of diarrhea, especially in neonates. It has been suggested that transmission of rotavirus to humans may be possible. The virus is shed in the feces and ingestion is the mode of transmission.

What are the symptoms?

Canines over twelve weeks of age are seldom affected. In the neonate, diarrhea is the most common sign. Poor appetite and lethargy may accompany the diarrhea.

What are the risks?

Most infections are mild; however, they usually involve infants. The diarrhea can lead to dehydration and death.

What is the treatment?

Treatment is aimed at maintaining hydration. Occasionally young puppies must be fed with a stomach tube. It is important to provide fluids to replace those lost through diarrhea. Currently, there appears little need for vaccine development against this disease, but this may change as the effects and incidence of rotavirus become more clear.

PARAINFLUENZA

Parainfluenza is a virus that has been implicated as an important cause of canine cough. It is spread mainly through the air.

What are the symptoms?

Coughing is the main symptom of parainfluenza. In severe cases a fever may be present. Coughing generally persists for seven to ten days.

What are the risks?

Parainfluenza is contagious and may infect several pets simultaneously in the same household or kennel. Deaths are rare.

What is the treatment?

There are no specific anti-viral drugs to treat parainfluenza. Most patients recover within seven to ten days from naturally developing immunity. An excellent vaccine is available and is generally included in the puppy and adult series of canine immunizations.

BORDETELLA BRONCHISEPTICA

Bordetella bronchiseptica is the most common bacterium implicated as a cause of canine respiratory disease. It is commonly involved in the development of canine cough.

What are the symptoms?

Coughing is the most common sign attributed to a bordetella infection. Frequently many patients within a household or kennel will be simultaneously infected. Death is rare.

What are the risks?

It is important to minimize bordetella outbreaks in areas where pets are in close contact. It is very contagious, spread through the air. Veterinary hospitals, boarding or grooming facilities and shows typically have many pets in close proximity. Outbreaks will be most common among pets frequently visiting the above areas.

What is the treatment?

Bordetella, being a bacterium, is responsive to antibiotics. Tetracycline antibiotics have been widely used in controlling infections. Vaccines are available to help prevent occurrence. It is especially important to utilize vaccines containing bordetella if a pet attends shows, performance trials or is a frequent visitor to boarding facilities.

LYME DISEASE

Lyme disease is caused by the bacterium *Borrelia burgdorferi*. These bacteria are spread from patient to patient primarily by several types of ticks, biting flies and fleas. It is possible for the disease to be spread in the urine with no biting vector included. Lyme has been identified in forty-eight states within the United States and is probably in all fifty, although not yet discovered.

What are the symptoms?

Lameness with a fever is characteristic of Lyme disease. It is possible to have Lyme without lameness or fever. The bacteria commonly colonize in joints, causing great pain and lameness. The degree of lameness will depend on the severity and the joints involved. Many patients test positive for the disease with no outward signs. It is possible a natural immunity develops in these patients.

What are the risks?

Lyme disease is always considered serious. Severe and permanent damage to the joints can occur if treatment isn't provided early in the course of the disease. Irreversible neurological damage has also been attributed to Lyme disease.

What is the treatment?

Early in the course of the disease, patients can be treated with good success. Various antibiotics including tetracycline, doxycycline and amoxicillin have been used with good results. Unfortunately, even with treatment, some patients suffer irreversible damage to the joints, resulting in chronic lameness. Vaccines are available to reduce the incidence of Lyme. Although not 100 percent successful in prevention, vaccines have greatly reduced the incidence of Lyme in problem areas. Good flea and tick control is *essential* in minimizing the likelihood of a Lyme outbreak.

RABIES

Rabies is the most feared and famous disease affecting companion animals. Rabies is a virus transmitted by a bite from an infected animal. Wild, warm-blooded animals including squirrels, raccoons, bats, skunks and foxes all serve as reservoirs for the virus.

What are the symptoms?

Domestic dogs afflicted with rabies typically exhibit neurologic symptoms which include difficulty swallowing, excess salivation, staggering, seizures, aggression or stupor.

What are the risks?

The disease is always fatal. The greatest risk is to humans. Dogs in the latter stages of the disease are highly contagious to humans. The virus is prominent in the saliva of the affected patient, especially in the latter stages of the disease. It is important to avoid all contact with an animal exhibiting any abnormal behavior attributable to rabies.

What is the treatment?

There is no treatment for canine rabies. *It is always fatal.* It is mandatory to isolate all animals, including humans, from any animal suspected of harboring rabies. In every suspected case, contact a veterinarian for proper isolation, testing and control measures. Excellent vaccines are available and usually legally mandatory for the vaccination of healthy dogs. These vaccinations are preventatives, not treatment. The only true test for an animal suspected of having rabies is by autopsy.

Glossary of Terms

Abscess—a pocket of infection filled with white blood cells.

Acute—of short and quick course. An acute illness is generally of rapid onset.

Alopecia—a loss of hair or baldness.

Anemia—a condition resulting from abnormally low numbers of red blood cells.

Antibiotic—a drug used to treat bacterial infections.

Anticonvulsant—a drug used to prevent or decrease the severity of convulsions.

Antihistamine—a drug used to treat the symptoms of allergies.

Atrophy—a decrease in size or wasting of tissues such as muscle or other organs, usually due to cell death.

Autoimmune—a condition in which the body destroys its own cells.

Benign—a mild illness or non-malignant form of cancer.

Biopsy—the removal of tissue for analysis to help with a diagnosis.

Birth defect—an abnormality present at birth.

Calcified—the hardening of tissue through the influx of calcium, usually as a result of chronic inflammation.

Carcinoma—a term used to describe various malignant and serious cancers.

Castration—a complete removal of the testicles, commonly referred to as neutering.

Cesarean section—a surgery performed to deliver infants unable to be born vaginally.

Chemotherapy—the treatment of diseases through the usage of chemicals. A common term used to describe the treatment of cancers.

Cherry eye—a term used to describe an eye with an enlarged third eyelid.

Chronic—of long term. A chronic illness is one of long duration.

Comedo—a blackhead, usually the result of a plugged gland within the skin.

Congenital—a condition which exists at birth.

Contagion—the transfer of a disease from one individual to the next. If a disease can be spread to other individuals, it is said to be contagious.

Culture—to grow an organism, commonly used to identify bacteria. Culture and Sensitivity test.

Cyst—An abnormal sac structure containing fluid.

Dehydration—a loss of fluids from the cells and tissues to a below-normal level.

Dermatitis—an inflammation of the skin.

Diuretic—a drug used to increase urine production and remove excess fluid from the body.

Dry eye—an eye with inadequate lubrication due to abnormally low tear production.

Dysplasia—an abnormal tissue development, common in the bones of the canine.

Echocardiogram—an image produced by ultrasound to aid in the diagnosis of heart abnormalities.

Edema—an abnormal accumulation of fluid within the cells, commonly the cause of swelling following trauma.

EKG—an electrocardiogram; a measurement of the electrical conduction of the heart; used to detect cardiac abnormalities.

Enteritis—an inflammation of the intestines.

Enzyme—a protein produced by certain cells that helps break down or change other substances such as sugars and fats.

Epiphora—an overflow of tears upon the cheeks due to a blockage or narrowing of the tear ducts.

Fertility—a term used to describe the ability to reproduce.

Foreign body—any abnormal substance within the body. Examples include wood slivers, ingested cloth, balls, glass in the feet, etc.

Granuloma—the formation of a nodule as a result of inflammation.

Hematoma—a mass of blood within the tissues. Generally the result of trauma to the blood vessels or abnormal blood clotting.

Hemorrhage—to bleed excessively; may be the result of injury or blood clotting abnormalities.

Hernia—the protrusion of an organ through an abnormal opening.

Hormone—a chemical substance produced by one organ and carried by the bloodstream to affect another organ.

Hyperplasia—an increase of the number of cells within an organ.

Icterus—commonly referred to as jaundice. A yellowing of the tissues, usually as a result of abnormal liver function.

Intravenously—to administer into the blood vessel, specifically a vein.

Intussusception—the folding of one intestinal segment into another, obstructing the flow of intestinal contents.

Lactation—the act of milk production and secretion.

Lethargy—to be without energy almost to the state of unconsciousness; to feel drowsy.

Metabolism—the process of energy utilization by the cells.

Mucus—a clear, thick secretion produced by mucous membranes.

Palpation—to examine with the hands or fingers.

Paralysis—loss of movement through inadequate nerve supply.

Parasite—an organism which lives upon or within another and feeds upon it.

Pheromone—substance secreted by one individual and detected by another, usually through smell.

Pyoderma—an infection of the skin; usually the result of a bacterial invasion. (Hot spot)

Radiograph—the creation of a picture through the usage of X-rays.

Regurgitation—the backward flow of material; commonly used to describe the expelling of food.

Ringworm—a condition resulting from a fungus. The circular appearance of a fungus lesion resembling a worm. However, *ringworm is not a worm.*

Sclerosis—a hardening of tissue, usually the result of chronic inflammation.

Seizure—an attack or sudden onset of symptoms; generally related to the nervous system of individuals affected with epilepsy.

Sphincter—a band of tissue or muscle which constricts to regulate the flow of material through an opening.

Stenosis—the narrowing of an organ of passage such as a blood vessel or intestine.

Symptom—a term used to describe a deviation from normal. If something is not normal in appearance, function or sensation then it may be described as a symptom.

Torsion—the twisting of an organ.

Ulcer—a lesion in which the tissue surface is eroded away.

Ultrasound—using ultrasonic vibrations to detect tissues of different densities; frequently used to determine pregnancies and aid in the diagnosis of cancer.

Umbilicus—the area of the body where the umbilical cord is attached; the belly button.

Vitamin—substance usually derived from food that are necessary for cell metabolism.

Wheezing—a noise made as air passes through the larynx or trachea, due to an abnormal narrowing.

Appendices

BLOOD TESTS AND BLOOD CHEMISTRIES

Occasionally veterinarians utilize sophisticated blood and urine tests to provide an indicator of health. An understanding of what these tests and their interpretation is helpful and is provided here.

THE COMPLETE BLOOD COUNT (CBC)

This is a measure of blood quantity. The cells are counted to provide indicators of health. In anemia, the red blood cells (RBC) are low. In many infections, the white blood cells (WBC) become elevated. Leukemia is a situation in which the white blood cells are too low. Below is a chart exemplifying how a CBC commonly appears with its normal values for the canine.

Packed Cell Volume (PCV)

The amount of blood that is composed of red blood cells. Red blood cells carry oxygen to the tissues. Usually expressed as a percent. Normal is 37 to 55 percent.

Platelet Count

Platelets allow blood to clot. Normal is 200,000 to 900,000.

White Blood Count (WBC)

White blood cells fight infections. Normal is 6,000 to 17,000.

THE BLOOD CHEMISTRY

The blood chemistry does not measure cells within the blood; rather, it quantifies proteins, enzymes, sugar, etc. The measurement of these elements yields important information as to how organs function. Below are commonly measured indicators.

Bilirubin

Yields information about the liver and red blood cells. Normal is 0 to 0.6 mg/dl.

Glucose (Blood Sugar)

Significantly elevated levels indicate diabetes mellitus. Normal is 70 to 140 mg/dl.

Blood Urea Nitrogen (BUN)

A very commonly utilized indicator of kidney function. Normal value is 10 to 25 mg/dl.

Total Protein

An indicator of liver function. Normal value is 0.1 to 0.6 gm/dl.

Creatinine

A by-product of muscle metabolism. Elevated levels indicate possible kidney impairment. Normal value is 0.5 to 1.2 mg/dl.

The Urinalysis

The constituents comprising urine can lead to useful information regarding kidney function as well as other organs.

Specific Gravity

This measures how concentrated the urine is. The more concentrated, the higher the specific gravity. The ability to concentrate urine is an indicator of kidney health. Normal value is 1.001 to 1.060.

Urine Sugar (Glucose)

Used to diagnose diabetes mellitus. Normal value is 0.

Urine pH

This determines the acidity of the urine. A low-acid or basic urine is referred to as an elevated pH, which can indicate an infection of the urinary tract. Normal pH is 5.5 to 8.0.

Other Physiological Data

Temperature—Normal is 100 to 102.5 degrees Fahrenheit.
Pulse—Normal is 60 to 180 beats per minute.
Respiration—Normal is 10 to 30 breaths per minute.

The above values are for patients at rest. Exercise will cause increased values.

Approximate Daily Caloric Requirements for Adult Dogs

The following chart represents an average. Needs may vary depending on activity, pregnancy, lactation, age, nervousness and actual breed. Small breeds tend to have a higher metabolism than medium breeds and may actually require more calories.

	weight in pounds	approximate daily caloric need
SMALL BREEDS:	5	225
	10	475
	15	725
	20	800
MEDIUM BREEDS:	25	650
	30	800
	35	1150
	40	1300
	45	1450
	50	1600
	55	1800
	60	2000
	70	2200
	75	2300
LARGER BREEDS:	80	2000
	85	2100
	90	2200
	95	2400
	100	2500
	105	2700
	110	2900
	115	3100
	120	3300

Index